DATE DUE

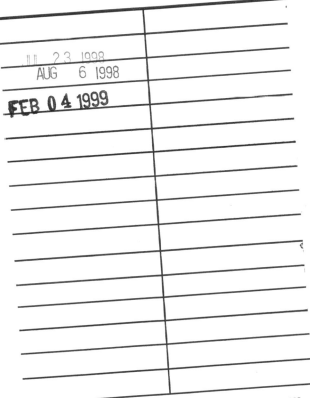

Teaching Within the Rhythms of the Semester

Donna Killian Duffy
Janet Wright Jones
· · · · · · · · · · · · · · · · · ·

Teaching Within the Rhythms of the Semester

Jossey-Bass Publishers
San Francisco

Substantial discounts on bulk quantities of Jossey-Bass books are available to corporations, professional associations, and other organizations. For details and discount information, contact the special sales department at Jossey-Bass Inc., Publishers. (415) 433-1740; Fax (800) 605-2665.

For sales outside the United States, please contact your local Paramount Publishing International Office.

Table 1.2, adapted from Fox (1983), is used by permission of the publisher, Carfax Publishing Company, PO Box 25, Abingdon, Oxfordshire, OX14 3UE, England.
In Chapter Two: "Halfway Down," from WHEN WE WERE VERY YOUNG by A. A. Milne, illustrations by E. H. Shepard. Copyright © 1924 by E. P. Dutton, renewed 1952 by A. A. Milne. Used by permission of Dutton Children's Books, a division of Penguin Books USA Inc., and of Reed Consumer Books Ltd.
Figure 5.3 is adapted from Svinicki, M. D., & Dixon, N. M. (1987). *College Teaching*, 35(4), 141–146. Reprinted with permission of the Helen Dwight Reid Educational Foundation. Published by Heldref Publications, 1319 Eighteenth St., N.W., Washington, D.C. 10036–1802. Copyright © 1987.

TCF Manufactured in the United States of America on Lyons Falls Pathfinder Tradebook. This paper is acid-free and 100 percent totally chlorine-free.

Library of Congress Cataloging-in-Publication Data

Duffy, Donna Killian
   Teaching within the rhythms of the semester / Donna Killian Duffy & Janet Wright Jones. — 1st ed.
     p. cm. —(The Jossey-Bass higher and adult education series)
   Includes bibliographical references (p.   ) and index.
   ISBN 0-7879-0073-7 (alk. paper)
   1. College teaching—United States I. Jones, Janet Wright. II. Title.
III. Series.
LB2331.D83 1995
378.1'25'0973—dc20
94-41810
CIP

FIRST EDITION
HB Printing   10 9 8 7 6 5 4 3 2 1   Code 9532

The Jossey-Bass
Higher and Adult Education Series

• •

To my parents,
Matt and Jay Killian,
for years of caring and encouragement

To
Paul, Peter, and David Jones,
my main men

Contents

· ·

Although they reflect the reality of our experience as teachers, the narratives, the professors, and the students in the vignettes and skits are all entirely imaginary.

Preface

*V*ignette: Professor Fellows has taught Biology II for fifteen years. She knows her subject well, has read extensively, and has just published a review of current research on the pancreas. One of the most successful professors at her college, she has chosen to stay in teaching rather than to join the corporations that have wooed her, both because she enjoys her students and because she believes in teaching. Professor Fellows feels that she can truly make a difference in the classroom, and she is secure in her certainty that Biology II is a foundation course for several of the most popular majors at the college. Yet today, as she stands behind the lectern, Professor Fellows is tired.

For the past several semesters, Professor Fellows has not been able to summon her usual enthusiasm for her courses or for her students. She has felt mired in a kind of listlessness, and she has worried that she is burning out. She recognizes that her classes are not going as well as they have in past years, but she is not sure exactly why. She knows, however, that they are not the same.

True, her classes are full, full to overflowing, but they are different. The students are different—their ages, their heritages, their priorities, their clothing, their attention spans, their interests, and thus their questions. They appear distracted, unconnected, or overwhelmed—she isn't sure which. They talk when she is talking and are often late to class; their papers and tests are not so fine as they once were; they have even questioned the value of the information she gives and the ways in which she presents it.

Clearly, her old approaches to teaching are no longer as effective. Professor Fellows needs time to rethink and to rekindle. She wants a chance to talk to her colleagues. How can she reforge the successful environment of her previous classrooms? Must she reorganize her course? Does she have the time or the energy to tackle changes? Indeed, can she even keep working successfully as a vigorous member of the fellowship of teaching?

By the late 1980s, it was clear to a number of people at Middlesex Community College that the Professor Fellowses were multiplying—not just in Biology II, and not just at our particular college. Beleaguered by spiraling costs, dwindling funds, changing demographics, and new expectations, frustrated administrators, faculty, and staff began to ask questions: Who are our students? In what ways do they learn? What should we teach? Which are the most effective teaching methods, the most appropriate teaching tools? Where is the support system? What will work? Can we still endorse individual approaches to teaching?

Supported by then president Evan Dobelle and led by Charmian Sperling, dean of staff and program development, the authors joined six other faculty members from across all disciplines of the college to analyze these challenges and to create new materials for our individual classes. As we met and discussed different approaches, it became clear to us that we, like Professor Fellows, needed to learn more about our own teaching styles and the ways in which students learn. Although we were experts in our own fields, most of us had had little or no training in educational philosophy, nor in many cases had we previously valued it. It was time to begin.

A Title III grant made it possible for us to investigate the scholarship of teaching (Boyer, 1990) and to create a multifaceted, inquiry-based (Fideler, 1991) instructional development program.

We urged that the leaders of the new program come from within our own college community so that they would know our requirements and would be readily available for questions, suggestions, even confrontations.

As work by Kuh and Whitt (1988) has suggested, in order to be effective, academic programs must reflect the unique culture of the particular college community. When a visiting expert presents a lecture or a daylong workshop or a group of professors attends a longer seminar away from the campus, a seed is planted. But it is difficult for the initial energy and excitement created by the new ideas to bear fruit. After the speaker is gone, there is generally little, if any, follow-up. The momentum is quickly lost in the pressure of the return to daily routines, and the new ideas fail to become an integral part of the curriculum.

In 1989, the authors—a professor of psychology and a professor of English and humanities (a most successful balance of areas of expertise and approaches to teaching, we have found) became the co-designers and the co-coordinators of an on-the-spot instructional development program. Believing in the philosophy that "how something is taught is as important as what is taught" (Cross, 1990) and wanting to reflect Professor Fellows's and others' frustration with a stagnant classroom, we named the program Activating Learning in the Classroom (ALC).

We began by considering not only the obvious components of a classroom—the professors, the information, and the students—but also two other components common to all teaching experiences— the classroom space and the envelope formed by the time frame of the semester. Considerable work is available that discusses the factors involved in effective teaching (Lowman, 1984; McKeachie, 1986; Katz & Henry, 1988; Brookfield, 1990). We felt that it was important to study these factors, but we also felt that this investigation was only the first step. Professors must translate how these factors fit with their own style, their own course content, and their particular group of students; and they must then go on to consider the dictates of their classroom space and the impact of the time patterns of a semester.

The ALC program, we felt, needed to allow time for investigation, for heated discussion, and for feedback. It needed to keep alive conversations about the scholarship of teaching and the improvement of student learning, while providing a vehicle for the introduction of philosophical and pedagogical research and a forum for the practice and critique of new ideas and methods. In addition, we felt that, given the new emphasis on faculty accountability (Boyer, 1987; Sykes, 1988; Edgerton, 1993), it was important that faculty leave the program with a completed end product.

In the initial ALC program, eight professors from each of the divisions of the college volunteered to redevelop a course that they planned to teach within a year's time. We met with the professors in regularly scheduled seminars to discuss a variety of topics including teaching styles, learning styles, gender differences, and critical thinking skills; multicultural, interdisciplinary, and global issues; the use of writing and collaborative learning; the multitude of assessment techniques and ways in which to handle stress; the arrangement of space within the classroom and the effect on learning of the rhythms of the semester; as well as ways to connect to the students' experiences and careers. During the summer and fall, each ALC seminar participant created a course guide. Since the inception of the Activating Learning in the Classroom program in 1989, ALC course guides have been used by more than five thousand students in 210 courses from across the academic disciplines.

Over the past five years, the ALC program, with the vigorous support of President Carole Cowan, has become an amalgam of information and ideas presented by the professor-coordinators, methods piloted by the practitioners, and new materials (of which course guides are only one kind) continually created and recreated by the individuals of the college community.

Theodore Marchese (1993) has written about the impact of Total Quality Management (TQM) on higher education. ALC has incorporated many of the ideas behind TQM but without touting itself as a TQM program, and perhaps fortunately so, at least for those who are doubters. The idea of benchmarking, defined by Marchese as "the systematic search for best practice" (p. 12), undergirds our program. There is no administrative directive that requires faculty, staff, or administrators to undertake the rethinking processes of ALC—attendance at the seminars is voluntary. Yet members of the faculty, the staff, and the administration have regularly come together to share their teaching discoveries and to benefit from their colleagues' suggestions. ALC participants have helped to establish "a collective sense of obligation toward or avidness about the improvement of student learning" (Marchese, p. 12).

The ALC program is at the heart of our discussion in this book. It is within ALC's many forums, and within our own classes, that we have been able to research our answers and test our conclusions. We have learned from those who have attended the sessions, and we have gained feedback from students who took the ensuing courses.

Audience

We hope that *Teaching Within the Rhythms of the Semester* will open avenues for those who confront the realities of teaching, whether it be as faculty, staff, graduate students, administrators, or corporate classroom trainers. We hope that individual faculty members and graduate students will read the book and be sufficiently intrigued with the philosophies and ideas presented that they will go forth and create their own approaches; that deans of the faculty and chairs of departments will be excited enough by it to share the ideas with their faculty; that directors of instructional development programs will see this book as a point of departure in the crafting of their own programs; and that leaders in the training of business and industry personnel will turn to it for insight into the ways of teaching, learning, and connecting new knowledge to external objectives.

Overview of the Contents

We have organized this book to follow the rhythms that occur within the envelope of any teaching configuration, whether the instructional period consists of a day, a few weeks, two semesters and summer sessions, three semesters, or four quarters.

We have divided the contents into two major parts. The three chapters in Part One address the prelude to the semester—the preparation for the opening of the semester. Each of these chapters explores areas that not only absorb professors before the semester begins but continue to absorb them once they have entered its time frame: teaching styles, the elements of a successful teaching experience, and the creation of an enriched syllabus.

The three chapters in Part Two explore the tempo of the semester, focusing on three distinct periods within the semester—the opening weeks, the low periods around the middle, and the closing weeks. Some readers may perceive this tempo as a fractal pattern that is repeated in many of the units integral to the teaching experience: in a single class, during several weeks devoted to a single topic, over a longer section of the course, or throughout the course itself. Our exploration addresses the implications of this pattern both for teaching and for learning.

Every chapter in *Teaching Within the Rhythms of the Semester* is organized around three elements: first, we present a vignette of a teaching experience that sets the stage for a situation which we hope is recognizable to anyone who has taught; second, we discuss the educational, cognitive, and affective theories reflected in the vignette; and third, we develop examples of specific techniques and materials that we and our colleagues have found helpful during the time period that the chapter explores. Each chapter concludes with a brief *replay* of the topics discussed in the chapter. These replay notes have proven useful for orientation, for review, and as a stimulus for creating individualized approaches to teaching and learning.

In Chapter One, we present an overview of various teaching

styles, discuss the avenues that lead to teaching effectiveness, suggest how you can use a teaching portfolio, and describe the structure of a course guide.

In Chapter Two, we describe the moment when the classroom community comes together and learning is cemented. We discuss six catalysts that can make this happen and identify specific tools to activate each catalyst.

In Chapter Three, we portray student reactions to a simple syllabus on the opening day of class. We then discuss the stages of cognitive development found in college students and show how those stages relate to the elements, uses, and benefits of an enriched syllabus. Chapter Three includes a section-by-section comparison of a simple syllabus and an enriched syllabus.

Chapter Four, which begins Part Two of the book, describes the opening weeks of the semester and discusses the nature of the community of the classroom as we discovered it to be through our participation as students in each other's classes. We explore five factors at work in these opening weeks and suggest ways to juggle these factors in order to create an effective classroom community.

In Chapter Five, we depict the doldrums, the low period that seems to occur in every teaching configuration. We discuss typical patterns and ways of learning and suggest teaching approaches that can recharge both students' and professors' energies.

Finally, in Chapter Six, we describe the closing weeks of the semester. We analyze the characteristics of end-of-the-semester student and professor stress and suggest techniques for combating this stress. We specify ways to design effective tests, particularly final exams, and we explore methods of unifying the course experience and of achieving closure.

Acknowledgments

We would like to thank those who lent us support and guidance throughout this adventure: Dean Charmian Sperling, without whose unfailing encouragement and willingness to go to bat, we would not have succeeded; President Carole Cowan, whose confidence made this book possible; Vice President Carl Schilling, director of faculty visions and fellow presenter; Dean Pamela Edington, friend, colleague, and leader; Peyton Paxson, designer of superior syllabi and guru of legal matters; June Barnes and Theresa Corso, staunch supporters in so many ways; Fred Hinkley, wizard of the machines and keeper of the roses; Rob Kaulfuss and Roger Flahive, patient guides through the mazes of computer interfacing; Barbara Levesque, searcher for texts; and our fellow ALC alumni, who laughed with us and taught us much—Sandi Albertson-Shea, Peg Bloy, Mary Cabral, Yvonne Dunkley, Beth Fraser, Darlene Furdock, Joe Gardner, Stan Hitron, Joan Kleinman, Bob Layden, Elaine Linscott, Don Margulis, Anne Miller, Jeanne Newhall, Lynne Osborn, Peyton Paxson, Marie Ryder, Ray Shea, Nancy Smith, Barry Werner, and Sheila Willard.

We want also to thank the members of our own personal support systems: the Duffy contingent—John for his equanimity, helpful suggestions, and unconditional support; and sons Sean and Ryan for innumerable favors, humor, and flexibility; and Paul Jones for his perspicacity, unflagging encouragement, and willingness to nosh on take-outs.

Bedford and Lowell, Massachusetts　　　　　Donna Killian Duffy
January 1995　　　　　　　　　　　　　　Janet Wright Jones

The Authors

Donna Killian Duffy is professor of psychology and co-coordinator of the Activating Learning in the Classroom (ALC) program at Middlesex Community College, Bedford and Lowell, Massachusetts. She earned her B.A. degree (1970) in psychology at Wheaton College (Massachusetts) and her Ph.D. degree (1976) in psychology at Washington University (Missouri). Duffy began her career as a psychologist at the Alberta Children's Hospital in Calgary, Alberta, and at present continues clinical work in a group practice. She has been involved in programs for students with learning disabilities from preschool to college and is interested in ways to integrate affective and cognitive development in academic settings. She has published several articles on the ALC program and has presented more than twenty workshops and papers for professional organizations. In 1991, she received an International Award for Teaching Excellence presented by the International Conference on Teaching Excellence at Austin, Texas, and student and administrative awards for teaching excellence at Middlesex Community College.

Janet Wright Jones is professor emeritus of Middlesex Community College and former co-coordinator of the Activating Learning in the Classroom (ALC) program at Middlesex Community College, Bedford and Lowell, Massachusetts. She earned her B.A. degree

(1956) in English at Smith College and her A.M.T. degree (1957) in English at Harvard University.

Jones has taught at nearly every level of education. Most recently, her focus has been equally divided between teaching English and creating the ALC program for faculty, staff, and administrators. She has directed a remedial reading program at the university level and taught English and humanities at the community college and high school level. From 1974 to 1979, she served as the coordinator of a multicultural, multiethnic program that bused urban students to a suburban school, where she designed and developed a multicultural curriculum, trained personnel, and opened avenues of discussion among the faculty, parents, and students.

Jones has coauthored a monograph, *The Black History of Concord,* published several articles on the ALC program, and presented more than twenty workshops and papers to professional organizations. In 1991, she received the International Award for Teaching Excellence presented by the International Conference on Teaching Excellence in Austin, Texas, and an award for teaching excellence at Middlesex Community College

Teaching Within the Rhythms of the Semester

Exploring Teaching Styles

Know thyself.
—*Inscription at the Delphic Oracle*

Vignette: It is the third week of the spring semester, early February, a time of cold winds, snow and icicles, and an occasional bright, sunny day. In the college's required course Introduction to Literature, four professors have elected to begin a section on Robert Frost. Each professor plans to cover the same core of information, and each has selected many of the same poems to discuss, yet each professor approaches the initial class on Frost in a quite different way.

Professor Capriani entered the room, opened his worn manila folder, took out his notes, placed them carefully on the podium, and smiled to himself. Teaching Robert Frost was almost always a pleasure. Capriani had spent time studying Frost and had published a well-received essay on Frost's use of darkness. Capriani knew his subject well, and he was deeply concerned that his students understand his insights into the complexities of Frost. He began: "Robert Frost, the poet of rural New England, was not born in New England; he was born in San Francisco, in 1874." Without looking up, the students wrote in their notebooks as Capriani continued on with selected details of Robert Frost's early life. He was careful to include the fact that although Frost tried college (Dartmouth and Harvard), he left quickly because he was unhappy with the academic approach, turning to the trades, then to teaching school and to farming, and finally to writing. "*Mountain Interval* was published in 1916 and included a poem that is probably familiar to you, 'The Road Not Taken.'" Professor Capriani looked up from his notes to give the members of the class time to finish writing and then asked them to turn to page 248 in their texts. "As is the case in much of Frost's poetry, the message of this poem is ambiguous, but if you read with care, you will see that the most reasonable interpretation of the often quoted final two lines is . . ."

Across the campus, Professor Freneau was also about to begin a section on Robert Frost. She, too, had researched Frost, felt comfortable with her understanding of his complexities, and was enthusiastic about the students joining with her in the upcoming discussion. She climbed the stairs to Room 216, walked in, letting the door swing shut behind her, put down her briefcase, dug out the literature textbook, opened it to the premarked section on poetry, waited a few seconds for the three students in the front to finish their conversation, moved away from the podium, the book, and her notes, and began: "We are about to start our discussion of Robert Frost. I look forward to this discussion, for there is much to talk about. Many of you are familiar with Robert Frost, so let's begin today with what you know. Take out a blank piece of paper and make a list—be sure that it is a list—of all that you know about Robert Frost. Then we will put the points on the board." Professor Freneau stayed standing just in front of the podium as her students began to write down bits of information.

Elsewhere, Professor O'Reilly was already in her classroom. She had just finished a class in composition the period before, and she was eager now to begin on the mysteries of Robert Frost and to encourage the students to explore these mysteries with her. She waited at the podium as the students came in and settled into their seats. Several of the students spoke to her as they walked by. One threw down his coat and his backpack and went forward to talk to her. Professor O'Reilly looked concerned and nodded. The student returned to his seat less agitated.

Professor O'Reilly dug into her briefcase and pulled out a small stack of white paper, putting it down on the podium. She picked up the worn textbook already on the table next to the podium, but did not open it. Instead, moving in front of the table, she began her class with a question: "Who was Robert Frost?" She paused, looked around, and asked the question again: "Who was Robert Frost?" The second time, she stressed the "who" rather than the "Robert Frost." Professor O'Reilly did not leave space for anyone to reply; instead, she leaned forward, smiled, and went on, "Take a couple of minutes to write down whatever you know about Robert Frost." She waited by the table next to the podium until most of the students had finished writing and had looked up. Professor O'Reilly then moved back to the podium and picked up the stack of paper, asking the class to break into groups of three. She planned to give each group a sheet that she had divided into two columns, one labeled "Accuracies," the other "Inaccuracies."

Just four rooms down the hall from Professor O'Reilly, Professor Nordstrom hurried into his classroom. He had stopped to talk to a student on the way up to the third floor and was a little out of breath, but he knew his course well and like the three other professors of literature, had spent time the previous evening thinking about the best way to introduce the enigma of Robert Frost and to guide the students toward their own well-supported conclusions. He left the door open for the time being—one student, Matt Goldstein, was always a couple of minutes late for reasons understood by both Matt and Professor Nordstrom—put his briefcase down beside the blackboard, pulled out the textbook, and opened it to the index card marking "The Road Not Taken."

The students, who had been talking among themselves, quieted quickly and turned as Professor Nordstrom, standing at the side of the room where he had put his briefcase, looked up and began to read the poem aloud. He read it all the way through. After a pause, he read the final stanza aloud once again. "Robert Frost was clearly saying something here. Take a minute to think about what he was saying and then write it down." When they had finished, Professor Nordstrom broke the class into small groups and asked the students to share their ideas and to find a connection between the poem and their own experiences.

Discussion

Professors Capriani, Freneau, O'Reilly, and Nordstrom have each chosen to discuss the same poem at the same point in the semester. In this way, their classes follow a similar path, but there the similarities stop. Their teaching styles differ, as do the environments of their classrooms, and the intensity with which they interact with their students. Professor Capriani lectures from behind the podium. He does not initially ask his students for their ideas, nor does he move out into their space. Professor Freneau, on the other hand, puts down her notes, walks away from the podium, and asks her students to list what they already know about Robert Frost. She will then begin her discussion by writing their information on the board.

Across the campus, Professor O'Reilly also asks her students to write down their ideas, but rather than gather the ideas together on the board herself, she will ask the students to break into small discussion groups to record their thoughts on sheets of paper that she has previously structured. Professor Nordstrom hurries into his room leaving the door open and not only moves away from the podium but begins his class from the far side of the room. He, too, asks the students to gather their thoughts, and like Professor O'Reilly, he will divide the students into small discussion groups. There the similarity ends, for Professor Nordstrom does not intend to structure the nature of the small-group discussions, just the outcomes.

As teachers, each of us brings his or her own teaching style, personality, experiences, goals, and educational philosophies into the classroom. It is essential that we continue to do so, just as it is essential that students be given the chance to experience a number of teaching approaches. Still, it is also essential that periodically we find time to confront our particular teaching styles and to explore possible changes. If we do not, we risk burnout, falling into the trap encountered by Professor Fellows in the preface.

William Reinsmith (1992) suggests that "when a teacher comes together with a student or students in a given way, a teaching encounter is born. Within that encounter certain predictable (in the midst of other more sporadic) energies unfold which constitute or reflect a specific teaching form" (p. xiv). Reinsmith maintains that there are eight archetypal forms of teaching at the college and university level and has arranged these archetypes along a continuum of increasing individualization of learning and interaction between professor and student. (See our depiction of the continuum, in Figure 1.1.) He describes this interaction as a "gradual interiorization of a teaching presence until in the last mode the distance between the two is collapsed" (p. xxiii).

The focus of the first four forms—Disseminator/Transmitter, Lecturer/Dramatist, Inducer/Persuader, and Inquirer/Catalyst—is teacher centered. The fifth form, Dialogist, is a transitional stage between teacher-centered and student-centered forms of teaching. In the Dialogist form, learning revolves increasingly around partic-

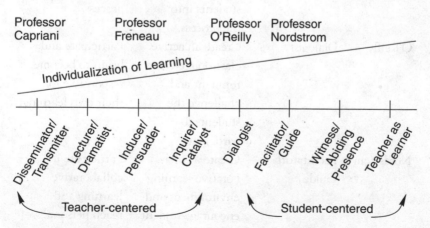

Figure 1.1. Continuum of Individualization of Learning.
   Source: Based on Reinsmith, 1992.

ipation among class members. The focus of the final three forms (Facilitator/Guide, Witness/Abiding Presence, and Teacher as Learner) is student centered.

Professors Capriani, Freneau, O'Reilly, and Nordstrom each reflect one of these forms of teaching (Table 1.1). Professor Capriani, who lectures from the podium, falls into the category of the Disseminator/Transmitter—along with the Lecturer/Dramatist, the most typical form of college teacher according to Cross (1986). The Disseminator/Transmitter sees his or her task as presenting essential information to students in a straightforward manner. Professor Capriani has reflected carefully on Robert Frost's poetry, and he

Table 1.1. Some Characteristics of Four of Reinsmith's Forms of Teaching.

Professor	Type of Professor	Responsibility of the Professor	Responsibility of the students
Capriani	Disseminator/ Transmitter	Provide the information.	Record the information.
Freneau	Inducer/ Persuader	Direct the flow of the information while inviting the students into the process.	Share their background knowledge and participate in the learning process.
O'Reilly	Dialogist	Create an active classroom environment and challenge the students to participate.	Participate and begin to become responsible for their own learning.
Nordstrom	Facilitator/ Guide	Create a collaborative learning environment and encourage student discovery.	Participate in collaborative learning and reach personal conclusions.

Source: Based on Reinsmith, 1992.

enjoys teaching Frost. He has gathered his ideas into a neat and well-used folder and has attempted to organize his lectures in a way that is clear and challenging to his students. He has chosen to focus on the content of his course rather than on personal encounters with his students. He therefore feels comfortable in telling the students how to interpret the final lines of the poem. But it has been suggested that "education is not a process of stuffing the mind with facts . . . not merely the imparting of knowledge but the cultivation of certain aptitudes and attitudes in the mind of the young" (Harvard Committee, 1945, p. 64).

Professor Freneau, who walks away from the podium and then records the students' points on the board, suggests Reinsmith's third approach to teaching, the Inducer/Persuader. In this mode, a professor does not give the answer but rather begins to listen to student responses and tries to adapt presentations in ways that will involve the students in the learning process of the course. As an Inducer/Persuader, Professor Freneau is interested in how the content of the course relates to the students' world. She sees her role as inviting or persuading students to begin to join in the learning process and personalizes her classroom in an effort to incorporate the existing knowledge of her students. She therefore urges her students to think back and then to create a list for themselves of what they already know. Professor Freneau will, however, maintain control of the presentation of that information by writing and organizing it on the board herself.

Professor O'Reilly, who uses small, directed groups, goes still further in her focus on interaction with students. She fits the description of Reinsmith's fifth and pivotal form of teaching, Dialogist. She has begun to consider the individuality of her students and is therefore able to calm an agitated student before class and then readily divide the class into working groups. In contrast to Professor Capriani, who is primarily interested in the presentation of information, Professor O'Reilly is also concerned with the process of the presentation. In contrast to Professor Freneau, who feels that students need to be involved in their own learning, she feels that students need to go further—not only do they need to be involved, they need to become responsible for their own learning. She asks her student groups to arrange what they know about Robert Frost into columns of accuracies and inaccuracies. By asking her students to sort fact from embroidery and then to share their ideas in groups, she hopes to raise uncertainties and to introduce conflict. Some of her students may find this approach uncomfortable if they have not yet developed the skills to work with discrepancies. Thus, in order for this approach to be successful, Professor O'Reilly will need to have a clear understanding of the level of her students' cognitive and emotional responses so that she stimulates but does not overwhelm.

Professor Nordstrom, who reads from the side of the room and then turns to the students, views himself as a Facilitator/Guide, Reinsmith's sixth form of teaching, and agrees with Galileo's view that "you cannot teach a man anything; you can only help him to find it within himself." Professor Nordstrom sees information as a jumping-off point. He locates himself among his students, standing at the side of the room, and opens his class first by reading aloud "The Road Not Taken," and then by rereading its final stanza. Unlike his colleagues, Professor Nordstrom makes no further comments and provides no further structure. He has introduced the topic, indicated the direction, and started the momentum; learning is now the students' responsibility. By shifting the control to the student groups, Professor Nordstrom plans to facilitate student discovery and to help students make the information their own.

Each of the four humanities professors in our vignette falls into one of Reinsmith's forms of teaching. But fortunately, professors are an elusive breed not willing to be categorized. Those who teach in the sciences might well describe teaching styles in a way quite different from those who teach in the humanities, a possibility that Dennis Fox (1983) at Trent Polytechnic in Nottingham, England, confronted in his paper on personal theories of teaching. Fox explored the views of professors at his technical institution by asking them to explain what they meant by "teaching." He then divided their responses into categories that he labeled personal theories.

Fox suggests that professors fall into two modes of teaching: the "simple modes," which he divides further into "transfer" and "shaping" theories; and the more "developed modes," which he divides into "traveling" and "growing" theories. According to Fox, transfer theory, the first of the simple modes, involves transferring a given commodity of knowledge from one container (the professor) to another (the student), rather like the method of Professor Capriani, who carefully organizes the material and then presents it to his students for them to write down and absorb. Shaping theory, the second of the simple modes, involves the act of shaping students into a predetermined form and is quite similar to Professor Freneau's approach of asking for student input but still maintaining control by organizing their ideas and writing them down on the board herself.

In the more developed modes, professors see teaching not as transferring or shaping, but as enabling. Professors using the traveling theory see teaching as an exploration with the professor as expert guide for the journey. This theory is similar to Professor O'Reilly's approach in directing students to organize their ideas into accuracies and inaccuracies and then encouraging them to structure their group discussions around this focus. In the growing theory, the focus is on working with the intellectual and emotional development of the learner, nurturing growth in these areas as a gardener nurtures growth in plants. Professor Nordstrom's approach is closest to this theory: first he plants an idea by simply reading the poem aloud, and then he nurtures the idea by encouraging his student groups to discover the connections to their own experiences.

Fox places these four theories on a matrix and then illustrates how a professor's theory of teaching influences his or her views on a number of issues in the classroom. (Table 1.2 summarizes this information.)

Table 1.2. A Summary of Fox's Four Theories of Teaching.

	Transfer Theory	Shaping Theory	Traveling Theory	Growing Theory
Verbs commonly used	Convey, impart, imbue, give, expound, transmit, put over, propound, tell	Develop, mould, demonstrate, produce, instruct, condition, prepare, direct (give orders)	Lead, point the way, guide, initiate, help, show, direct (show the way)	Cultivate, encourage, nurture, develop, foster, enable, help, bring out
The subject matter	Commodity to be transferred to fill a container	Shaping tools, patterns, blueprints	Terrain to be explored, vantage points	Experiences to be incorporated into a developing personality
The student	Container to be filled	Inert material (clay, wood, metal) to be shaped	Explorer	Developing personality, growing plant
The teacher	Pump attendant, food processor, barmaid	Skilled craftsperson working on raw material or selecting and assembling components	Experienced and expert traveling companion, guide, provider of traveling aids	Resource provider, gardener
Standard teaching methods	Lectures, reading lists, duplicated notes	Laboratory, workshop, practical instructions like recipes,	Simulations, projects, exercises with unpredictable outcomes,	Experiential methods similar to those for traveling

Table 1.2. A Summary of Fox's Four Theories of Teaching, *cont'd.*

	Transfer Theory	Shaping Theory	Traveling Theory	Growing Theory
		exercises with predictable outcomes	discussions, independent learning	theory but less structured and more spontaneous
Measuring progress	Measuring and sampling contents vessel	Checking size and shape of product	Comparing notes with traveling companion	Listening to reflections on personal development
Explanations of failure— teacher's view	Leaky vessels, small container	Flawed, faulty raw material	Blinkered vision, lack of stamina, unadventurous, lethargic	Poor start, inadequately prepared, no will to develop
Explanations of failure— student's view	Poor transfer skills, poor aim	Incompetent craftsperson, poor or missing blueprint	Poor guides, poor equipment, too many restrictions on route	Restricted diet, unsuitable food, incompetent gardener
Attitude to training	Need simple skills of transfer	Need shaping to British Standard Teacher	Need skills of expert guide as well as knowledge of terrain	Need skills of diagnosing needs of individual plants

Source: Adapted from Fox, 1983, p. 163.

Interestingly, both Reinsmith and Fox conclude that as teaching styles move along a continuum from simpler to more developed forms, the interactions with students increase. The less complex modes are more teacher centered and group oriented; the more complex modes are more student centered and individualized. One of the participants in Fox's study supplied this teacher's eye view of the progression: "I now see myself less in the driving seat and more as a mechanic helping to keep the engine of learning running smoothly" (p. 161).

As we have noted, each of the four professors in our vignette fits roughly into one of Reinsmith's or Fox's forms of teaching. With that fact understood, this important question arises: Is any one of these approaches more successful than another at keeping the engine of learning running smoothly? Not necessarily. Lowman (1984) suggests that the quality of instruction depends not so much on the teaching style of the professor, as on the professor's method of using this style and on the classroom environment that is created. In his model of teaching effectiveness, Lowman argues that the ability to generate intellectual excitement in the students as well as positive interpersonal rapport with them is the essence of an effective classroom community. These results can happen within many styles of teaching. In our opinion, the issue is not to name the styles and then to determine in the abstract which style is the most effective, but rather to become aware of one's own personal style and then to discern ways in which to enhance the effectiveness of that style.

In our work with colleagues during the past five years, we have discovered that in order for professors to feel comfortable with the process of exploring different approaches, they must first be given time to reflect on their own strengths (Jones & Duffy, 1991; Duffy & Jones, 1991). Confronting your personal teaching style means that you must question what you do and have been doing, in many cases for a significant period of time. This is an exciting process, but it is an exhausting process. If professors begin from the knowledge that they know how to teach, which indeed they do, and that they know how to teach certain information and skills effectively, then they are comfortable in considering the next step. They are open to investigating new methods and to expanding their repertoires for the classroom. Nevertheless, adjusting one's teaching approaches means taking risks. Garvin (1991) has effectively described these risks by focusing on three fundamental steps that he calls "shifts."

> The successful practice of discussion teaching—or for that matter, any other form of education aimed at active learning—requires three fundamental shifts. The first is a shift in the balance of power: from an autocratic classroom, where the instructor is all-powerful, to a more democratic environment, where students share in decision making. The second is a shift in the locus of attention from concern for the material alone to an equal focus on content, classroom process, and the learning climate. The third is a shift in instructional skills: from declarative explanations rooted in analytical understanding and knowledge of subject matter, to questioning, listening, and responding, which draw equally on interpersonal skills and a sensitivity to group development [p. 10].

In our seminars, we urge faculty members to consider these shifts, yet many professors come to the classroom with a mental set that the lecture format is the best way to teach, for in most cases that is the way they were taught. As you begin to contemplate your own style and how you might embellish it, both Reinsmith's archetypes and Fox's personal theories are most helpful, for they provide a concrete outline of teaching approaches to serve as a reference point.

Application

As you examine your own teaching style and begin to contemplate possible changes, you will need a way to keep a record of your ideas and your materials, and you will need an avenue for direct feedback from your students. The teaching portfolio and the course guide are two possible methods. Each will allow you to reflect upon your experiences and to reinforce your discoveries. Each will provide a record of your approaches and will involve your students in the evolution of your style.

Teaching Portfolios

During the 1980s, a number of national reports stressed the need for a rethinking of the direction of higher education (*To Reclaim a Legacy*, Bennett, 1984; *Involvement in Learning: Realizing the Potential of American Higher Education*, National Institute of Education Study Group, 1984; and *Integrity in the College Curriculum*, Association of American Colleges, 1985). In response to these reports, academic institutions moved to find ways in which to reassess the process of classroom teaching. Leaders sought new methods that would encourage teachers to explore their personal teaching styles.

Edgerton, Hutchings, and Quinlan (1991), Seldin (1991), and Urbach (1992) have suggested that faculty members use teaching portfolios, adding to and building these portfolios throughout their teaching experience. Like the portfolios of artists, architects, or inventors, the portfolios of professors should be representative of the professors' philosophies and of their work. But what should be included? What is effective? What is safe? Edgerton, Hutchings, and Quinlan; Seldin; and Urbach all agree that to be effective a teaching portfolio should include three kinds of entries.

- Materials used in the course

- Comments on how the materials worked

- Reflections on the process of using the materials

Urbach elaborates further, explaining that in order to create a fully documented teaching portfolio, you must consider seven dimensions of the classroom experience.

- What you teach
- How you teach
- What changes you make
- What standards you use
- Your use of student feedback
- Your efforts to develop your skills
- Your colleagues' assessments of your teaching

Urbach also suggests that your portfolio be multilevel. It should include not only materials pertaining to each dimension, but also your ongoing commentary on the changes that you are considering, as well as the results of these changes. Perhaps a bit daunting, initially, but do not despair. If you consider beginning a portfolio, remember that these suggestions are just that—a list to start the process. The purpose of a portfolio is to be helpful to you. You are the explorer. Your portfolio is a personal document and a private invention.

Clearly, a teaching portfolio is always in progress. Never fully completed, the portfolio becomes a record of a personal journey, filled with ruminations, observations, and results. If a teaching portfolio is to be used for evaluation, or is linked to tenure, the purpose and the nature of the portfolio will be significantly changed. It will no longer be a self-assessment tool. The author will not be free to fail—an essential privilege in all creative work. If the portfolio is designed primarily for outside viewers, each entry must be weighed with care and shaped in a way that is presentable. Each entry must have been tested and evaluated. Not so if the portfolio remains private, shared only when the author wants it to be.

Just as the right to share or not to share the content of a teaching portfolio is best protected, the decision to create such a portfolio needs to be voluntary. Only then does the portfolio become a safe haven for the bits and pieces of ideas (as messy or as organized as your style dictates) that have not yet been finalized. Only then can the portfolio become a complex chronicle of an individual's changing approaches to teaching as well as a vehicle for private reflection.

In our short seminars, we structured a way for professors to give the teaching portfolio a fair trial. We asked them to follow these steps:

- Select a brief classroom or homework activity.

- Consider its structure and presentation with care.

- Design your newly conceived activity.

- Execute it with your students.

- Garner written feedback from your students.

- File the feedback.

- Add your own comments.

- Bring all of these materials to the second session of the seminar.

- Share and discuss these materials with your seminar colleagues.

- Garner written feedback from your colleagues.

- File all of the information from this seminar session.

- Some time later, when your reactions have had sufficient time to percolate, make a record of possible changes in the activity.

- Be sure to include your reasons for considering these changes.

When they had completed these steps, nearly all of our colleagues opted to continue their teaching portfolios. They particularly liked the portfolio's flexibility, its fluidity, and its space for commentary. Several commented that they wished that they had started such portfolios earlier in their teaching careers.

As you consider the possibility of beginning such a record of your teaching, it is useful to review Urbach's dimensions, keeping in mind that you are free to select only those that are helpful to you. The first dimension centers on what you teach: the content of your course, your goals, and your objectives. Here you could include a syllabus, study guides, or a list of your goals (see Edgerton, Hutchings, & Quinlan, 1991, pp. 15–17, for an example of a portfolio entry on course descriptions).

If you are considering restructuring the goals for a particular class, Angelo and Cross (1993) have created a helpful Teaching Goals Inventory that contains fifty-two goals to be rank ordered for a specific course. The goals are organized into six "clusters" (higher-order thinking skills, basic academic success skills, discipline-specific knowledge and skills, liberal arts and academic values, work and career preparation, and personal development) that focus on teaching priorities (p. 22). Angelo and Cross have discovered that professors in the same academic discipline often share similar teaching priorities, priorities that may be significantly different from those of professors in other disciplines. Thus, even though Professors Capriani, Freneau, O'Reilly, and Nordstrom use varied approaches in creating their classroom environments, and should certainly be free to continue to do so, it is likely that their overall teaching goals for Introduction to Literature are the same. Their different styles would become clear from the materials that they chose to illustrate the second dimension of the teaching portfolio—how you teach. Here is the place to do your own critical thinking, to reflect on your style of teaching, and to explore your personal theory of teaching. The work of Reinsmith (1992) and of Fox (1983), discussed earlier, provides a helpful guide for defining your perspective and for demonstrating how that perspective relates to the broader continuum of teaching styles.

To describe how you teach, you may want to include notes from one day's lecture, a description of a class when you used a group approach or tried to incorporate music into the discussion, or possibly a videotape of your teaching. For example, Professor Nordstrom's classroom (the final classroom presented in our vignette, in which he opened the class by reading the poem aloud) has a loosely structured agenda with a clear emphasis on student participation. Should he decide to create a teaching portfolio, Professor Nordstrom might want to include an explanation of why he begins by asking his students to share their ideas and then to connect them to their own experiences. Professor Nordstrom might also refer to work by Angelo (1993) on the value of interaction among students and the importance of linking new information to students' prior knowledge.

The third dimension of a teaching portfolio, the classroom experience, involves you in documenting the changes in your teaching and in your courses. In this section, you might want to point out that although one model of teaching was effective for a certain course, it was not nearly as effective for another. For example, you might use the Disseminator/Transmitter mode effectively to cover the content in an introductory course, but you might find that this approach does not work at all in an advanced seminar. In your portfolio, you might include additions or deletions of teaching activities, with notes (they need not be neat—they are, after all, notes) reflecting reasons for your changes, time lines showing how you modified teaching skills and models, or descriptions of successful and unsuccessful innovations. For instance, this year Professor O'Reilly used cooperative learning groups with a structured worksheet for each group. Last year, she tried asking similar groups to discuss Robert Frost without using group worksheets but found that her students had difficulty focusing on important points. Now, she is able to include her structured worksheet in her portfolio to show the refinement of an earlier activity.

Urbach lists academic standards as a fourth classroom dimension that could be represented in your portfolio. To document this dimension, you explore your standards, how you apply them, what models of learning you use, how students respond, and how you evaluate your assessment procedures. Consider including a discussion of your grading standards from your syllabus, statements regarding your expectations for student performance, or examples of testing materials. Be selective; this is your record of your procedures and your style. Professor Capriani finds it essential to understand the life experiences of poets in order to interpret their poetry. He lists knowing background information about the poets discussed in class as one of the objectives of his course and includes questions on the poets' lives in each of his three exams. Professor Capriani might decide to include a description of this course objective in his portfolio and to support the description with a discussion of how he is assessing that objective. He could include copies of his exams or student papers or a narrative about a class that suddenly came alive as they talked about the background of one of the poets.

The fifth dimension focuses on student impressions of your teaching. Under this heading, you consider how you use student feedback to monitor your teaching and how you deal with the needs of individual students. Material for this dimension might include student evaluation forms, summaries of incidental student comments, dated documentation of course changes, or descriptions of methods used to deal with different student learning styles. Unfortunately, we often discover that students do not own the basic information required to understand certain course content. Professor Freneau might learn that students have no knowledge of a key historical event that is central to understanding a poem. She may well have assumed that they were familiar with this event, but they are not. What changes will she make in her presentation to address the missing knowledge? One of the strengths of a teaching portfolio is that it reflects the "complexities of teaching" and can "foster . . . a new discourse about it" (Edgerton, Hutchings, & Quinlan, 1991, pp. 4–6). By documenting her solutions, Professor Freneau advances the conversation about ways to teach our increasingly diverse students.

The sixth dimension focuses on your efforts to develop your teaching skills. In this section, you delineate the attempts you have made to expand your teaching repertoire (see Weimer, 1990, for helpful suggestions) and the studies you have made of your own teaching style. You might decide to include descriptions of workshops you have attended, new teaching strategies you have learned, discussions you have led, or copies of your research on teaching.

The seventh and last dimension of the teaching portfolio includes examples of colleague assessment of your teaching. In this dimension, you consider the assessment information that you have gathered and discuss the ways in which you have incorporated this information. You might choose to include reports of classroom visits by colleagues, discussions with your director, annual evaluation reports, or teaching awards.

As the direction of higher education comes under greater scrutiny and as the nature of the college population continues to change, it behooves all of us as teachers to find the time and the energy to think critically about what we do and to explore our individual approaches to teaching. It is an appropriate moment to consider Garvin's "shift in the balance of power: from an autocratic classroom, where the instructor is all-powerful, to a more democratic environment, where students share in decision making."

Yet how does one do this with some measure of safety? The teaching portfolio provides a tangible method of demonstrating how teaching effectiveness evolves. Gathering your materials (whether they illustrate all of Urbach's dimensions, or just a few) immediately reminds you that you are documenting something that you already know a good deal about and at which you have already been successful. But there comes a time for change. As you explore new methods, new approaches, and new materials, you can keep a record of your efforts in a private folder for future reference. You are then free to stand back when time permits and to contemplate your teaching portfolio and the constantly evolving process that is teaching.

Course Guides

As you explore and amend your teaching style, you may well discover that you want to use new materials and to reframe those you have been using. This is the moment to consider a course guide, for it allows you to design a road map for your course that will lay out what is ahead, will empower students to work with the materials of the texts, and will encourage them to explore their own ideas before they come to class. A course guide is an excellent place to try out the materials and to test the ideas stored in your portfolio.

You need not contemplate a guide for every course. Try it for one course that you enjoy teaching and that you have the time and energy to rethink. By the time you have completed the guide, you will have cemented your teaching style for the semester.

Generally housed in a loose-leaf notebook, a course guide is your own invention. It serves as a supplement to your course and is filled with whatever printed materials you select and create. It is a tool that you have chosen to give your students and that you hand out as you introduce your course. It connects your students to your teaching methods, asks them to think about highlighted materials, directs them to answer certain questions, and provides them with a concrete link to you and your approaches while they are studying outside the classroom—a subtle (or sometimes not so subtle) support that is particularly effective at the beginning of the semester. The guide can be as interactive and inventive as you want, and because it is shared by all members of the classroom community, it becomes a common ground for discussion and exploration.

Whether it is as long as two hundred pages or far briefer, the course guide reflects your teaching approaches and extends the conversation of your individual classroom community. The basic elements of all course guides are generally the same, but the ways in which the elements are presented and the additions made to them are entirely up to the individual professor. Just as there is no one right way to teach a class, there is no one right way to create a course guide.

A guide begins with an introduction to the course that may include a course description, a discussion of the professor's goals and objectives, perhaps an explanation of the professor's teaching methods and philosophies, and an extended or enriched syllabus (see Chapter Three). Reading questions on the course materials and focus questions (thought questions that relate course material to interdisciplinary and multicultural issues as well as to the students' experiences) generally account for the bulk of a course guide.

The reading questions (see Anderson and others, 1983, and the discussion of cue words in Chapter Six) are assigned ahead of class and are usually incorporated into the course grade. Reading questions check and reinforce understanding of the text. In an environmental science course, the graded reading questions for a chapter on groundwater might ask for direct responses to the material presented and then for summary definitions of specific terms.

The reading questions may follow any pattern you want. You may choose to use them extensively at the beginning of the semester and then phase them out as the semester progresses, or you may decide to be specific and directive at the onset of the semester and become less directive and less specific toward the end.

The focus questions have a different purpose and allow for greater individuality of approach. Focus questions aim to connect course material to students' experiences and are often ungraded. They usually precede the reading questions for a topic or introduce a new topic and are more far-reaching and less centered in the specifics of the assigned material than reading questions. They focus the students on their personal connections to the information, personal skills, or concepts about to be studied. A focus question on the groundwater chapter in the environmental science class could direct students to measure their use of water for a day—cooking, dishwashing, showering, and laundering—and draw up the results in the form of a chart; or it could ask students to conduct a personal survey by testing the flavor of three different sources of water—at least one of them to be a commercial brand—and then to write an argument for or against filling their water bottles with "natural spring water."

The focus questions can be serious or humorous; they can incorporate music, photographs, cartoons, poetry, or skits. They may be assigned either before, during, or after class.

Course guides can also include text previews; letters to the students; reminders of upcoming course commitments; encouraging words or warnings about difficulties looming ahead; directions for labs, journals, papers, or tests; maps, calendars, and cartoons; and as one professor wrote, "occasional pithy, personal, wise, and whimsical comments from me."

Just as a course may change its form from semester to semester, a course guide is also a protean creation that is rarely finished. Yes, it does take time to create—a considerable amount of time—but it is an engaging creation that reflects your vision of your course, your humor, and your methods of teaching. It follows the journey of your course to its finish and forges continuous personalized links among the components of the classroom: professor, information, and students.

As you explore your personal teaching style, as you reach new insights into the ways in which your students learn, and as you consider new techniques and decide to test new approaches, your teaching portfolio can be a place to file these experiments, and the course guide can be a place to execute your ideas and then to gain almost immediate feedback.

Replay

Each chapter ends with a replay. The replay can be used in a number of ways: as an introduction to the content of the chapter, as a guide through the progress of the chapter, as a reminder of the ideas integral to the chapter, or as a place to add your own thoughts. The replays are notes—visually accessible, verbally terse—rather like an index. The figure that is placed at the top of each replay illustrates how the five essential classroom components are interrelated within the envelope of the semester.

Professors

Review the continuum of teaching styles

- From teacher centered
- To student centered

Consider how these teaching styles

- Transfer knowledge
- Shape knowledge
- Develop skills
- Mold learners

Determine your own style

Consider and reconsider your approaches

Create a teaching portfolio

Create a course guide

Information

Is placed in teaching portfolios that are

- · Private
- · Personal
- · Flexible
- · Never complete

Is placed in teaching portfolios that include

- · What you teach
- · How you teach
- · What standards you use
- · Student feedback
- · Colleague comments
- · Changes you make
- · Ideas in progress

Is placed in course guides that

- · Reflect your teaching style
- · Map your course
- · Provide a connection
- · Encourage immediate student involvement

Is placed in course guides that include

- · An extended syllabus
- · Reading questions
- · Focus questions
- · Inventions of your choice

Students

Are cast in the role of

- · Containers
- · Clay
- · Travelers
- · Participants
- · Fellow learners

Benefit from

- Clarity of plan
- Variety
- Involvement
- Reinforcement

2

. . . .

Creating Magic in the Classroom

*Make no little plans; they have no magic to stir men's
blood.*
—Attributed to Hudson Burnham, 1846–1912

Vignette: On a cloudy day in early April, Professor Yamaguchi
began his introductory class in retailing with a recap of a story
that had recently been in the news. The incident centered around
a disruptive complaint brought by a customer who was infuriated
by the faulty tools sold to him at a local hardware store. During the
encounter, minor damage had been done to the store, a saleswoman
had been traumatized, the police had been called in, the tools—not
the store's own brand—had been thrown down on the counter and
new ones demanded. The problem that Professor Yamaguchi posed
to his class was, "Where do the responsibilities lie?" Peter, in the far
left-hand corner, shrugged in his down jacket; but Bernard, next to
him, remembered trying to return a can of paint that had dried up
after a day's use. Lee, in the first row, worked in a department store
and thought of last week when a particularly aggressive customer
would not be satisfied, no matter what. Three friends, who sat near
the middle of the room and who felt that they had been rooked on
a set of weights, turned toward each other, clear in their minds that
it was the store's responsibility; yet Angie, who had started her own
business recently, thought of the damage done to the store. The

class was silent as they waited for Professor Yamaguchi to tell them
The Answer so that they could write it down in their notes and
spout it back on the next test. But Professor Yamaguchi had not
asked his question in order to answer it himself. Instead, he shifted
his weight, smiled, shrugged, leaned toward the class, and waited.

It worked. The center three students twisted in their chairs;
Bernard spoke out; Angie loudly disagreed; others joined in; Professor Yamaguchi moved away from the front of the class and asked
another question; Lee spoke with conviction about difficult cus-
tomers as some classmates nodded in recognition; Michael commented that that particular brand of tools was well known to be
faulty and clearly it was the manufacturer's responsibility. The
period went by. In the far left-hand corner, Peter took off his down
jacket without even noticing that it was almost time to leave for
the next class. The classroom had come alive.

Discussion

On that April afternoon, a magical moment happened in Professor
Yamaguchi's class—a moment when the elements of the classroom
came together, when the instructor felt good, the students were
excited, and the information became important. What is this
moment about? What is happening with the instructor? What is
involved in the presentation of the material? What is going on with
the students? What has sparked the moment?

Csikszentmihalyi (1990) has studied the psychology of optimal
experience, focusing on the different types of inner experiences that
people feel make life worthwhile. He has found that the best
moments in a person's life tend to occur when the person's body or
mind is "stretched to its limits in a voluntary effort to accomplish
something difficult and worthwhile" (p. 3). Csikszentmihalyi
describes these optimal experiences using the concept of *flow*. A
"flow experience" is "the state in which people are so involved in
an activity that nothing else seems to matter; the experience itself

is so enjoyable that people will do it even at great cost, for the sheer sake of doing it" (p. 4). And so Peter shrugged off his down jacket—a first for him that semester. We cannot formulate this magic precisely, but it has been described as "elusive and mercurial, something felt rather than seen. However, we have all experienced magic in the form of a palpable sense of vitality that seems to energize everything and everyone in the classroom. Sometimes it's a bubbling, exuberant kind of energy. Other times it's a powerful, quiet kind of energy. Either kind transforms lessons into learning and creates the charged atmosphere in which we also become transformed. Our perceptions shift, and we comprehend significant things about the world outside us and the world inside us" (De Felice, 1989, p. 640).

When a flow experience, or a magical moment, occurs in a classroom filled with a teacher and a group of students, they draw together into a community of successful learners, and the information and the skills of that particular class change from being unknown and orphaned into being understood and owned. Magic ought not to be too stringently analyzed, however, because, after all, it is by its nature a happening. But happenings do not happen unless the surroundings are ready and unless a catalyst is present. If the professor has not forged a receptive environment, and if the professor does not provide appropriate catalysts, there will be no magical moment.

Let us first look, therefore, at what is involved in readying the classroom environment and then turn to discussing a number of possible catalysts. A thorough knowledge of one's subject and an awareness of the current research surrounding it are, of course, the foundation of all courses (Angelo, 1993; Creed, 1993). But subject proficiency is not enough. What are the principles behind the successful teaching of the content? Katz and Henry (1988), Angelo (1993), and Chickering and Gamson (1987) have each analyzed this question and made important suggestions. Katz and Henry list seven principles and Angelo fourteen principles that focus on how learning takes place in the classroom, and they isolate practices that facilitate learning. Chickering and Gamson focus on the seven "good practices" of undergraduate education.

Table 2.1 arranges these principles and practices to show their areas of commonality. It is interesting that four principles are common to all three lists and six principles are common to at least two of them: encouragement of communication among students and provision of an avenue for student-faculty interaction (A), tools for early and frequent feedback on learning success (B), a high expectation for student achievement (C), a vehicle for active rather than passive learning (D), a recognition of individual styles of learning (E), and an understanding that learning requires a great amount of focused time (F). These six principles are also reflected in the American Psychological Association's discussion of learner-centered psychological principles (1993).

Clearly, these principles for effective learning involve an interaction among the classroom components of professors, information, and students; but the responsibility for sparking that interplay varies. It is the professor's responsibility to initiate interaction with students (principle A) and, as Lowman (1984) suggests, establish different levels of interpersonal rapport. It is the professor who must provide early and frequent feedback (principle B) and maintain high expectations for student learning (principle C). It is also the professor who creates the environment for active learning and cooperation, but it is the student who must be willing to enter into the process of learning (principle D) and to commit the necessary time (principle F). Similarly, the professor needs to recognize and to appeal to different styles of learning, but students must try to discover and then make use of their own learning styles and strengths (principle E).

What is the energy that makes possible this transformation of lessons into learning? Katz and Henry (1988) argue that it is intense emotion. In *Turning Professors into Teachers*, they emphasize that this energy must come from both professors and students: "We have interviewed countless students who have told us that even in large

Table 2.1. Principles Behind Successful Teaching.

"Teacher's Dozen" (Angelo, 1993)	Basic Learning Principles (Katz & Henry, 1988)	Seven Principles for Good Practice in Undergraduate Education (Chickering & Gamson, 1987)
A. Interaction between teachers and learners is one of the most powerful factors in promoting learning; interaction among learners is another. (14)	A. Ability to inquire with other people. (4)	A. Good practice encourages student-faculty contact. (1) A. Good practice encourages cooperation among students. (2)
B. To learn well, learners need feedback on their learning, early and often; to become independent, they need to learn how to give themselves feedback. (7)	B. Participation. (5)	B. Good practice gives prompt feedback. (4)
C. High expectations encourage high achievement. (11)		C. Good practice communicates high expectations. (6)
D. Active learning is more effective than passive learning. (1)	D. Transformation of student passivity into active learning. (1)	D. Good practice encourages active learning. (3)

Table 2.1. Principles Behind Successful Teaching, *cont'd.*

"Teacher's Dozen" (Angelo, 1993)	Basic Learning Principles (Katz & Henry, 1988)	Seven Principles for Good Practice in Undergraduate Education (Chickering & Gamson, 1987)
E. Information organized in personally meaningful ways is more likely to be retained, learned, and used. (6)	E. Individualization. (2)	E. Good practice respects diverse talents and ways of learning. (7)
F. Mastering a skill or body of knowledge takes great amounts of time and effort. (9)		F. Good practice emphasizes time on track. (5)
Learning requires focused attention and awareness of the importance of what is to be learned. (2)	Process of inquiry. (3)	
Learning is more effective and efficient when learners have explicit, reasonable, positive goals and when their goals fit well with the teacher's goals. (3)	Support. (6)	

Table 2.1. Principles Behind Successful Teaching, *cont'd.*

"Teacher's Dozen" (Angelo, 1993)	Basic Learning Principles (Katz & Henry, 1988)	Seven Principles for Good Practice in Undergraduate Education (Chickering & Gamson, 1987)
To be remembered, new information must be meaningfully connected to prior knowledge; it must first be remembered in order to be learned. (4)	Recognition that learning is an intensely emotional experience. (7)	
Unlearning what is already known is often more difficult than learning new information. (5)		
The ways in which learners are assessed and evaluated powerfully affect the ways they study and learn. (8)		
Learning to transfer, to apply previous knowledge and skills to new contexts, requires a great deal of practice. (10)		

Table 2.1. Principles Behind Successful Teaching, *cont'd.*

"Teacher's Dozen" (Angelo, 1993)	Basic Learning Principles (Katz & Henry, 1988)	Seven Principles for Good Practice in Undergraduate Education (Chickering & Gamson, 1987)
To be most effective, teachers need to balance levels of intellectual challenge and instructional support. (12)		
Motivation to learn is alterable; it can be positively or negatively affected by the task, the environment, the teacher, and the learner. (13)		

Note: Capital letters are used to indicate related items; numbers in parentheses following the items indicate the placement of each item in the original list from which it was taken.

Source: Adapted from Angelo, 1993, pp. 3–13; Katz & Henry, 1988, pp. 6–7; Chickering & Gamson, 1987, pp. 3–7.

lecture courses the empathic attitude of the professor to them could make the difference of how much they wanted to learn. It is sad to realize how the fortuitous encounter in an introductory course with a noncaring or a hostile-aggressive teacher can turn students away from a subject matter—even the choice of a major—that they might otherwise have wanted to pursue" (p. 8).

Parker Palmer (1983) takes this approach a step farther and states that to "teach is to create a space" where students and pro-

fessors can be honest in expressing feelings and can then more easily recognize truths. Palmer states that "our feelings may be more
vital to truth than our minds, since our minds strive to analyze and
divide things while our feelings reach for relatedness" (p. 85). For
a magical moment to happen, therefore, the connections among
professor, information, and students must be not only vital and
interactive but also emotionally charged (compare Katz and Henry's
seventh principle).

As professors at a community college, we often see students for
whom the magic in learning is dead. These are students who have
met with failure in the earlier years of their education (Cohen &
Brawer, 1989). They frequently associate academic settings with feelings of inadequacy and disappointment. For these students, learning
has been a struggle. Our college, or a similar one, may be their last
chance to feel comfortable in an educational environment. It is this
challenge—the last-ditch stand to reignite a zest for learning and to
reinforce a belief in success—that has helped to make community
colleges great centers of teaching. But community colleges are not
alone in the struggle to unlock the processes of learning for an often
underprepared and frequently disillusioned student body. Other colleges and universities are faced with the same challenges. It is essential that we make it possible for our students to gain confidence in
themselves as learners. Only then will Peter be able to take off his
coat and Professor Yamaguchi's class be ready to carry a discussion.

Leo Buscaglia (1982) quotes Nikos Kazantzakis's observation
that "ideal teachers are those who use themselves as bridges over
which they invite their students to cross, then having facilitated
their crossing, joyfully collapse, encouraging them to create bridges
of their own" (p. vii). For a brief, shining moment, Professor Yamaguchi was able to create such a bridge and to establish a sense of
magic during one of his classes. Can he expect such magic to happen repeatedly throughout the ebb and flow of the semester? All
classroom experiences are shaped by a rhythm inherent in the pro-

gression of a semester, and all professors must work within this time constraint as they ready the classroom environment.

In 1970, Mann and others studied what they labeled "the natural [emotional] history of the college classroom" (p. 243). We have conducted a similar although far more informal study. Our colleagues readily acknowledge the existence of an emotional rhythm in a semester; in fact, they are relieved to hear that others also feel its presence, but they have not often considered plotting it. Yet, as they describe their class histories, these histories consistently follow the pattern discovered by Mann and others.

Mann and others found that there is a typical emotional progression of a college class throughout a semester. As a class begins, the possibilities are vast. Energies and expectations are high, and professors and students are anxious about the new beginning. Even experienced professors enter the classroom with concerns about being accepted and successful with their students. Students start the class hopeful that it will be their best class yet. Inevitably, as the semester progresses, assignments, tests, and outside commitments clash. As the initial high energies are taxed, a vague feeling of discontent surfaces in the classroom environment. Professors can begin to doubt the effectiveness of their teaching, and students can become overwhelmed, questioning the applicability of the course. As we looked at this rhythm of the semester, we too consistently came up against such low moments. In recognition of the fate of the crew in "The Rime of the Ancient Mariner," we named them the doldrums—a shared drop in morale (discussed further in Chapter Five).

As professors, we are particularly influenced by these down periods, for when the course begins to drag, we realize that as the masters of ceremonies, we are ultimately responsible. As our stress increases, we search for ways to relieve it. Despite all that we have discussed— a mastery of one's subject, the thoughtful use of teaching principles, an understanding of the emotional energies of the classroom, and an awareness of the low points of the semester—magic cannot happen when the master of ceremonies is working under excessive stress. The classroom environment is not fully ready. What are some of the sources of this stress, this inhibitor of magical moments?

Gmelch (1987) reviewed data from the National Faculty Stress Research Project to identify factors that contribute to faculty stress. He listed excessive tension among students as one of the factors. Again, the rhythms of the semester come into play. Particular time periods are devastating to the community spirit in a classroom: the four- to six-week doldrums documented by Mann and others, the return from spring break, and the days before the end of the semester are likely to trigger increased student tension. Yet if both faculty and students recognize the ups and downs of the semester and learn to work within them, the level of stress in the classroom can be reduced and a sense of common purpose can replace it. One way to combat these down periods is to confront them head on. If a professor walks into his or her class and announces at the start, "Hey, this a down period for us all; it's almost midsemester; it's rained five days in a row; and we all feel at loose ends," the students may be jolted into understanding that they are not alone, that this is a low point for everyone. Misery loves company, and the realization that it is a shared misery often results in a united effort to dispel it.

If talking about a down period is not appropriate or not your style, then why not try a lecture, a lab, a video, or another activity that breaks into the doldrums by changing the pace? Gmelch (1987) recommends noting the high payoff (HIPOs) and low payoff (LOPOs) activities of each course and then injecting a HIPO when needed. He also points out that in addition to down times, another factor of time—limited time—contributes to faculty stress. The fixed number of weeks of a semester places constraints not only on the daily interactions within the classroom, but also upon the goals that the professor has set for the course. A professor is doomed if he or she plans to cover too much. As the weeks go by, we often hear professors worry that they will not be able to cover everything and that they are unable to stay within the syllabus-listed course outline. Yet many students look at the syllabus as a contract to be fulfilled, willy-nilly. As a result, the environment grows tense, colored by a feeling from both professor and students alike that there is never enough time. Once again, Gmelch has a suggestion. He encourages faculty to make more use of planning, organization, and time-management techniques: to write lists, to draw flowcharts, and to keep records (see Gmelch, 1993, for additional suggestions).

Finally, Gmelch (1987) lists excessively high self-expectations as a cause of inhibiting stress for faculty. He points out that these high self-expectations are self-defeating, for they are closely linked to a faculty member's identity as a successful teacher. Every professor is known to students by his or her course. If a professor's expectations about the information that it is possible to cover within the time frame of a course are unattainable or the number of students expected to be excited by the topic is unrealistic, that particular piece of his or her identity is threatened, teaching suffers, stress skyrockets, and the classroom environment around the professor tenses. And as Whitman, Spendlove, and Clark (1986), Greenberg (1987), and others have documented, accomplishable course goals and realistic expectations not only empower the professors, they also reassure the students, thus readying the classroom climate for magic.

In his book *The Skillful Teacher* (1990), Stephen Brookfield discusses techniques for surviving the experience of college teaching. He emphasizes the importance of developing a personal vision of teaching, stating that "until you begin to trust your inner voice, until you accept the possibility that your instincts, intuitions, and insights often possess as much validity as those of experts in the field, and until you recognize that in the contexts in which you work *you* are the expert, there is a real danger that a profoundly debilitating sense of inadequacy may settle on you" (p. 14).

Throughout this book, we encourage you to find your own vision; to consider your instincts, intuitions, and insights as the semester progresses; and to create your own individual classroom environment.

Application

As we have discussed earlier, the classroom is composed in large part of three interactive components: professors, information, and students. Each of these components is a complete entity with its own characteristics, structures, and requirements, but each component is also shaped by the nature and the needs of the others. To depict this interdependence, we have drawn arrows between the components, making them double pointed in order to stress that the interaction flows both ways. To complete the image, we have surrounded the components and their arrows with structures that represent two aspects common to all courses: the physical space of the classroom and the envelope of the time frame. Although the actual components and the classroom space differ with each class, the envelope remains a constant. It unifies the teaching experience (see Nash, 1991).

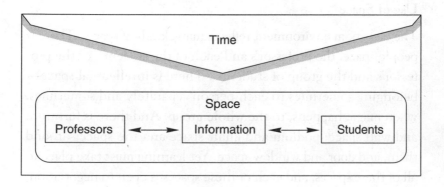

Ideally, each of these elements, except calendar time, will expand during the semester beyond its original form. In each course, the professor must reach out in different ways to teach a diverse group of students; the content must move from the territory of the unknown into a body of knowledge and skills experienced by the students; the students must listen, react, absorb, respond, and learn; and the metaphorical walls of the classroom must come down, freeing those who sat within them.

How does this change and growth come about? Magic is one of the ways that it happens, and when it happens, it happens for the whole. It creates a sense of soul within the classroom: boundaries are stretched, connections are made, knowledge and skills are newly owned. What will spark a magical moment in a receptive environment? What are the catalysts?

We have used the fishbone (Figure 2.1) here as a visual way in which to organize our discussion of possible catalysts for magic in a receptive classroom environment. A complete discussion of the nature of each of the ribs is impossible, for that would be a volume unto itself, but there is space to mention a few important resources for specific ideas and to describe some techniques that can be adapted and applied to many classrooms.

Use of Space

The classroom environment reflects many kinds of spaces. There is people space: the professor's and each of the student's or the professor's and the group of students'. There is intellectual space—belonging sometimes to each person separately and sometimes, when magic happens, to the whole group. And there is furniture and wall space: podium and chair space and the spaces around them, and door and window space. Yet learning must take place in all of these spaces, and each of these spaces is open to negotiation, to manipulation, and to ownership. How the spaces are used, as well as who owns them, can affect the speed and the success of that learning. We professors may not often think of taking the time to consider all these spaces, but it is worth the time, for a change in the use and the ownership of space can trigger a magical moment.

The typical classroom arranged with chairs in rows that face forward toward either a podium or a table sets the stage for the professor to be the focus of visual and auditory attention. In this

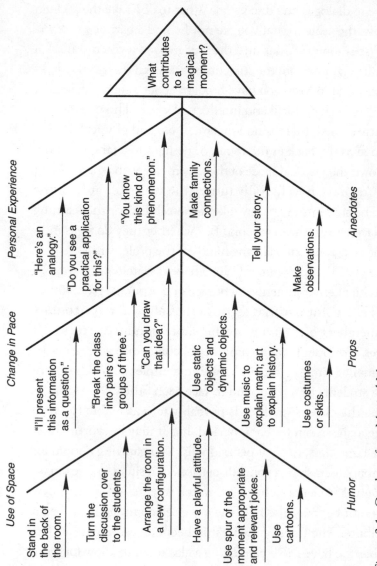

Figure 2.1. Catalysts for a Magical Moment.

Note: The Ishikawa Fishbone Diagram (1986) is a Total Quality Management tool that encourages creative participation and is generally used as a method for exploring the causes behind a problem. First, the problem is named and printed within the arrowhead of the fish. The primary types of causes are then listed and connected by lines to the backbone, thus creating the skeleton of the fish. Finally, the people involved in discovering the causes for the problem and therefore ultimately in arriving at possible solutions brainstorm about the contributing factors behind the primary causes, attaching their ideas to the appropriate ribs.

configuration, the professor owns the entire space of the classroom in that he or she controls what is said. Excellent for a lecture, not as conducive to dialogue and discussion. What to do? Take the podium away, move the table so that you are not behind a barrier when you begin a discussion; walk out into the students' area when you ask a question. If you move into the students' space, even though the desks are still arranged in rows, you have brought about a subtle change in ownership of both physical and intellectual space. Those spaces are now jointly owned; there is no longer a visual and physical barrier. If you move to the back of the room, or perhaps to a far corner, the students own the physical space of the classroom, even when you are talking. You have now literally turned the tables (or at least the chairs). The students must now take responsibility for the learning taking place within the classroom. But whether they do so as individuals or as a group still is in the hands of the professor.

Steele (1973) and Sommer (1969) have researched the ways in which physical environments encourage or discourage group interaction. They point out that settings that allow for eye contact among members of a group are far more conducive to social exchanges. Consider breaking up lines of chairs into a large circle, several smaller circles, or a circle within a circle. If the chairs are fixed, ask students to turn around to face each other.

Unless the class is small, it is probably unreasonable to try to rearrange a classroom for each period, but it may be worthwhile, even in a large class, to try it occasionally. Reorganizing a room for a large-group discussion, a panel discussion, or a simulation exercise not only gives students a chance to watch interactions from a new vantage point but may also help the more reluctant members begin to contribute. The lines of ownership become less apparent, less rigid. When we have tried rearranging a classroom to allow for more informal contact, students who typically did not readily move verbally into the communication spaces of the classroom began to talk; perhaps hesitantly, but they started. The change in the physical pattern of the class seemed to encourage students to change their personal patterns and to open the door to that magical moment that engenders a new learning situation.

In the poem "Halfway Down," A. A. Milne (1952, p. 83) wrote about space:

> Halfway down the stairs
> Is a stair
> Where I sit.
> There isn't any
> Other stair
> Quite like
> It.

When a student walks into a class on the first day, he or she selects a seat, and it becomes "the chair where I sit." Rearranging that chair's space by turning it around or moving it into a group, changes the nature of that chosen space. Asking students to leave their chairs and to move across the room for a discussion, or even asking students to stand up, alters the chosen spaces. Renner (1983) emphasizes that we should not limit our use of space just because of the size or shape of a particular classroom, pointing out that many possibilities exist for new and inventive ways to arrange the space, even in a small classroom. Renner supports his ideas with useful diagrams of desks and chairs rearranged into long tables, circles, semicircles, squares, and small groups (see also Meyers & Jones, 1993).

Use of Humor

In *Playful Activities for Powerful Presentations*, Bruce Williamson (1993) quotes Albert Schweitzer as saying, "I know of no other manner of dealing with great tasks, than as play" (p. 138). When used thoughtfully, a playful attitude on the part of the professor can help to improve communication with students and can serve to reactivate that sense of wonder that Schweitzer reveres. But humor must be used with care so that it does not move into the realm of sarcasm and thus intrude into the personal spaces of the students with ad hominem remarks. Joel Goodman (1992), director of the Humor Project in Sarasota Springs, New York, suggests the use of the "AT&T" test when using humor in the classroom. His AT&T test asks whether a remark is "appropriate, timely, and tasteful." Goodman also emphasizes the importance of relating classroom humor to the subject matter at hand.

Research into the effectiveness of humor in teaching college classes has been limited, but a recent review by Edwards and Gibboney (1992) states that the use of humor "correlates positively to perceived appeal, effectiveness, and delivery" (p. 1) of presentations. However, Edwards and Gibboney point out this is true for male instructors only. "The jury is still out on how female instructors' use of humor influences students" (p. 23). In their review of the research, Edwards and Gibboney cite fifteen principles for humor in the college classroom. Many of these principles, such as using humor to help build a sense of class unity and to increase comprehension of lecture material, are supported in other sources (Civikly, 1986; Loomans & Kolberg, 1993). Some of the principles, however, such as avoiding humor in tests or in anxiety-provoking situations, are not supported in our own experiences or in work that considers the healing power of humor (Klein, 1989). In our psychology and literature classes, we have incorporated cartoons into directions and tests, used humorously worded questions on exams, and written an AT&T joke on the board before a test, all with consistently positive results. Our students, too, have contributed their own humorous comments on exams. At the end of the course, they have expressed appreciation for the infusion of a lighthearted perspective to break the tension of the evaluation process.

Humor is effective, however, only if the humorist is comfortable with it. It cannot become a part of a class setting unless it fits with the style and the personality of the instructor. Goodman (1992) suggests that teachers work toward what he calls a "prepared flexibility" (p. 20), in which they think ahead to anticipate the situations where humor will be helpful. In one of our seminars, a professor of nursing talked about the difficulty of helping students through their first experiences with giving injections. She knew that the students worried about the importance of the task, the fears of their patients, and their likelihood of messing up, and so they took the practice all too seriously and could not start. Their intensity and anxiety were interfering with their performance. She remembered humorous incidents from her own training and realized how much these events had helped her to cope. By telling some of these past, often colorful personal anecdotes, she was able to help students laugh and relax and begin the process of mastering how to give a painless injection. In this way, she introduced into her classroom the prepared flexibility that Goodman discusses, making appropriate and timely humor a successful element of a presentation.

The primary benefit of the use of humor in the classroom may be the creation of an environment in which students feel free to take risks and to have fun. Comedian Steve Allen captures this idea effectively: "As I look back at the years of my formal education—sketchy as it was—I find that three teachers stand out in my recollection. What they all had in common was a good sense of humor. Whether they taught their subjects any better than their relatively humorless equivalents I don't really know, but their geniality and their general good nature set a social context within which I felt comfortable" (Loomans & Kolberg, 1993, p. ix).

Use of Props

If you walk into an elementary, middle, or high school classroom, you will find a variety of props used to enrich the classes that are taught there: boxes; bulletin boards; places to work with tools, clay, pens, or computers; flowers to smell; books and cassettes to read or listen to. But college classrooms are generally bare: four walls with a board and an occasional window, few if any pictures or books, often not even a map, and no supplementary objects with which to expand upon a point. True, many professors use audiovisual tapes and discs in their classes, but how about simple props, concrete objects to illustrate non–lab based discussions? Such tools may well be seen as either distracting or irrelevant to the college classroom environment. Yet props make a number of important connections: they momentarily change the pace of the class, they soften tension, they add humor, and they enlarge the sensory experience of a course.

Research in the area of accelerated learning (Rose, 1985; Jensen, 1988) states that each person has a dominant sensory system that is either visual, auditory, or kinesthetic. According to the accelerated learning approach, individuals prefer to communicate or to learn new information using their dominant sensory system. In K–12 classrooms, the variety of teaching materials typically allows for processing in a visual, auditory, or kinesthetic manner. Yet in most college classrooms, with the exceptions of labs, the focus is primarily on auditory and visual modalities. The addition of concrete objects to illustrate ideas can help to incorporate the kinesthetic modality, as well as to enhance the visual and auditory presentations. The addition of props can also break up the monotony of the classroom, relieve the doldrums, and add an opportunity for playfulness and imagination. Suppose that Professor Yamaguchi had pulled a bunch of tools out of his briefcase at the start of the class and thrown them down on the desk, much as the enraged customer had at the local hardware store. Would this action have added emotion and created focus? Would the class have leaned forward into the common space of the classroom and Peter have taken off his coat at the beginning of class? Possibly. Possibly it would have been a way into a magical moment.

Thus, by connecting an abstract and complex concept to a concrete and often mundane reality, props are often able to open up the process of understanding. Each student in a literature class was asked to bring in a kitchen utensil that he or she particularly valued for its form or for its textures rather than for its usefulness, and each student was asked to share why he or she liked it. The tactile presence of a beautifully shaped Lucite ladle contrasted with the equally beautiful, though crudely carved, wooden spoon that another student brought stimulated a discussion of poetic form in a way otherwise not possible.

There are countless ways that props can be incorporated into a classroom setting. When she begins a discussion of cause and effect, an English professor sets up and topples a line of dominoes and then removes one domino and tries again. She claims that after students see that the chain fails to fall when one domino (cause) is omitted, they never forget the importance of a carefully constructed causal chain. A math professor hands out bags of M&Ms to small groups as part of an exercise to calculate probability—in this case, the probability of obtaining a certain color—and then, of course, the students add another more playful experience: they eat the props. History professors play music or display art from a specific time period to capture the atmosphere of that time. Professors from all disciplines use costumes or skits to illustrate experiences and ideas in a more concrete way.

Use of Anecdotes

Work by Peter Frederick (1990) has focused on the power of stories, or anecdotes, to make connections in the classroom. He suggests that the use of students' personal narratives can provide an effective way of acknowledging student thoughts, feelings, and experiences throughout the course. When students are asked to elaborate on their insights by sharing personal anecdotes, the students feel valued, they are recognized, their space is vital, their previous experiences are credited, and then, if the stories are pertinent, the classroom community comes together in recognition and appreciation.

In an interview for *Common Boundary*, the writer van der Post discusses the dearth of community, the serious alienation and isolation that he feels exists in individuals and in our society because of a lack of stories. He states: "The more collectivist and materialistic man becomes, the more the storytelling pattern is reduced. You see it in the increase of world unrest. It's not the sort of unrest one has in wartime, but it's a deep unrest in the spirit of man. People don't know who they are. They've lost a sense of identity. The person who still has his story never feels that he is unknown. He always feels he's a person; he's known and he knows" (Simpkinson, 1993, p. 35).

In his autobiographical book *The Call of Stories: Teaching and the Moral Imagination* (1989), Robert Coles points out that we all have stories that need to be heard. He looks back to one of his many conversations with fellow physician and poet William Carlos Williams, who reminded Coles that "their story, yours and mine—it's what we all carry with us on this trip we take, and we owe it to each other to respect our stories and learn from them" (p. 30). Coles elaborates on this point by suggesting that in our human interactions it behooves us to elicit stories and then to listen carefully and to comprehend as fully as possible (p. 25).

Many students in college courses complain about a sense of being a number and an unimportant component in a classroom. By incorporating stories or personal anecdotes into a class and encouraging students to know themselves through their stories and the stories of peers, the space for "obedience to truth" that Palmer describes (1983, p. 88) as essential for a productive educational environment may happen.

The power of anecdote to enhance the human connection between faculty and students is not limited to the students' stories. If professors are comfortable in sharing their own stories "we all carry with us," the class will become more immediate. As it did in the nursing class, a story about how a professor has coped with a difficult subject or skill or even an unreasonable teacher gives a struggling student a new perspective and a vital sense of hope. But anecdotes are not for everyone, for not every one of us is a storyteller. There are, however, other catalysts for magic that bring the world into the classroom environment and dignify the students' experiences.

Use of Personal Experiences

In order to become active learners, students need to develop a personal commitment to the process of learning. In order to develop this personal commitment, students need to be shown the links between the everyday events of their lives and the ideas and information in their classes. Boehrer (1990–1991) states that "without engagement in the problem, without some personal sense of investment in reaching a solution, the individual is poorly motivated to withstand the disturbance that accompanies genuine learning" (p. 2).

By consistently encouraging students to make connections between the abstract material of a course and the concrete material of their lives, professors can open the way for even reluctant students to invest in the learning experience. When students discover a connection between the course and their own knowledge, they have involved themselves; they are part of a flow experience and the classroom can become filled with that "palpable sense of vitality that seems to energize everything and everyone" (De Felice, 1989, p. 640).

We witnessed examples of this vitality during a semester in which we were participant observers in each other's classes. As all of us discussed "The Rime of the Ancient Mariner" in Introduction to Poetry and the need of the Ancient Mariner to retell his tale, a student raised his hand and said that was just like Harry introducing himself at an AA meeting and then telling his story. Poetry had become real for that student and for his classmates. They will remember the albatross. As we all discussed characteristics of the Type A personality in Abnormal Psychology class, a student remarked that his boss, Mr. O'Neil, talked rapidly, was impatient with little mistakes, and had blown up at Alice when she had bent a corner of her timecard. Suddenly, the student understood his Type A boss a little better. He may stay on at that job and may be a better boss when his time comes.

Such moments in the classroom when the students link the material to their personal lives vividly confirm Cantor's view (1953) that we must recognize that it is not the professors' mastery of the material but the student's struggle with it that is the issue; we must remember to keep the students' experience, not simply our own involvement, at the center of the process.

Use of Changes in Pace

At some time, all of us have wanted a change in pace. Whether it was because we had become mired in routine or because the material was not connecting or because we had that day faced a class that just did not seem to come together, or whatever the cause was, we needed a change in the rhythm of that class. At this time, each of us longed for the catalyst that would create magic, that would make the dullness go away and change the class from negative to positive.

Visitors to Disney theme parks are familiar with the use of surprise and novelty in attractions. At these parks, visitors are transported to fantasy worlds where anything is possible and openness to new experiences is a given. You may not be able to create a Disney setting in your classroom, nor may you want to, but you can imitate Disney's success a bit and think about how you can present ideas using new, imaginative, and creative approaches. Ask students to draw an idea rather than to describe it verbally. Ask students to worry a problem together and reach a joint solution. Ask students to come up to the board and list their questions. Ask students to use clay to create a model of a system.

You could also ask students to use a fishbone diagram to investigate cause and effect. We have found that this critical thinking tool can spark magical moments in a number of ways. For instance, in a class that has found working in small groups difficult, try handing each group a blank or partially blank fishbone diagram. The whole class may already have worked together on a possible arrow-head question, but the labeling of the ribs is now the responsibility of the groups. Or a professor, anticipating long silences during a dis-cussion of a difficult chapter could assign a fishbone diagram of the chapter, or perhaps a part of the chapter, to each student. The stu-dents will then come to class fully armed and ready to talk or at least to ask questions, and the professor can begin the class's discussion with the students' interpretations. Writing instructors have used the fishbone diagram as one method of helping students understand the logical divisions of an outline, and individual students, finding this method helpful, have used it as a personal review tool. Professor Yamaguchi could have used it to involve all his retailing students in an active discussion of the causes behind the hardware store inci-dent, or of the reasons for the reactions of each of the participants, or even of ways in which to avoid future similar incidents.

For us, the fishbone diagram sparked a magical moment in our seminar with colleagues from the Moscow State Pedagogical Uni-versity. After three intense, often exhausting days and an inter-rupting weekend, we had hit one of those stress-inducing low moments. We knew that we needed a change of pace to revitalize the sense of community that had been begun in our seminar, and we knew that we needed a review tool that would involve us all. Before the beginning of the final day, we hung a giant fishbone dia-gram on one of the classroom walls, labeled the ribs with the major themes that we had discussed so far, handed out Post-Its, and invited the Soviets to write their ideas in Cyrillic on the Post-Its or directly on the fishbone itself. It worked. Ideas were shared, enlarged upon, and cemented; participants argued, laughed, and redesigned. The fishbone became covered with two kinds of alphabets, and the room was filled with both Russian and English.

There are a number of manuals available that describe other novel ways to present material, among them *deBono's Thinking Course* (1985), which includes a series of thinking techniques that can be adapted to any subject matter. For example, in an approach called Plus, Minus, Interesting (PMI), participants list what is positive, negative, and interesting about a particular idea. The technique is a simple one that can be adapted to any setting and can stimulate brainstorming when students are not open to considering possibilities. James Adams's book *Conceptual Blockbusting* (1986), which contains suggestions for dealing with perceptual, emotional, cultural, and environmental blocks, includes exercises on visual thinking and the use of other sensory languages. And Herbert Leff's *Playful Perception* (1985) encourages the reader to develop new ways of perceiving and thinking about the world through a variety of activities and exercises. In one of the activities, Leff suggests that people try to view everyday things as if they were art exhibits.

It is true that activities involving creative ways of viewing a topic are a change of pace and are useful for students, but they are also a change of pace for faculty members who are facing a monotony of days. Indeed, the greatest value of pace-changing activities may be in helping faculty regain their faith in teaching—their original sense of wonder and enthusiasm in a course that they are now teaching for the thirtieth time. By standing back and looking through a different lens, professors may recapture a sense of magic for themselves. Even Professor Fellows might well feel the debilitating symptoms of burnout fading away.

Replay

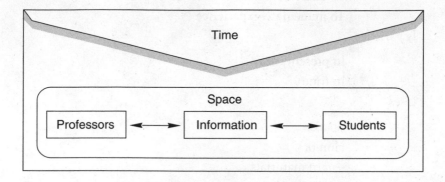

Space

Should offer new learning contexts:

- · Move around the room
- · Rearrange the furniture
- · Group the students

Professors

Freshen outlook

Allow emotion, generate emotion

Diminish unnecessary stress

Encourage participation

Make use of the classroom

Vary tone with humor

Consider props

Tell stories, ask for stories

Change pace

Information

Stretches horizons

Makes connections

- To other bodies of knowledge
- To immediate experience

Is varied

- In presentation
- In tone

Uses

- Space
- Humor
    In materials
    In tests, exams
- Props
- Anecdotes
- Personal experiences
- Changes in pace

Students

Discover their strengths

Take risks

Join in

Connect their experiences

Tell their own stories

Stand up for their opinions

3

. . . .

Stalking the Superior Syllabus

> *I wish he would explain his explanation.*
> —Lord Byron, *Don Juan*

V*ignette:* It was Wednesday, September 6, the first day of classes. By 10:58, Professor Sanchez's class in Room 34 of the Social Science Building was nearly full. Students had climbed the three flights of stairs—the elevator was broken—opened the door which Professor Sanchez had adjusted so that it would shut quietly after them, taken the syllabus (Exhibit 3.1) from the neat pile that he had stacked next to the podium, and found a seat. The class was Government 216, Constitutional Law; it satisfied the requirement for a social science elective.

Natasha arrived early and chose a front-row seat. She had selected Government 216 because it would complete her core requirement. Still, the title of the course seemed worrisomely broad, and so she turned to the two-page syllabus for further explanation. She was disappointed to find that the course description given in the syllabus was the same as the one printed in the college catalogue. It was very general. Natasha was uncomfortable with generality and uncertainty; she liked information to be specific and rules to be absolutely clear. She read on. Good, a course outline was included. That was helpful, but unfortunately, it was arranged by assignments from the textbook and listed only chapter numbers and no dates. The outline did not name the specific topics to be covered. The assignments included two papers and case briefs, but what were their topics, were they going to require extensive research, and how did each one fit into the grade? Natasha hoped that Professor Sanchez would explain all this right away, today, so that she could understand the direction of the course.

Brian, a government major, had also taken a seat near the front of the room, but his reason for taking the course was different from Natasha's. He had talked to a number of friends who reported that Gov 216 was a demanding course that went beyond memorization, and he was happy about that. The course also filled a time slot that he wanted to fill, at a time convenient for him. He had to leave for his job by noon each day. Brian needed a good grade, yet he did not have too much time to give to this class. The shortness of the syllabus reassured him. He turned to the bottom of the first page to check out the grading system. Two papers and a couple of tests were listed, but it was not clear when they were due or how much they would count. Unlike Natasha, he was not overly worried about the topics for the papers, the professor would probably change them as the course went along, anyway. Brian was, however, concerned about the form and the length of the papers; he had to plan his calendar now.

Thon was excited about the topic of Government 216. Born in Cambodia, he had been ten when his family had immigrated to Lowell, Massachusetts. The adjustment had been difficult, but now, at twenty-five, Thon felt comfortable in the college environment. He had had some personal experience with other legal systems and wanted very much to be clear about the American Constitution. He looked forward to a variety of assignments and especially to the class discussions that he expected to follow. As he read over the syllabus, the skeleton of the course seemed clear enough to him—the prerequisites, the catalogue course description, the required text, the attendance policy, the assignments with chapter numbers (though no titles), and the written assignments, although they were not specific. But when he searched the syllabus for some insight into the style of the professor, he could find no indication. Thon became concerned that the class might be as dry as the syllabus.

Alicia was returning to college from a career in business. She was an outstanding student, with a 3.9 grade point average, yet during the opening days of the semester, she was always uneasy. She could fulfill the requirements of the course; she was certain of that. And just as the other three students were clear about their personal reasons for taking this course, Alicia knew hers. While Natasha wanted an interesting course that completed her core requirements, Brian needed a government course in the right time slot, and Thon wanted to expand his understanding of the philosophy of the Constitution, Alicia's reasons went further. She had been a part of the workplace, seen legal situations that she had been uncomfortable with, and now knew that in order to be clear about one's rights one must know the law. But to gain as much from a course as she wanted, Alicia needed to understand the purpose of the course— the professor's objectives, goals, and expectations.

As she scanned the syllabus, Alicia was not reassured. The brief listing of the course objectives was content specific; no skills were mentioned. The professor's goals were not discussed. Alicia reasoned that a syllabus is a professor-designed guide to a course and serves as an initial opportunity to understand the soul of that course. Yet the nature of Government 216 was unclear to her. There was no personal connection evident in the syllabus. Alicia worried that she might have to find another course.

Exhibit 3.1. Professor Sanchez's Original Syllabus.

Constitutional Law, Government 216—Victor Sanchez
3 Credits; EN 1103, required; EN 1105, preferred
Office Hours: M–F, 9:30–10:30, Social Science Bldg., Rm. 39

Course Description: Case analysis of the development of federalism, the separation of powers, and the role of federal and state courts in constitutional development and contemporary control.

Course Objectives: To familiarize you with the roles the
                       federal and state constitutions play in

the administration of criminal justice.

To examine the concept of federalism among the states and federal government, as well as the separation of powers among the various branches of government.

To understand defendants' constitutional rights.

To examine the laws that enforce and protect these rights.

Required Text: John Smith and Jacqueline Schwartz, *Constitutional Law,* 3rd edition (New York: Legal Publishing, 1993).

Grading:

Papers (2)	35%
Case Briefs	5%
Tests	30%
Participation	5%
Final Exam	25%

Attendance: If you miss more than three successive classes, or a total of four classes for the semester, the result can be a diminished course grade, or even failure.

Course Outline:	Date	Assignment
	Week 1	Introduction and Chapter 1
	Week 2	Chapter 2
	Week 3	Chapters 2 & 3
	Week 4	Chapter 3
	Week 5	Chapter 4
	Week 6	Chapter 4
	Week 7	Chapter 5
	Spring Break	
	Week 8	Chapter 6
	Week 9	Chapter 7
	Week 10	Chapters 7 & 8
	Week 11	Chapter 8
	Week 12	Chapter 9
	Week 13	Chapters 9 & 10
	Week 14	Chapter 10
	Week 15	Semester Review

Discussion

Natasha, Brian, Thon, and Alicia enter Professor Sanchez's course with different needs and interests. Each, however, has specific concerns about the syllabus that may influence his or her continued attendance in class. Professor Sanchez is prepared for class on the first day with his neat stack of syllabi, but is he ready for the cognitive diversity represented by such students as Natasha, Brian, Thon, and Alicia? What information about adult development would be helpful for Professor Sanchez as he considers ways to clarify his syllabus so that students will connect to and commit to his course from day one?

William Perry began to answer this question in his classic study of adult development that examined how students change during the college years. Perry (1970) interviewed male undergraduates at Harvard during the 1960s and arrived at nine developmental positions that depict intellectual and ethical development throughout the undergraduate experience. In the late 1970s, Belenky, Clinchy, Goldberger, and Tarule (1986) began to interview women from diverse academic institutions and family agencies to consider how Perry's developmental scheme fit with the experiences of women. More recently, research by Baxter Magolda (1992) at Miami University in Ohio has focused on intellectual development in college and has included interviews with both male and female undergraduates from the freshman year to the year following graduation. The developmental models generated by all these studies show definite patterns and trends in the ways that students change during the college experience. Although the theorists differ somewhat in their explanations, they describe similar general patterns of developmental stages that students experience. These stages are simplified and summarized in Table 3.1. In our discussion, we use the developmental scheme developed by Baxter Magolda (1992), because the sample upon which it was based includes both male and female students.

Baxter Magolda found that the majority of freshmen in her study (68 percent) were in the stage of absolute knowing, while the majority of juniors (83 percent) and seniors (80 percent) were in the stage of transitional knowing. In the year following graduation, 57 percent of the former students had reached the stage of inde-

Table 3.1. Summary of Research on Student Development.

Stages of Adult Development (Perry, 1970)	Stages of Adult Development (Belenky, Clinchy, Goldberger, & Tarule, 1986)	Stages of Adult Development (Baxter Magolda, 1992)
Dualism. Knowledge is seen in true-false, good-bad dichotomies. Authorities have "The Answer."	*Received knowledge*. Women do not have their own "voice." They see themselves as receiving knowledge from external authority but are not able to create knowledge on their own.	*Absolute knowing*. Absolute answers exist in all areas of knowledge. Students use receiving or mastery patterns in their approaches to learning.
Multiplicity. Students begin to recognize that the world may not be divided dichotomously into right and wrong elements. Certainty may exist in a few select areas, but very little is known conclusively.	*Subjective knowledge*. Truth and knowledge are conceived as personal and private. People "know" things subjectively. Students may become anti-intellectual and distrust scientific areas.	*Transitional knowing*. Knowledge can be separated into certain and uncertain categories. Students use interpersonal or impersonal patterns in their approaches to knowing.
Contextual relativism. Students gain the ability to see knowledge in the context of a particular situation. A student applies rules of adequacy and evaluation not only to opinions of others but to judgments of self.	*Procedural knowledge*. Students become invested in learning. They apply objective procedures for analyzing and evaluating information (separate knowing), or they try to understand another person's perspective	*Independent knowing*. Knowledge is open to many interpretations. Students use inter-individual or individual patterns in dealing with knowledge.

Table 3.1. Summary of Research on Student Development, *cont'd.*

Stages of Adult Development (Perry, 1970)	Stages of Adult Development (Belenky, Clinchy, Goldberger, & Tarule, 1986)	Stages of Adult Development (Baxter Magolda, 1992)
To make meaning of different choices it is necessary to narrow down possibilities.	by relating ideas to personal events and meanings (connected knowing).	
Commitment within relativism. Students comprehend that truth is relative and that they must make decisions based on their own values and sense of identity.	*Constructed knowledge.* Students view knowledge as contextual. They see themselves as creators of knowledge, and they value both objective and subjective strategies for knowing.	*Contextual knowing.* Individuals create their own perspectives by judging evidence in a context.

Source: Adapted from Perry, 1970; Belenky, Clinchy, Goldberger, & Tarule, 1986; Baxter Magolda, 1992.

pendent knowing, and 12 percent the stage of contextual knowing (pp. 70–72). The earlier studies of Perry (1970) and of Belenky, Clinchy, Goldberger, and Tarule (1986) show similar patterns.

It is important for professors to be aware of these patterns of development if they are to gain more insight into the frustration and the confusion that students may be experiencing in the classroom. It is even more critical for professors to create learning materials that not only will engage students who are at different stages of development but also will foster thinking at increasingly complex levels. Baxter Magolda organized her findings and the comments of students at each of the four levels of cognition into a table (Table 3.2) to present student suggestions about ways professors could improve six areas of the classroom experience.

Table 3.2. Students' Advice for Curricular Education.

	Absolute Knowing	Transitional Knowing	Independent Knowing	Contextual Knowing
Professor's attitudes	Demonstrate helpfulness	Relate to and demonstrate care for students	Treat students as equals	Engage in collegial relationships with students
Professor-student interaction	Provide opportunity to know professor	Engage in positive interactions with students	Establish genuine relationships with students	Engage in collegial relationships with students
Teaching strategies	Make classroom active	Get students involved	Connect learning to real life	Create opportunities for mutual responsibility Look at the "big picture"
Classroom structure	Make classroom relational	Build in peer involvement	Create opportunities for independence, critical thinking, and peer collaboration	Create opportunities for interdependency
Evaluation	Help student understand grading	Promote thinking rather than memorization	Allow for freedom of expression	
Knowledge discrepancies		Introduce contradictory views	Value contradictory views	

Source: Baxter Magolda, 1992, p. 229, Table 8.1. Reprinted by permission.

Had Professor Sanchez studied Baxter Magolda's stages of development and her table of student advice, how would they have helped him relate to his students' attitudes and needs on the first day of class? Natasha, the first student to enter Professor Sanchez's class, represents a person in the absolute knowing stage of development. She wants specific information, and she wants class rules that are clearly spelled out. She sees Professor Sanchez as a dispenser of knowledge; it is his job to communicate clearly so that students understand the information in the course. Thus, Natasha was anxious on the first day of class when she felt that critical information was missing.

Within her absolute knowing approach, Natasha might have adopted either a receiving or mastering pattern of learning. Although women and men used both patterns of learning in Baxter Magolda's study, the receiving pattern was employed more frequently by women while the mastery approach was more typical of men. In the receiving pattern, the role of the learner is to listen and to record as much information as possible from the instructor. These students prefer to use a structure provided by an authority and are uncomfortable in coming up with an approach independently. In the mastery approach, students see their roles as participating in activities and as showing the instructor that they are interested in the subject matter. Students using this approach expect the instructor to be entertaining, but they also expect to participate more in the learning process. Professor Sanchez's syllabus needs to be structured and specific to meet the needs of the absolute knowers, yet it also needs to convey his own expectations and methods of evaluating student participation. If the syllabus can entertain as well as inform the students, it may allow the student in the absolute knowing stage to feel more comfortable about making a commitment to the course on the first day. Such an initial commitment by students can begin the process of their growth to the next stage, transitional knowing.

According to Baxter Magolda, students in the absolute knowing stage want the chance to know their professors, and they prefer professors who show helpfulness. They look for an active classroom and consider it essential to understand grading policies. Professor Sanchez's syllabus does not include any welcoming remarks, and it does not provide any information about the possibility of obtaining extra help. The requirements of the course and the grading policy are vague. Students who require specific information to feel secure may find Professor Sanchez's general syllabus poorly suited to their intellectual and emotional needs on the first day of class.

Brian, the second student in the vignette, has been around the academic environment for some time and has more tolerance for the variability of courses. He knows that professors tend to make changes as the semester progresses; his major concern is that he understand the content of the course. As a person in the stage of transitional knowledge, he appreciates that some knowledge is certain and some is uncertain. He is beginning to figure out how to deal with discrepancies. If he uses the impersonal pattern for learning that is typical of the majority of males in the Baxter Magolda study, he will be most concerned with the challenges of the learning environment. Brian will want a course where he can think about the material and not just memorize it for a test. He looks for a teacher who is fair and balanced.

The majority of women at the same stage of cognitive development as Brian, the state of transitional knowing, use an *inter*personal rather than an *im*personal pattern of learning. According to Baxter Magolda (1992), in the *inter*personal pattern, "relationships are central to the learning process because knowing others promotes sharing perspectives and sharing perspectives increases knowledge. If instructors are uncaring, teaching (and thus learning) is ineffective" (p. 134). In order to appeal to Brian, Professor Sanchez needs to show how he will challenge students to think in his course, but he also needs to provide evidence of a caring attitude for his women students who may focus more on the relational aspects of the learning environment (Jordan et al., 1991).

Thus, Professor Sanchez needs to reframe his syllabus to meet the needs of both kinds of learning patterns. Those students in his class who learn through an interpersonal approach will not find any collaborative activities or group projects listed, nor will they find any evidence of a teaching philosophy. They will have to guess whether interaction is valued in Government 216. Professor Sanchez lists assignments, cases, tests, and papers in his syllabus, but he explains neither their nature nor their purpose. The papers may well deal with the controversies that are central to constitutional law and thus give his students an opportunity to work with contradictory viewpoints. But students such as Brian, although anxious to work with conflicting opinions, still need guidance in how to resolve discrepancy. The description of the papers in the syllabus does not make the content clear nor does it give guidelines for what is expected.

The third student in the vignette, Thon, has lived in a variety of cultures and is well aware that knowledge is open to many different interpretations. He has become a critical thinker, is able to think for himself, and can create his own perspective when evaluating new information. He looks for a professor who encourages independent thinking and the exchange of opinions in a classroom. Thon appreciates someone who connects learning to real life and who treats students as equals. As an individual at the stage of independent knowing, Thon also uses the individual pattern for learning that Baxter Magolda found most typical for males who are independent knowers. Thon's primary concern is his own thinking; he appreciates the independent thinking of others but does not see connecting with others as essential for his learning process. In contrast, the majority of women at the independent knowing stage use an interindividual pattern, in which sharing and comparing interpretations with others is a necessary ingredient for learning. Women at this stage often require connection and relationships with others to move forward in their learning.

Professor Sanchez has not reflected on his teaching philosophy anywhere in his syllabus. Thon wonders whether he values the independent thinking of students, whether he treats students as equals, and whether he makes any attempt to connect course material to real life. For students such as Thon, some indication of Professor Sanchez's general approach would be helpful. Thon does not need the absolute clarity and specificity in a syllabus that is essential for Natasha, but he does want to know whether his thinking will be expanded if he puts forth his usual effort throughout the semester. Will he have a chance to take part in discussions, and will he be respected for the ideas and experiences he has been thinking about during the past few years, or will he have to listen to some authority drone on and on from behind the lectern?

The fourth student in the vignette, Alicia, has many of the same concerns as Thon, but her needs for integration and application are even greater than his. Alicia has been working in a business setting for the past five years and has realized that she must expand her understanding of the law. Alicia is accustomed to exchanging and comparing perspectives in her work at the office; she is adept at solving problems and applying knowledge to specific settings. As an individual who generally uses contextual knowing, she wants a professor who will value her contributions, not one who will tell her what she should think. Alicia is focused and motivated and does not want to waste her time and money on a course that will add little to her goal of gaining more insight into the workings of the law. The topic of Government 216 sounded intriguing to Alicia, but her initial impressions, shaped by the uncommunicative syllabus, have dulled her enthusiasm.

Clearly, Professor Sanchez's syllabus cannot be summarily dismissed just because it fails to meet the needs of some of his students. It does present essential information. Moreover, a syllabus is only a small component of any course. However, many of the questions raised by the four students in the vignette can be readily answered by expanding some sections of this syllabus and adding others. Research on the college experience (Tinto, 1987; Kuh, Schuh, Whitt, & Associates, 1991; Pascarella & Terenzini, 1991) indicates that faculty-student connections that are cemented early in the semester lead to increased commitment on the part of students. As the diversity of the college student population expands, it is becoming critical for faculty to figure out new ways to establish these connections with students. A syllabus that responds to the needs of students who are at different cognitive levels is not the only answer to creating connections, but it is a concrete beginning.

Baxter Magolda (1992) summarizes four approaches that she thinks faculty can take to become more responsive to students' different ways of knowing in higher education. First, validating students as knowers is essential to promoting students' voices. (Compare our remarks in Chapter Two about the essence of magic in the classroom.) Second, situating learning in the students' own experience legitimizes their knowledge as a foundation for constructing new knowledge. (Compare Tom Angelo's fourth principle for successful teaching, summarized in Table 2.1.) Third, defining *learning* as meaning that is jointly constructed will empower students to see themselves as the constructors of knowledge. Fourth, validating students through relationships (the relational component evident in all of the first three findings) is an essential component of empowering students to construct knowledge.

Baxter Magolda (1992) makes a critical point when she states that "lack of connection hampers *some* students, and a relational approach reaches *most* students" (p. 390). As professors, we cannot reach all students, but we can aim for most of them. The concrete document of the course syllabus provides such a connection to the professor and to the information for most students, for it informs and reassures students about what is ahead and therefore empowers them to continue the process of constructing knowledge.

Application

Congratulations! You have been given a widget and have just opened the carton. On top of the wrapping, you find a manual that you expect to explain a bunch of hows: how to set it up, how to use it, how not to use it, how to maintain it, how to repair it. As you pick up the manual, you decide instantly whether or not to look inside it. If the manual is very short, flimsy, in tiny print, or poorly laid out, you will probably put it aside. On the other hand, if it is comfortable to hold, not overly long, and on good quality paper, you will probably open it. What will keep you reading? Crispness of lay-out, clarity of wording, specificity of directions, respect for the unini-tiated user, enthusiasm about the many uses of the widget, humor, and relevance. Once you have read the manual, will you refer back to it? Perhaps—if it caught your attention, met your immediate needs, and included suggestions for possible future uses.

What if this new item is not a widget, but is a course, the car-ton a classroom, and the manual the syllabus? Are the students' expectations for the syllabus that different from your expectations for the manual? Not really. A student turns to a syllabus looking for many of the same qualities: crispness, clarity, specificity, respect, enthusiasm, humor, and relevance. But these expectations are not easily met. They demand considerable time and energy from the designer, as well as a certain amount of risk. For just as a course is never absolutely the way one wants it, so the syllabus that reflects it is never absolutely perfect.

According to Altman (1989), the purpose of a syllabus is to make clear to both faculty and students where they will "wind up" at the end of the semester (p. 1). It puts the plan of the semester in writing for the student and the professor. It is also a road map that on the one hand can simply answer the most frequently asked stu-dent questions—"What do I have to do in this course?" and "When must it be completed?"—and on the other hand can reveal the essence of the professor's educational philosophy and teaching style.

The difference between a simple syllabus and an enriched syl-labus lies in the kind of map that is drawn. A simple syllabus is rather like a soliloquy that outlines the information essential to a student's progress within the course. An enriched syllabus also out-lines the course but with embellishments; it allows for commentary and digression along the way. No longer a soliloquy, an enriched syllabus becomes a conversation. Both varieties of syllabi present a written plan that binds the students and the professor to a proposed progression, but the enriched syllabus establishes an annotated plan that allows for the changes and additional connections that can take place within a college semester.

From the start, the conversation of an enriched syllabus introduces a learning community into the classroom environment. It unites the professor and the students in a documented conversation, and in this way it holds both professor and students accountable for that classroom community. Gabennesch (1992) has suggested that such a syllabus can encourage a student to make the critical connections with other bodies of knowledge that will move that student toward becoming a lifelong learner and an educated man or woman. Yet there are other less altruistic and more personal reasons for you to consider the enriched syllabus. To write such a document, you must find a comfortable space in which to reflect on both the purpose and the form of your approach to teaching—a challenging task, perhaps a lonely task, but certainly an energizing and enriching task. It is also a liberating task, for the enriched syllabus frees you from certain constrictions. You are licensed to chat. You may carry on about what seems important to you. You may comment briefly or at greater length. You may add drawings, rearrange the order of the sections, or expand the document in whatever way suits your vision. Thus your syllabus becomes a personalized manual, designed by you to connect with each student; a discussion that explains your material, teaching approaches, and expectations.

Most of the recent reports on undergraduate education (National Institute of Education Study Group, 1984; Astin, 1985; Association of American Colleges, Task Group on General Education, 1988) emphasize that students are not active participants in their own education. They are not involved in the process of learning, and in many classrooms the vital connection between professor and student is weak if not broken. Yet the National Institute of

Education Study Group and Astin both stress that "the effectiveness of any educational policy or practice is directly related to the capacity of that policy or practice to increase student involvement" (Astin, 1984, p. 306). A syllabus is a document that is common to most first days of class. It can provide a tangible incentive for this involvement. As Rubin (1985) has suggested, "the syllabus is a small place to start bringing students and faculty members back together. . . . [I]f students could be persuaded that we are really interested in their understanding the material we offer, that we support their efforts to master it, and that we take their intellectual struggles seriously, they might respond by becoming involved in our courses, by trying to live up to our expectations, and by appreciating our concern" (p. 56).

The following list contains a number of topics that can be profitably covered in a course syllabus. It is a reference document, not necessarily a checklist. Some of the topics are standard; some are not. Some of the items can be quickly entered; others will take more time.

- Course number, section number, course title

- Prerequisites/corequisites

- Credit hours

- Contact hours per week: number of lectures, laboratories, individualized instruction, conferences, clinics, field placements, or co-op hours

- Instructor's name

- Office location; college telephone number and instructor's extension number; voice mail, E-mail, and fax numbers

- Office hours

- College catalogue course description

- Instructor's course description

- Instructional goals and objectives

- Student goals and objectives

- Instructor's educational philosophy

- Teaching procedures

- Attendance and tardiness policies

- Classroom atmosphere

- Required texts: annotated list

- Supplementary reading: material on reserve or recom-
  mended reading

- Bases for student grading; explanation of instructor's
  evaluation instruments: class participation, quizzes,
  tests, papers, reports, labs, projects; policies on late
  papers; make-ups, work for extra credit, plagiarism

- Support services: libraries; labs; tutors; transfer, career,
  and personal counseling

- Course outline

- Extras: grade-recording sheet, student sign-off sheet,
  letter to students, textbook preview, calendar, maps,
  timelines

In the following discussion, we have organized the list into categories and then suggested ways to enrich each entry. The suggestions are just that. They may or may not be appropriate for
a particular class or comfortable for a particular professor, for just
as there is no one right way to teach, there is no one right way
to design a syllabus. The challenge for you is to discover the syllabus that is best for your course and for your unique classroom

community.

The description of each category of topics will be followed by a comparison of the relevant material that was presented in Professor Sanchez's original syllabus and the material that might be presented in an enriched and extended syllabus. (The complete enriched syllabus is shown in Exhibit 3.2.)

Preliminary Considerations

Try to plan the layout of your syllabus with great care, so that all salient bits of information stand out, even to the cursory glance. Avoid hiding data in the middle of sentences; think about the possibility of using columns, spacing, bullets, bolding, icons, and charts. Consider incorporating a cartoon to change the flow or to emphasize a point. Think carefully not only about the tone of your comments, but also about where you include them. The flow of a syllabus is important.

It is also important to consider several features of the paper stock you will use. Should it be with or without holes? Why bother with that kind of detail? Consider the purposes of a syllabus. It is your first connection with your students. From it, you want your students to understand the organization, the progression, the skills, and the requirements of your course, so that you can get on with it. You want students to keep the syllabus, to appreciate it, to refer to it, and to learn from it—not to lose it. Yet syllabi do get lost; handouts are stuffed into pockets, spiral notebooks, or textbooks, particularly on the first days of class. You have carefully organized the structure of the course, why not help students organize the content of the course? (Natasha will be grateful.) How about suggesting that students use a folder? Or how about requesting that your syllabus be printed on three-hole punched paper and requiring that students use a three-ring notebook for course handouts?

That folder or that notebook, however, is going to fill rapidly with your handouts and perhaps handouts from other courses. Your thoughtfully constructed syllabus is in there, but where? Consider printing the syllabus on colored paper. It will then be easy for students to locate and easier still for students to return to. There are other possible benefits to using colored paper. A professor of Fundamentals of Math, wise to the math phobias of her students, commented in one of our seminars that she always printed her syllabus on green paper because, as she tells her students, "It's the color of hope." A psychology professor who teaches 7:30 A.M. classes chooses yellow paper for her syllabus because, she tells her students as she looks around the room, "It is the color of cheerfulness." Whether the color enhances students' emotional reactions to a course is a matter for debate, but certainly colored paper does make the syllabus stand out among the rest of the students' handouts.

As you plan the appearance of your syllabus, you need to consider the Americans with Disabilities Act (ADA), passed in 1990. It requires that the needs of students with disabilities be met. The act does not mention syllabi specifically, but because the syllabus is central to your course, it is important that it be easily accessible to every student. When you have finished writing your syllabus, consider putting it into large print for students with impaired vision or transcribing it onto a cassette or a diskette to be available for those students who, for whatever reason, find handling papers difficult.

Specific Course Information

Course Number, Section Number, Course Title; Prerequisites/Corequisites; Credit Hours; Contact Hours per Week (Number of Lectures, Laboratories, Individualized Instruction, Conferences, Clinics, Field Placements, or Co-op Hours); Instructor's Name

These initial entries are similar to the initial entries in a résumé. They should be crisp, concise but complete, and arranged in a logical and visually effective order. They need to be well-centered, well-spaced, easy to read, and perhaps selectively bolded or in a font of a different style or size from the one used in the rest of the doc-

ument. Students tend to scan these first items quickly, often over-
looking essential information. If, for instance, students do not note
the prerequisites/corequisites, they may well find themselves in a
class for which they are not prepared. If they fail to notice the
every-other-week study-group meeting, they may not be able to
meet that requirement. Both misreadings result in muddles that will
have to be unwound at a future date.

Fortunately, each of the four students in this chapter's vignette
will be all right with this initial information. Natasha and Brian,
each for different reasons, will read it and record it in their personal
filing systems—Natasha on her neat calendar, Brian in his mental
daily schedule. Thon will skim over it, having already researched it
and learned it. Alicia will remember that the information is there
and refer back to it as necessary. But there are other, less organized
members in Professor Sanchez's class, such as Rick, who simply
jumps in and swims through life, noticing only those life preservers
placed clearly and directly in his way; or Helen, who reverses everything—numbers, letters, directions—especially in tense situations;
or Christl, a free spirit, who will focus on something only if it is in
front of her and she is reminded that it is important. It is helpful,
therefore, to plan the visual presentation of this part of the syllabus
with an eye to making the information stand out.

Compare the specific course information sections of Professor
Sanchez's original and enriched syllabi.

Original Syllabus
Constitutional Law, Government 216—Victor Sanchez
3 Credits; EN1103, required; EN 1105, preferred

Enriched Syllabus
Constitutional Law, Government 216–01
Tuesday, Thursday 9:30–10:45
Victor Sanchez
. . . .

Prerequisites:	EN 1103 (English Composition)
	EN 1105 (English Literature) helpful, but not required
Credit Hours:	3

Office Information

Office Location, College Telephone Number and Instructor's Extension Number, Voice Mail, E-mail, Fax, Office Hours

This is still basic, required information, essentially pretty cut and dried. The cardinal rules of crispness, conciseness but completeness, careful arrangement in a logical order, and ease of reading still hold. However, is there more to these entries? Ought they to be only names and numbers? Baxter Magolda (1992) points out that students in every stage of development value helpful and collegial connections with their professors. These early entries are a concrete place to begin this connection. Do you want to include a home telephone number? Do you want to rely on an answering machine to screen your calls? What kind of calls do you consider reasonable? Do you want to include a fax number or permission to reach you by modem? If so, it is essential that you specify just what is acceptable: on the day Brian decides his job takes precedence over class, would you accept a final draft of his paper if it was electronically transmitted at midnight, just under the wire? What about a fax of a drawing that Helen belatedly realized should face the other way? An E-mail question about an assignment that Christl lost? Alicia's E-mail list of thoughtful additional insights relating to a philosophical debate that was cut short by the end of class?

Office hours are the final item listed in these entries. The days and the times are certainly essential for a student to note and then to use effectively; office hours can be more than a scheduled time to talk with either individual students or small groups of students. Less formal and more personal than the classroom, office hours are another way to encourage students to enter into the process of their own education and thus to become more thoroughly responsible for it. What is your feeling about office hours? What are your rules? Do you require all conferences to be held during office hours? Do you want to encourage students to drop by with questions? Do you want to point out that you enjoy talking with students? Why not explain your philosophy in an extended entry? Such a discussion would not only reassure Thon and give Alicia insight into the fiber of your course, it might also encourage less focused students to explore the material of your course.

Compare the office information sections of Professor Sanchez's original and enriched syllabi.

Original Syllabus
Office Hours: M–F, 9:30–10:30, Social Science Bldg., Rm. 39

Enriched Syllabus

Office and Phone:	Social Science Bldg., Third Floor, Rm. 39	
	Telephone:	(999) 333–4444
	Voice mail:	(999) 333–4444
	E-mail:	SanchezV@OAK.UML.EDU
Office Hours:	M, W, F:	9:30–10:30
	T, Th:	1:00–2:00 or by appointment

These are my official office hours, but the door is open. I enjoy teaching, and I enjoy talking to you, so if you have questions that we did not answer in class, or if you want to explore an idea ☆, come by. The best times to reach me are early morning and lunch time. If I am not in my office, leave a note either on my desk or in my office mail; I will get back to you.

Course Descriptions

College Catalogue Course Description; Your Course Description

Many departments require that the syllabus course description duplicate the description in the college catalogue, but by its nature, the catalogue description must be terse. The number of words is limited by the space available, and the content is generally dictated by departmental requirements. There is no room for explanation, commentary, or humor. Yet the tone and the presentation of each course are different. A course is shaped by the personality, the particular interests, and the philosophies of the professor who is teaching it. As we suggested in Chapter One, four sections of a required course such as Introduction to Literature will be taught in four different ways. In the same way, Government 216 will be governed by the insights of Professor Sanchez.

Natasha, an absolute knower, as are 68 percent of our freshmen and 46 percent of our sophomores, according to Baxter Magolda (1992), searched Professor Sanchez's syllabus for an extended course description precisely because she found the constricted catalogue description confusing. Thon and Alicia, independent and contextual knowers, respectively, also found it insufficient. Rick and Christl, both unaccustomed to questioning the given, probably did not spend much time with it. Still, the course description begins it all. It sets the tone. It is the grabber that seizes the students' attention and helps them to anticipate the journey. The college catalogue is not in the business of previewing this journey, but an extended course description can clarify the content, the progress, the connections, and the individuality of the course, and the journey it represents. An extended description can explain what will be taught and how best to learn it. It can touch upon how the course will be useful in the future. It can challenge and entice. In such a description, professors are free to make a personal connection by explaining what is glorious about their individual courses.

Compare the course description sections of Professor Sanchez's original and enriched syllabi.

Original Syllabus

Course Description: Case analysis of the development of federalism, the separation of powers, and the role of federal and state courts in constitutional development and contemporary control.

Enriched Syllabus

Catalogue Description: Case analysis of the development of federalism, the separation of powers, and the role of federal and state courts in constitutional development and contemporary control.

Extended Description: Welcome to Constitutional Law, or Gov 216, as it is generally known. In this course, we will begin at the beginning; for after all, it is the U.S. Constitution that shaped our federal government and dictated both its powers and its limitations. Throughout the semester, we will concentrate on judicial interpretations of the Constitution and how those interpretations affect our everyday lives.

Instructional Goals and Objectives

Pedagogical theorists, educational institutions, academic divisions and departments, and individual faculty members may all hold differing interpretations of the words *goals* and *objectives*. In some instances, instructional *goals* are set by academic deans or by a curriculum committee; in some, by individual faculty members. In some courses, both the instructional goals and the instructional objectives will be measurable and attainable; in other courses, the goals will be neither, and only the objectives will be measurable. In some courses, instructional goals will refer to a brief period of time and instructional objectives to an even briefer period. In other courses, instructional goals will predict the future, whereas instructional objectives will frame the present.

Whatever the reigning policies and interpretations, a clear, concise, and brief listing of instructional goals and objectives is an essential ingredient of any syllabus, and one that must consider the needs of students at each stage of cognitive development. For students like Natasha, instructional goals and objectives can supply the confidence in the professor as the dispenser of ordered knowledge that she needs before she can move on toward an ability to handle contradictory knowledge. For students like Brian, goals and objectives provide an anchor to which he can return periodically in his progression toward understanding discrepancy. And for Thon and Alicia, goals and objectives fulfill their expectations for an explanation of the integration and application of the knowledge and skills of the course.

Writing instructional goals and instructional objectives is a demanding task, for you cannot successfully write them before the design of the whole course is clear in your mind. They will not jell until you have had time to step back and reflect on the course as a whole. To add to the challenge, they are impossible to write at the last minute, and once you have put them down on paper, you will probably want to rewrite them. Goals and objectives, therefore, are almost always under construction. Nevertheless, Alicia, an outstanding student, searches for them immediately, and each of the other students will benefit from them.

In the parlance of the enriched syllabus that we are describing, instructional goals and instructional objectives are two discrete entities. The instructional objectives are concrete and attainable. They are content based and delineate what can and will be measured both of the knowledge and of the skills that are to be learned in the course. Instructional objectives may be organized in a number of ways—by topic, by progress through the course, or by final outcome—but however you choose to organize them, they need to be clearly listed and positioned, possibly bulleted and placed one above the other. Then, at some point in the syllabus, perhaps at the time the objectives are listed or perhaps in your section on grading policies, the ways in which these objectives will be tested need to be clearly stated.

Goals, on the other hand, are more abstract, less content based, and less time specific than objectives; they may be unmeasurable and not necessarily attainable. They are more likely to be predicated on the joys rather than the structures of learning. Instructional goals describe what one wants to achieve and to accomplish and are like the golden nuggets in the pot at the end of the rainbow: they embody the crucial connections that the professor hopes will be made, if not right away, then in the months that follow the course. Try writing a list of what you would like your students to remember from your class in two years and then in five years. Then include that list in the discussion of your goals.

Instructional goals will incorporate the philosophical as well as the practical uses of the instructional objectives and will make clear the connections between the body of knowledge acquired in the present course and other bodies of knowledge. Goals can become the ultimate motivators for students in a course, for they are the soul of the course, a clearly stated, unifying list to which all students connect according to their energy and their ability. Goals are wonderful to write but often wrenching to put into print, particularly if they are not met with immediate cheering on the opening days of class. Still, goals are what Thon and Alicia will look for, what Natasha, Rick, and Christl will respond to, and what all of the students should ponder.

Once written, your instructional goals and objectives are not merely a list to be discussed on the first day. Like the course outline and other pieces of the syllabus, goals and objectives can be referred to throughout the progression of the semester. The instructional objectives can be discussed periodically, even physically checked off as they are introduced and learned, thus helping students to build their confidence in their ability to learn, to solidify their understanding of the progress of the class, or even to rekindle their interest and effort during the down periods inevitable in the rhythms of the semester. You can also use the list of objectives as a review tool to elicit questions and to begin a discussion before a test. A final discussion of the objectives on the last day of class not only serves as a review of the totality of the course, but perhaps even more important, dignifies the effort students have put into the course. Such a discussion reassures the bottom-line-focused students of the 1990s such as Brian that their "consumer expectations" (Levine, 1993, p. 4) for a course have been met and that it has been a "quality" course (Cornesky, 1993; American Association for Higher Education Continuous Quality Improvement Project, 1994).

Finally, a rereading and discussion of the instructional goals moves students beyond the specific skill and information structure of a class into the broader connections made during the course. The goals underscore for the students the span of the learning that took place during the semester and the potential of that learning for future use.

Original Syllabus

Course Objectives: To familiarize you with the roles the federal and state constitutions play in the administration of criminal justice.

To examine the concept of federalism among the states and federal government, as well as the separation of powers among the various branches of government.

To understand defendants' constitutional rights.

To examine the laws that enforce and protect these rights.

[No discussion of Course Goals]

Enriched Syllabus

Course Objectives: You should be able to demonstrate in your questions, your papers, case briefs, and tests:

- Familiarity with the roles the federal and state constitutions play in the administration of justice

- Ability to examine the concept of federalism among the states and federal government, as well as the separation of powers among the various branches of government

- Understanding of defendants' constitutional rights:

  Freedom of speech, press, and assembly

  Freedom against unreasonable searches

  Privilege against forced self-incrimination

  Privilege against double jeopardy

  Right to federal and state due

process

Right of counsel

Right to a fair and speedy trial

Right to a jury trial

Right to confront adverse witnesses

Freedom from cruel and unusual punishment

- Familiarity with the laws that enforce and protect these rights

Course Goals: Course goals lie beyond objectives. They are the nuggets in the pot of gold at the end of the rainbow: not always immediately attainable, but always worth working toward. Let's hope that by the end of the semester, we all will have a good understanding of the purpose of the federal and state constitutions in our society, and that we will be aware of the most important constitutional provisions.

Student Goals and Objectives

Student goals and objectives? A section on student goals and objectives may not seem appropriate to a typical syllabus at first glance. However, researchers (Stark, Shaw, & Lowther, 1989) have discovered that "based on their prior preparation and self-views, students have broad goals for attending college, narrower goals for achievement in particular courses, and even more specific goals as they approach each learning task" (p. vi). As we have discussed, the process of trying to articulate goals and objectives for a course requires the professor to think ahead and to place the materials and skills to be learned within the greater continuum of acquiring knowledge. If students are asked to consider their personal reasons for taking a course and then to verbalize these reasons, they must also think ahead, and they must then inevitably step into the process of their own learning and be motivated to play an active part in the final outcome of the course.

According to Cross (1988) and Stark, Shaw, and Lowther (1989), helping students clarify their goals encourages them to monitor and thus to gain control of their learning process—certainly an important consideration, and one that is most appropriate for the beginning of the semester. There are many possible ways to involve students in the process of framing their own goals and objectives. Some professors introduce their discussions of their own instructional goals and objectives by stating that certain of their goals and objectives are nonnegotiable but that others are more fluid and are negotiable. They then encourage students to make suggestions for a final, redesigned class list. This activity does not mean that the professors lessen their control over the direction of the course—the final say is still theirs—rather, it opens the classroom to a conversation about the direction of the course and from the first day, lays the foundation for a community of learners.

Still, this kind of interplay is only one possible method and is not appropriate for everyone. Some professors do not feel it appropriate to renegotiate the goals and objectives listed in the syllabus but do feel it is important to include the students in the goal-setting process, and so they leave a blank space in the syllabus for students to write in their own lists of goals and objectives—either immediately or as the course progresses. Students are generally surprised by this exercise. They may be hesitant or reluctant to create such a list, doubting either their ability to be accurate or the importance of their input. Yet verbalizing their reasons for being in the course not only helps them build their confidence and begin the process of thinking critically about the course, it also clarifies for them their personal interest in the course content.

Some professors may find that it is helpful to involve students in specifying their own goals and objectives, but they feel that these goals and objectives should not become part of the course syllabus. Instead, during the opening class, these professors may invite each student to make a list of his or her course objectives on an index card (the size of the card limits the number of objectives that can be listed) and then ask students to share ideas as the basis of a class discussion. Or they may ask students to begin framing such a list in class and to hand in a final version later as part of an assignment. There are many ways to contemplate.

This gathering of student goals and objectives at the beginning of a course, whether for inclusion in the syllabus itself or for classroom discussion, is a dignifying exercise for students. It is also helpful for professors. Through it, professors learn more about the diversity of knowledge and of motivation within their classrooms and are, therefore, better able to emphasize the teaching approaches that seem most appropriate for each unique classroom community. And should they find this sort of student activity particularly useful, they can expand it into a more complex and ongoing process of classroom assessment and research (Angelo & Cross, 1993).

Original Syllabus
[No discussion of Student Goals or Objectives]

Enriched Syllabus

Your Goals for This Course: You will notice an enticingly empty space below. Use it to list your goals for this course. We will return to discuss them together throughout the semester.

-
-
-

Educational Philosophy and Teaching Procedures

Once you have designed and listed your instructional goals and objectives, the next logical question is how can they best be achieved? The nature of college classrooms is changing rapidly. Professors today are confronted with new situations that challenge them to revisit their educational philosophies and to reconsider their choice of teaching procedures (Stull, 1992). As one settles into teaching, the pressures of contractual obligations, the need to research and to publish, and the minutiae of daily academic life absorb one's energies. There is little time left or space available to step back and ask why and how. Yet in the past decade, the student body has become far more diverse, the academic community's understanding and acceptance of the many ways in which students learn has deepened, the required core of knowledge has burgeoned, and the rhythms of our society have changed.

As we work to absorb this new complexity, we need to consider the expectations of our present students, for whom "higher education is not the central feature of their lives, but just one of a multiplicity of activities in which they are engaged every day. For many, college is not even the most important of these activities. Work and family often overshadow it" (Levine, 1993, p. 4). In order to meet the needs of this newly emerging student body, we must relate the course material to the other activities that engage these students, and we must more actively involve all the players (Bonwell & Eison, 1991). Most students are no longer comfortable with the transfer or empty vessel approaches (described in Chapter One) in which a professor stands behind a lectern and fills the students with information that they then diligently record in notebooks to study for the next test.

Educational Philosophy

Even though students may ask to be included in the restructuring of higher education, they are generally unused to being invited into a dialogue about educational philosophy and possible variations in teaching approaches. They may have considered neither that an educational philosophy is integral to the progress of a course nor that the discovery of this underlying philosophy can enable them to enter the magic and the learning process of the classroom with far greater success. Not all students have reached the developmental level of Thon and Alicia or are as ready to join in as Christl. But one of the benefits of an enriched syllabus is that it can initiate a conversation between professor and students about education in general and about content and method in particular. Including a philosophical discussion in your syllabus is beneficial both for your students and for you. It franchises your students to look into the beliefs of the teaching academy. By its inclusion in the course contract—the syllabus—such a discussion draws the student into the totality of the educational experience and emphasizes the discovery and the learning that must take place in the classroom. And if you have been wondering where the students are "that value learning for learning's sake" (Schroeder, 1993, p. 21), this philosophical discussion liberates you to talk about the excitement integral to learning.

Teaching Procedures

A discussion of educational philosophy can spade and fertilize the ground, but teaching procedures are what bring forth results. Students like Natasha turn to the syllabus for specificity of procedure, and Brian searches for challenges beyond mere memorization. Thon and Alicia want to be certain that the learning will be relevant and active, and all students need reassurance that they are respected as learners. In a section on teaching procedures, the professor can clarify for students the expectations and the challenges that are ahead. Will the course be primarily lecture? Will critical thinking be stressed? Will there be a significant amount of writing? Will the course include cooperative learning groups, labs, panels, case studies, role-playing, free writing, debates, or review sessions?

Studies conducted during the past twenty years using the Myers-Briggs Type Indicator (MBTI) have looked at which of the four particular learning patterns students use: concrete active (the ES pattern), concrete reflective (IS pattern), abstract active (EN pattern), or abstract reflective (IN pattern). Nearly 50 percent of high school seniors fell into the concrete active pattern, 10 percent preferred the abstract reflective pattern, and the remaining 40 percent of the students were about evenly divided between the concrete reflective and the abstract active patterns (Schroeder, 1993, p. 24).

The 50 percent who are most comfortable in the concrete active pattern are "action-oriented realists," learning best when the "useful applications are obvious." The 40 percent in the concrete reflective and the abstract active groups are either, respectively, realists who prefer "to deal with what is real and factual" or "action-oriented innovators." Ninety percent of students, therefore, may learn best when presented with concrete material that is connected to reality and facts. Only the final 10 percent, the abstract reflective learners, are introspective, valuing ideas and knowledge for their own sakes (Schroeder, 1993, pp. 24–25).

What does this say about teaching procedures? Certainly, that from the very beginning of the course, professors need to give thought to ways in which to teach specific information linked to pragmatic, direct applications; the more abstract and theoretical information may then follow. The study also indicated that for the majority of students, learning is best accomplished through active involvement in processing the information. Consider using cooperative learning groups, panels, labs, cases, role-playing, free writing, debates, and review sessions. Ponder the inclusion of critical thinking activities and assignments. Should you decide to include such learning methods, it will be helpful to describe them in the syllabus. Include a brief explanation of what they are, why they are a part of your course, how they will be organized, when they will be used, and how they will be graded.

All of this information may seem lengthy and burdensome to produce, but it need not be. It may be presented in a simple chart or in a few sentences that clarify what is ahead. In this way, a student who needs specificity can see the linear progression of the course; a student who flounders in the presence of uncertainty can see the methods of the course; and the student wanting challenges can appreciate the active participation.

Original Syllabus
[No discussion of Teaching Philosophy]

Enriched Syllabus

Teaching Methods: This course is that interesting mixture—a lecture course in which participation and discussion is not only encouraged but is expected. I look forward to intelligent questions and lively and well-supported debates. Be sure to complete the assigned reading before each class; otherwise, you will be unable to take effective notes and to enter into the discussions. While lectures will cover the general topics, lectures and reading material are meant to complement each other rather than repeat each other; thus, attendance is critical.

Classroom Policies

Attendance and Tardiness Policies; Classroom Atmosphere

A syllabus, whether simple or enriched, is no longer simply an information manual given out during the first days of the semester. In an increasingly litigious society, there are those who view a syllabus as a binding and therefore contestable legal document. Students have brought suit over policies they felt were unclear or improperly administered and over material they have claimed was included in the semester outline but not covered in the course. What to do?

Point one: do not shirk the task of designing policies on such issues as attendance, grading, make-up, and extra credit, and then state these policies as succinctly as possible. If you do not put the policies of your course into print, you are vulnerable to students' claims that they did not know the rule, and even if you have explained, discussed, and reiterated a rule ad infinitum, administrators can not support you on it if it is not in print.

Point two: even a carefully worded policy statement may not be sufficient. We have colleagues who do not feel that it is. They find that they are still open to hurried or fuzzy readers and inattentive listeners who tend to misinterpret or who simply do not accept responsibility for knowing the rules. At the end of their syllabi, these colleagues include a tear sheet to be signed by each student. In effect, it states: "I have read and understood the requirements and policies stated in this syllabus." The professors then keep the signed tear sheets on file for several semesters. Other colleagues give a quiz on the syllabus (carefully noted in the body of the syllabus) at the end of the registration period; still others incorporate a question about the syllabus into their first test.

Attendance Policy

College attendance policies vary. Some institutions state a collegewide attendance policy in the student handbook and expect students to follow it. Other institutions indicate in their catalogues that attendance is essential to academic success, but leave the specifics up to the students and the professors. The attendance policy is then a matter of the philosophy and the personal energy of each professor. And there are many solutions.

Keeping a careful record of who is in class and who is not is the cardinal rule for all attendance policies. For professors who automatically open each class by taking attendance, record keeping is a simple task. For those who do not want to take up class time with attendance taking and who may use a roll call only during the first few weeks as a technique to learn names, record keeping is not a simple task. Should you decide to limit absences to a specific number before penalties are incurred—such as points taken off or conferences required—you are then left open to having to prove each absence. To protect yourself, take attendance, by some method.

Students may well feel that this is college; they have left attendance policies behind, and it is up to them to make their own decisions. True, in the best of all possible worlds, this would be absolutely
correct, but the external pressures on students today are many and
demanding. Jobs, families, illnesses, transportation, recreation, social-
izing—all press into students' schedules, not necessarily in that order,
and sometimes students need help in refocusing and reprioritizing.
If you want students to understand your feelings about the importance of attendance, write about it. Pointing out that not all of the
learning that is integral to a course is contained in the textbook may
seem obvious to you but not so to the students. A discussion of the
additional kinds of learning that are part of the interaction of a classroom experience—the discovery, the questions, the elaboration, the
collaboration—can be an eye-opener to students who feel that if
they read and study the material, that will be enough.

One possible solution is to involve students in setting the attendance policy. Some of our colleagues have found that if students help
set the policy, they stick to it. Other professors do not want to take
that time or do not feel this method appropriate. Still others do not
want an attendance policy at all. Solutions are as various as are
philosophies of teaching, but a printed directive is often a fine idea.

Tardiness Policy

Professor Sanchez has adjusted the door of his classroom to shut
after each student. Natasha, Brian, Thon, and Alicia have arrived
on time. Rick and his buddies probably will, although they may stay
out in the hall until the last minute, but what about Helen who gets
lost easily or Christl for whom time is not always relevant? There is
no question that students who enter after the class has begun are
disruptive, not only because they walk in front of others, shove
chairs out of the way, take off coats, shuffle papers, and even drop
an occasional book or pen but also because they break the flow and
the space of the opening of class, the time that sets the tone for the

remainder of the class.

There is a good reason for members of the audience being asked to remain in the rear of the theater until the end of the scene. A classroom is similar to a theater in a number of ways. Professors are metaphorically, sometimes actually, on stage (see Eble, 1976). They perform in front of an audience (the students) who have paid for the privilege of listening, learning, and enjoying. Some tardiness is inevitable and excusable. But if you have found that lateness has become more of a problem in recent years, or if you have found, as the semester progresses, that students begin to drift in later and later, especially on beautiful warm days, include a discussion of your feelings about tardiness in the syllabus. Your explanation of your attendance and tardiness policies can also be an effective segue into a discussion of the importance of classroom atmosphere.

Classroom Atmosphere

In each course, certain ground rules exist that shape the atmosphere, or environment, in that classroom, whether implicitly or explicitly. There are the small, personal dislikes each professor has about chewing gum, swigging soft drinks, munching on pastrami sandwiches, listening to Walkmans, knitting, or even wearing hats, that are useful to clarify from the outset. Then there are the more important rules relating to questions, interruptions, comments, and the reactions to and treatment of fellow members of the class. A discussion of how these situations shape the flow of the class period and how they influence the self-confidence of all participants—students and professors alike—is not often attempted in a syllabus. Such a discussion may seem unnecessary, even belittling, but in actuality, an explanation of ground rules that stress respect for others and receptivity to the input of others accomplishes several things. It sets the stage for the play to begin, clarifies the roles of all the players, underscores the dignity of the learning process, and shares the responsibility for the success of the performance with all the players.

Natasha wants to be certain the professor is in control but she also wants to participate. She will not attempt it if she feels her ideas will be pushed aside. Brian and other transitional knowers like him need to be challenged, but they also need an atmosphere in which they can feel comfortable that their input will be valued. Rick and Christl do not mean to be disruptive, but if they come in late, comment without forethought, or laugh inappropriately, the learning climate for that period may be shattered. Thon and Alicia searched the syllabus immediately for some sign that they would be able to share their perspectives and experiences and to learn from the other members of the class. That the classroom environment be interactive is central to their learning success.

A discussion of the classroom atmosphere and how it is shaped is one way Professor Sanchez can reassure them all. Such a syllabus entry also allows professors to celebrate the diversity of the classroom, to put into print their own belief in the dignity of the individuals in the classroom, and to remind students that the classroom is an incubator of lifelong learning that works only when the atmosphere is based on mutual respect.

Compare the classroom policies sections of Professor Sanchez's original and enriched syllabi.

Original Syllabus

Attendance: If you miss more than three successive classes, or a total of four classes for the semester, the result can be a diminished course grade, or even failure.

Enriched Syllabus

Attendance: Class attendance is required. Learning is an active process, and it is simply impossible for you to participate if you aren't here. I am not sympathetic to those who complain that the class is too early or the roads are too crowded at certain times of the day. If you weren't in class, you'd likely be working, and your boss wouldn't tolerate your inability to show up, either. You are allowed three unexcused absences. I will deduct semester points for additional absences.

Tardiness: When you make an appointment with a friend, you expect him or her to be on time. Your employer, too, depends on you to arrive promptly each day. Likewise, I plan to start class on time and expect that you will be there. Occasionally, you may find it necessary to be late. In that case, I would certainly prefer that you come after class has started rather than miss the entire hour. However, tardiness should never develop into a pattern.

Class Atmosphere: Any true discussion involves personal exposure and thus the taking of risks. Your ideas may not jibe with your neighbors'. Yet as long as your points are honest and supportable, they need to be respected by all of us in the classroom. Encouragement, questions, discussion, and laughter are a part of this class, but scoffing is never allowable, just as disruptive behavior is grounds for dismissal.

Texts

Required Texts—Annotated; Supplementary Reading Materials (Material on Reserve or Recommended Reading)

A listing of the required texts is a standard inclusion in all syllabi, but in an enriched syllabus, there is room to discuss the texts, to elaborate upon your choices. You can comment on such points as where to buy a particular text, possibly including the price (helpful to students on a tight budget). You can explain why you have selected a text, clarify its purpose in your course, and discuss when it is needed and whether all texts should be bought at the beginning of the course or whether some may be borrowed from a library. You can describe how the chosen text is seen by others and how it relates to the broader college curriculum. In addition, you can include a list of supplementary reading materials, clarifying whether a work is required reading, and thus placed on reserve in a specific place in the library, or whether it is purely optional for those who wish to explore further. In either case, an explanation of the content of the supplementary reading may direct students toward the required reading and also entice them to sample the optional reading.

Compare the textbook sections of Professor Sanchez's original and enriched syllabi.

Original Syllabus

Required Text: John Smith and Jacqueline Schwartz, *Constitutional Law,* 3rd edition (New York: Legal Publishing, 1993).

Enriched Syllabus

Required Text: John Smith and Jacqueline Schwartz, *Constitutional Law,* 3rd edition (New York: Legal Publishing, 1993).

Bookstore price: $78.95.

The Smith and Schwarz text is challenging and informative reading. As the authors state, this book has "never succumbed to the temptation of oversimplification" (p. xi). I chose this book because it is well organized and nicely combines text information with the actual cases. Former students have told me that they still use the book as a reference.

Supplementary Materials: Appropriate case studies and handouts will be used throughout the course. I also highly recommend a paperback law dictionary; several different ones are available at most bookstores. I prefer *Black's,* but any available law dictionary is probably fine.

Grading Policies

Explanation of Your Evaluation Instruments: Class Participation, Quizzes, Tests, Papers, Reports, Labs, Projects; Make-Ups, Extra Credit; Plagiarism

The bottom line. Every student turns to this section. Some read only it. Others do not pay enough attention to it. Some seem to forget the policies as the semester progresses. Others hold you to them throughout the semester. Given this diversity of approach, the bases for grading need to be presented as clearly as possible—they must be visually accessible, verbally concise, and mathematically understandable (see Milton, Pollio, & Eison, 1986; and Davis, 1993, for a more detailed discussion). Some of our colleagues, finding that students often fail to calibrate their course grade accurately, now include a blank grid in the syllabus and encourage students to record their marks there as the semester progresses. In this way, the professors hope to avoid those unhappy meetings with students who cannot understand why their final grade is not the A, or at least the B+, that they were sure was theirs.

Participation Policies

Some professors assign a percentage of the course grade to areas in which performance cannot be measured by quizzes, tests, labs, and papers, and therefore, these professors do not find a grading grid particularly helpful. Class participation is one such area. How does one define it? How does one grade it? What percentage of the course grade does one assign to it? "Some faculty use [participation] as a kind of 'swing vote,' cast only in borderline cases. . . . Some faculty try to be objective and precise with elaborate schemes of comment-counting" ("To Grade," 1989, p. 5). These professors maintain a checklist on which to record the number of times a student speaks out—ten times is the required minimum, fifteen times is good, twenty times is very good, and so on. Yet isn't it more likely that the nature and the quality of the participation are what is important and not the frequency of the participation?

Certainly, there is no question that for individuals to function effectively in this society, it is essential for them to learn how to participate constructively in a discussion, and equally certain that the classroom is an appropriate area in which to practice this participation. But in order for students to feel confident enough to take the risks, the classroom environment must be receptive and the atmosphere unthreatening. This is sufficient reason to include a discussion of class atmosphere in your syllabus.

Should you consider including class participation in your calculations for a course grade, you need to remember that participation equals risk. For you to participate, no matter in what form, the protective boundaries of your personal space must expand beyond yourself. Your ideas are suddenly exposed, and if you are uncertain, you may feel that you have lost a necessary kind of control. For many students, such as Natasha or even Brian, even taking part in a small group may initially present a threatening situation in which they must move from the security of their carefully preselected seat into an unfamiliar space, peopled with unfamiliar faces. For other students, such as Helen and perhaps Christl, presenting a required speech, participating in a panel, or even answering a question in class is an extremely scary prospect. Yet for many students such as Thon and Alicia, class participation is exciting, and a heated discussion may well be the catalyst for a magical moment.

There is no requirement that you assign class participation a percentage of your course grade; indeed, some of our colleagues argue that this kind of participation is ungradable and that to include it in the grade stifles any chance of real participation. Conversely, should you disagree and decide that including class participation in the course grade is important for your course and your style of teaching, it remains essential that you think with great care about two factors: the percentage of the mark that you will assign to participation and the explanation of what it will entail. Clearly, some courses by their very nature require a significant amount of active participation, such as speech, group dynamics, theater arts, and creative writing or seminars, lab, and design courses. The percentage of the grade assigned to class participation in these courses will be significant. But other courses are not as clearly based upon active class involvement. In these courses, class participation is a matter of the teaching style of the professor or the nature of the material being discussed at the moment; and the percentage of the course mark given to participation can be much less.

When it comes to the actual grading of student participation, a number of criteria have been suggested (Clarke, 1985; Lyons, 1989), but in reality both the methods and the criteria are up to each individual professor. Consider whether you will count the attendance record and small-group work as participation. Consider whether you will count answering questions, asking questions, and volunteering perceptions and tales of relevant experience. Will you include students' jumping into those long, awkward silences after a professor-posed question, whether or not the students have related material to offer? If you require a certain amount of participation, how will you calibrate the amount? Be as specific as possible.

Written Work Policies

In what other ways do you evaluate students? What are your expectations and what are your requirements? What is the grading schedule? Natasha wondered about the topics of the papers; Brian needed to know the dates; Thon and Alicia wanted to be sure that they would be given opportunities to demonstrate what they know; Christl and others would appreciate noncompetitive grading criteria; Helen might need extra time in testing situations. Given the variety of the ways that students learn and then respond to evaluation, and given the increasing diversity of educational sophistication in today's classrooms, it is clear that the more you can vary the nature of your evaluation instruments, the greater the number of students you will help to succeed. Similarly, the more specific you can be about your instruments, the more certain your students are to feel in control, and thus the more quickly they are likely to accept responsibility for their own success.

Clearly, there is not enough space in a syllabus for you to elaborate on each evaluation instrument, nor is it appropriate to include complete directions, but an indication of the nature of your grading tools helps those students who need to know from the outset how the bottom line works. Natasha can then relax, and perhaps Rick and Christl will take note. Will the quizzes and tests be multiple choice, fill in the blanks, short essay, or extended essay, and will there be choice? Will you allow extra time? (Under the Americans with Disabilities Act, you must allow extra time to certain students.) When and how often will tests be given? Will you incorporate contract grading—a prearranged, mutually agreed-upon contract of expectation for grades (see Fuhrmann & Grasha, 1983)? Will there be group projects? If so, how will you organize them; must everyone speak (one of the most frequently asked questions), and why? Is there a form for lab reports? Do the reports require original work, researched conclusions? What are the possible topics or areas for the written requirements in your course? Will written assignments include extensive research? Are you comfortable with indicating a preferred length for written assignments?

If putting such specificity in writing seems too binding, and you worry about the student who says, "But you said you would give only two tests and one group project. You can't stick in a quiz," you can include a qualifier, stating that you reserve the right to change the nature and the number of the evaluation instruments and that you may find it necessary to include an occasional quiz not mentioned in the syllabus.

Deadline Policies

There are other bugaboos of grading: missed tests, late papers, and partially finished projects. What is your policy about deadlines not met? This is a sticky area, one that raises a number of difficult questions and one therefore that like your attendance policy, needs to be spelled out in the syllabus to avoid future misunderstandings. Your policy will, of course, be based on your individual teaching philosophy, but you will probably want to distinguish at least two kinds of circumstances: the ones in which a deadline honestly cannot be met—an accident, a severe illness, or a family crisis; and the ones in which a student spins an improbable tale, procrastinates, fails to hand in an assignment, or tries to pass in a late assignment. What is your policy in the first situation, and what are your policies in the other situations?

Do you accept late papers at all? If so, do you mark them down and how much? Do you give make-up quizzes or make-up exams and if so, on what schedule? Do you assign extra-credit tasks for those wanting to raise their grades? How does your policy work, and why do you use it? In each case, your policies need to be clear and concise: no late papers will be accepted; or a late paper will be docked one-third of a point for each calendar day that it is late; or you are responsible for calling me to explain why the paper is late and for hand-delivering the late paper to me; or if your paper will be late, notify me ahead of the paper due date; or you are allowed a two-day grace period on any *one* of the assigned papers. Any other late papers will be down-graded one-third of a point for each calendar day that it is late.

Make-Up and Extra-Credit Policies

What is your policy about make-up tests? Again, it is important not only to be as clear and concise as possible but also to consider two kinds of excuses: a legitimate excuse (you may want to define what you mean by legitimate), which allows for a make-up, versus an illegitimate excuse, which does not. And what about extra credit? Here, you want to clarify your policy, as well as to explain the reasons behind that policy. A cogent explanation not only reinforces the nature of any course but also draws the student into the process of learning, prodding that student into accepting responsibility for the outcome of the course.

Plagiarism Policies

Finally, what is your policy about plagiarism: how do you define plagiarism, and what do you do about it? Some institutions establish an institutionwide policy and penalties and publish this information in the student handbook; other institutions state a general policy in the handbook but do not specify the penalties. Whether your college has a stated institutionwide policy or not, it is wise to specify a policy in your syllabus. Then, should a problem arise, the policy is there in print and you have made clear your intent to reinforce it. In her syllabi, one of our colleagues first defines plagiarism as stealing and then elaborates on its soul-corroding nature. She explains that a zero is given to an assigned document that is not handed in, but that any evidence of plagiarism will result in a double zero for the plagiarized document. Thus, a document that is assigned 10 percent of the course grade counts as 20 percent zero if it is plagiarized. (It is very difficult to pass a course when 20 percent of your grade is zero.) She says that she very rarely sees plagiarized material in her classes.

Compare the grading policies sections of Professor Sanchez's original and enriched syllabi.

Original Syllabus

Grading:		
	Papers (2)	35%
	Case Briefs	5%
	Tests	30%
	Participation	5%
	Final Exam	25%

Enriched Syllabus

Grading:	Requirements	Percentage of Course Mark
	Case Briefs	5%
	(Each Brief 1%)	
	Papers	35%
	(Paper 1 15%)	
	(Paper 2 20%)	
	Tests	30%
	(Test 1 10%)	
	(Test 2 10%)	
	(Test 3 10%)	
	Participation	5%
	Final Exam	25%

Grading Policies:

Case Briefs: Case briefs on assigned cases must be submitted at the start of class on the dates stated on the assignment schedule. These briefs will be submitted on preprinted forms that will be issued to you. They are graded on a pass/fail basis. Briefs may be up to one week late. Any brief more than one week late will not be credited. You will be assigned five briefs during the semester.

Papers: Papers must be submitted at the start of class on the dates stated in the assignment schedule. No late papers will be accepted unless you and I have mutually agreed upon an extension before the paper is due. Let me tell you now that extensions are not often granted. Each paper will involve some research, should be thorough, thoughtful, and at least six pages long. The topics of the papers will be assigned later.

Tests and the Final Exam: The tests and the final exam will each consist of objective questions (true/false and multiple choice), along with four short-answer questions and three essay questions. On the tests, you will be asked to select one of the essay questions; on the final exam, two. The final exam is cumulative.

Missed Tests: There are no make-up tests. Generally, if a test is missed, the other two tests then become 15 percent of the final grade. But if you miss a test for a whimsical reason (I will define whimsy), I reserve the right to score that test as a zero. Zeros are tough to overcome.

Participation: As a participant in this course, you are expected to contribute. This means being actively present in class—joining in discussions and raising questions. I will deduct a point for each unexcused absence beyond the allowable three. Should your course grade be on the cusp at the close of the semester, the fact that you have actively, appropriately, and consistently joined into class discussions will push your grade toward the higher mark. But don't join in just for the points. Discussion is one of the best ways to clarify your understandings and to test your conclusions. After all, the framing of the Constitution owes much to debate.

Extra Credit:	Completing all these requirements with distinction will keep you occupied. I do not give extra credit assignments.
Plagiarism:	Plagiarism is deliberately handing in another person's material as your own. It is stealing. It belittles you. Any evidence of plagiarism results in a double zero on that assignment (that is, an assignment that normally would count for 10 percent of the grade will be counted as 20 percent zero if plagiarized). Any evidence of repeated plagiarism will result in an *F* for the course.

Support Services

Libraries; Labs; Tutors; Transfer, Career, and Personal Counseling

Professors cannot be all things to all students nor should they be. Libraries, labs, tutors, and many kinds of counseling services are a vital part of the structure of teaching institutions, yet many students are only dimly aware of their existence or do not understand their importance. Supports are only supports when students know of them and use them. If you describe them in your syllabus, you help ensure that they will be used. A reminder that the research librarian is an extraordinarily good source of information is a useful addition to an annotated list of required readings. A description of the writing, math, and computer lab services, hours, and even locations may encourage students to make use of them. If your department has tutors available, you may want to include that information as well as the cost and a telephone number to call. If one of the counseling services works in conjunction with your course, specify the name, location, and telephone number of that service.

Even in classes in which writing is an important and integral part of the class, professors often cannot take the time to be writing instructors for their students. What is your policy about student papers that are littered with structural and grammatical mistakes? Some of our colleagues who teach in departments other than English, state in their syllabi that any student who receives a mark below a C+, must take that paper to the writing lab, rewrite it with the lab's aid, and then resubmit it to the professor within a specified amount of time, complete with commentary. Other professors arrange a system of feedback from tutors or labs and then indicate that any student receiving a mark below a C on a test or paper must report to the appropriate tutor or lab within the week in order to discuss the work and to rewrite the indicated sections.

For many students, just the fact that extra help is available is sufficient to keep them enrolled in a difficult course. Unless the extra help is required, they may or may not make use of it, but they are reassured by the fact that it is there and that it is valued by the professor.

Original Syllabus
[No discussion of Support Services]

Enriched Syllabus
Support Services: Free tutoring is available in the Writing Lab (Building 4) and from the Social Science Tutor in the Reading Lab (Building 5). The hours are posted each semester. There is no cost to the student. Do not hesitate to visit the labs if you have questions. The ability to write clearly and cogently is a skill that lies at the heart of being an educated man or woman. The ability to work easily within the text and assignments of this class is central to your success in the course. The writing and social science tutors are experts in helping you to achieve these goals. Give them a chance.

Course Outline

Think of a course outline as a travel schedule. Some of us are more attuned to using travel schedules than others. Some of us are lost without them. Others look at them once and remember everything. Some of us will lose them and have to call the travel agency, while others will rely on their fellow travelers to remind them what to do and when to be ready. But all of us expect the schedule to outline what lies ahead—dates, times, places, requirements, and highlights—and to do so in as visually accessible and verbally concise a manner as possible.

In his original syllabus, Professor Sanchez included a course outline that was succinct, visually accessible, and neatly arranged in columns. Yet Natasha, an absolute knower, found it insufficient and looked for more; she requires more data in order to be ready to proceed. If Professor Sanchez had included the chapter titles with the chapter numbers, Natasha would have immediately understood the topics of the course as well as have been given an anchor to return to periodically during the course. Rick and Christl would also have looked for more information in the original syllabus; they need to be made more aware of schedules and deadlines. Indicating calendar dates rather than just listing the weeks (few students think in semester weeks), and perhaps even bolding the dates, would help to center them in time. When they, or students like them, stop by Professor Sanchez's desk to ask when the chapter on search and seizure is due, he can remind them that they can look these dates up. Being able to say, "It is there in print," is certainly an effective stress-relieving technique for Professor Sanchez.

Obviously, the course outline, or schedule, will be defined by the timeline of the semester. Thus, the outline needs to present a chronological listing of the chapter headings, topics, or skills to be covered during the semester; the dates of the assignments and primary activities of the semester; and the dates of the tests, papers, reports, and projects that must be completed during the semester. This is not to say that a syllabus must state exactly what will be assigned for every day or exactly what activities will happen on every day. That kind of specificity is only appropriate for some courses and only comfortable for some professors. But the course outline must follow *some* clear form. It could be organized by days, weeks, or periods of weeks and then subdivided by individual assignments or by areas of assignments. Or it could be organized in some other course-specific way. But in some way, it must be organized and then divided.

If need be, you can also include a qualifying statement that makes clear that the nature of the topic, the tornado season, emerging discoveries, new laws in progress, or whatever is relevant may make it necessary for you to reorganize the content of the course while the course is in progress. That statement can help protect you from the litigious.

If you wish, you can certainly embellish the bare necessities of the course outline. Some of our colleagues include suggested ancillary activities, cartoons, asides, or qualifying comments. Other of our colleagues visually reinforce the course outline's organization by placing the units of the course outline in individual boxes or supplementing the list with a flowchart of the main topics and related activities. There are multitudes of methods but only one unifying principle: make the schedule as clear and specific as possible. No one wants to miss the trip.

Compare the course outlines in Professor Sanchez's original and enriched syllabi.

Original Syllabus

Course Outline:

Date	Assignment
Week 1	Introduction and Chapter 1
Week 2	Chapter 2
Week 3	Chapters 2 & 3
Week 4	Chapter 3
Week 5	Chapter 4
Week 6	Chapter 4
Week 7	Chapter 5
Spring Break	
Week 8	Chapter 6
Week 9	Chapter 7
Week 10	Chapters 7 & 8
Week 11	Chapter 8
Week 12	Chapter 9
Week 13	Chapters 9 & 10
Week 14	Chapter 10
Week 15	Semester Review

Enriched Syllabus
Course Outline and Assignments:

Date	Topic	Assignments
1/24	Introduction	None
1/26	Creation of the national government and the concept of federalism	Chap. 1
1/28	Creation of the national government and the concept of federalism (cont.)	Chap. 1
1/31	Speech, Press, Assembly *Hess* v. *Indiana*	Chap. 2
2/2	Speech, Press, Assembly (cont.)	Chap. 2
2/4	Speech, Press, Assembly (cont.)	Chap. 2
2/7	Speech, Press, Assembly (cont.)	Chap. 2
2/9	**Test 1**	
2/11	Authority to Detain and to Arrest	Chap. 3
2/14	Authority to Detain and to Arrest (cont.)	Chap. 3
2/16	Authority to Detain and to Arrest (cont.)	Chap. 3
2/18	Authority to Detain and to Arrest (cont.)	Chap. 3
2/21	*Presidents' Day (No class)*	
2/23	**Paper 1**	
	Search and Seizure	Chap. 4
2/25	Search and Seizure (cont.)	Chap. 4
2/28	Search and Seizure (cont.)	Chap. 4
3/2	Search and Seizure (cont.) *Mapp* v. *Ohio*	Chap. 4
3/4	Search and Seizure (cont.)	Chap. 4
3/7	Electronic Surveillance	Chap. 5
3/9	Electronic Surveillance (cont.)	Chap. 5
3/11	**Test 2**	
3/14–3/18	*Spring Break*	
3/21	Interrogations and Confessions	Chap. 6
3/23	Interrogations and Confessions (cont.)	Chap. 6
3/25	Interrogations and Confessions (cont.)	Chap. 6
3/28	Self-Incrimination: Testimonial v. Non-Testimonial Evidence *Schmerber* v. *California*	Chap. 7
3/30	Self-Incrimination: Testimonial v. Non-Testimonial	Chap. 7

	Evidence (cont.)	
4/1	*Professional Day (No class)*	
4/4	Self-Incrimination (cont.)	Chap. 7
4/6	Self-Incrimination (cont.)	Chap. 7
4/8	Assistance of Counsel	Chap. 8
4/11	Assistance of Counsel (cont.)	Chap. 8
	Edwards v. *Arizona*	
4/13	Assistance of Counsel (cont.)	Chap. 8
4/15	Double Jeopardy	Chap. 9
4/18	*Patriot's Day (No class)*	
4/20	**Paper 2**	
	Double Jeopardy (cont.)	Chap. 9
4/22	Double Jeopardy (cont.)	Chap. 9
4/25	Double Jeopardy (cont.)	Chap. 9
4/27	**Test 3**	
4/29	Defining a Fair Trial	Chap. 10
5/2	Defining a Fair Trial (cont.)	Chap. 10
5/4	Prohibition of Cruel and Unusual Punishment	Chap. 11
	Coker v. *Georgia*	
5/6	Prohibition of Cruel and Unusual Punishment (cont.)	Chap. 11
5/9	Semester Review	
5/11	Final Debate	
5/16–5/19	**Final Exam (exact date and time to be announced)**	

Extras

Grade Recording Sheet, Student Sign-Off, Letter to Students, Textbook Preview, Calendar, Maps, Timelines

More? Yes, probably. But while none of these possible inclusions is required in a standard syllabus and none is necessary, some may solve a problem that you have encountered in past semesters, and some may open up new areas, while others may not fit with your particular style at all. We have already mentioned the grade recording sheet, or grid, on which students can keep their own running record of their grades as a visual reminder of their progress in the course. And we have already discussed the legal reasons for including a student sign-off sheet that, once signed, indicates a student has read and understood the contents of the syllabus. But we have not yet described the letter to the students, the text preview, or the calendar, maps, and timelines.

Letter to Students and Text Preview

The letter is just that, an open letter to your students, generally attached to the front of the syllabus. The text preview, on the other hand, provides a more thorough explanation of the text than the text annotation suggested earlier. The preview might explain, for example, an author's use of headings, summary boxes, bolding, or abbreviations. It might encourage students to refer to the index or the supplementary glossaries. In essence, a text preview highlights what the professor has found useful or difficult about the text, and it reminds students about sections that they often neglect to use.

Several of our colleagues combine welcoming remarks and a text preview in an opening, informal letter. On an extra sheet stapled to the front of the syllabus, they write to their students introducing themselves, the nature of their course and the skills to be learned, their own love of the course, and the challenges ahead, as well as describing tricks for reading and learning the information that is presented. Such letters can be warm, humorous, encouraging, and/or dignified—reflecting your individual style.

Calendar

An increasing number of our colleagues are attaching a calendar to the end of their syllabus: one page for each month in the semester, with boxes marked off for the individual days. Deadlines for papers, reports, projects, tests, and other assignments, as well as college events and holidays, are noted on appropriate days. Reminders that a deadline is fast approaching may be written in. Several professors include drawings, icons, asides, and even warnings. It has been our experience that faculty enjoy creating these calendars (especially if calendar blanks are available), and that students are pleased to have them, often adding their own comments to them.

Maps and Timelines

For some of us, orientation within time and space is an easy task. We readily grasp chronological and spatial relationships, and once we have conceived them, we remember them. If we are actually or metaphorically put down in the middle of unfamiliar territory, we know which way is north. But for others, such awarenesses are not easy. We do not readily see proportions within time or relationships within space. We need visual clues as well as verbal directions. Maps and timelines are just such tools. They make connections and show proportions. They place the pieces within the whole.

Not many professors may think of including maps or timelines in a syllabus, yet if the purpose of a syllabus is to serve as the ultimate reference tool for a course, is any extended syllabus complete without a map or a timeline? Perhaps not. Whether your course covers large periods of time and refers to many parts of the world, or whether it deals with a small time frame and a particular area of the world, it is unlikely to be totally isolated from time and space. Maps and timelines enable students and professors to center the course within a larger frame and allow them to make connections from the course to the larger world.

Original Syllabus
[No Extras were attached.]

Enriched Syllabus
[Professor Sanchez attached two maps to his syllabus—one of the United States of America, the other of the United States Court of Appeals circuits.]

We began our discussion of the extended syllabus by comparing it to a successful manual; that is, a manual that introduces the product in a way that makes the new owner want to use the product and that then leads the reader through the salient points of using the product to get the desired results. In essence, a successful manual is one that sells (a word we have carefully avoided up to now) the product. Should you decide to create such a manual, how do you select what to include? That is your choice. The manual must be your creation, your sales tool. Consider your students: their level of cognitive development and their sophistication with your topic. Consider your expectations for your course and then begin to talk about that course in an orderly fashion. Should you say too much at first, you can always go back and edit.

Because you create it with specific considerations in mind, your extended syllabus becomes a personalized manual, one that introduces your students to your course and then guides them through it. (See Professor Sanchez's complete enriched syllabus in Exhibit 3.2). You and your students can return to the list of objectives as the objectives are met, refer to the grading policies as tests are approaching, rediscuss the section on attendance and atmosphere during a siege of the doldrums, haul out the calendar as a reminder of what is ahead, peer at the timeline or the map to clarify how a section just being introduced fits into the whole, and perhaps most effective of all, at the close of the semester, return to the syllabus for a final review of the course.

Exhibit 3.2. Professor Sanchez's Enriched Syllabus.

Constitutional Law, Government 216–01
Tuesday, Thursday 9:30–10:45
Victor Sanchez
••••••••••••••

Prerequisites:	EN 1103 (English Composition) EN 1105 (English Literature) helpful, but not required
Credit Hours:	3
Office and Phone:	Social Science Bldg., Third Floor, Rm. 39 Telephone: (999) 333–4444 Voice mail: (999) 333–4444 E-mail: SanchezV@OAK.UML.EDU
Office Hours:	M, W, F: 9:30–10:30 T, Th: 1:00–2:00 or by appointment These are my official office hours, but the door is open. I enjoy teaching, and I enjoy talking to you, so if you have questions that we did not answer in class, or if you want to explore an idea ★, come by. The best times to reach me are early morning and lunch time. If I am not in my office, leave a note either on my desk or in my office mail; I will get back to you.
Catalogue	Case analysis of the development of fed-

Description: eralism, the separation of powers, and the role of federal and state courts in constitutional development and contemporary control.

Extended Description: Welcome to Constitutional Law, or Gov 216, as it is generally known. In this course, we will begin at the beginning; for after all, it is the U.S. Constitution that shaped our federal government and dictated both its powers and its limitations. Throughout the semester, we will concentrate on judicial interpretations of the Constitution and how those interpretations affect our everyday lives.

Course Objectives: You should be able to demonstrate in your questions, your papers, case briefs, and tests:

- Familiarity with the roles the federal and state constitutions play in the administration of justice
- Ability to examine the concept of federalism among the states and federal government, as well as the separation of powers among the various branches of government
- Understanding of defendants' constitutional rights:
  Freedom of speech, press, and assembly
  Freedom against unreasonable searches
  Privilege against forced self-incrimination
  Privilege against double jeopardy
  Right to federal and state due process
  Right of counsel
  Right to a fair and speedy trial
  Right to a jury trial
  Right to confront adverse witnesses
  Freedom from cruel and unusual punishment
- Familiarity with the laws that enforce and protect these rights

Course Goals: Course goals lie beyond objectives. They are the nuggets in the pot of gold at the end of the rainbow: not always immediately attainable, but always worth working toward. Let's hope that by the end of the semester, we all will have a good understanding of the purpose of the federal and state constitutions in our society, and that we will be aware of the most important constitutional provisions.

Your Goals for This Course:

You will notice an enticingly empty space below. Use it to list your goals for this course. We will return to discuss them together throughout the semester.

•

•

•

Teaching Methods:

This course is that interesting mixture—a lecture course in which participation and discussion is not only encouraged but is expected. I look forward to intelligent questions and lively and well-supported debates. Be sure to complete the assigned reading before each class; otherwise, you will be unable to take effective notes and to enter into the discussions. While lectures will cover the general topics, lectures and reading material are meant to complement each other rather than repeat each other; thus, attendance is critical.

Attendance:

Class attendance is required. Learning is an active process, and it is simply impossible for you to participate if you aren't here. I am not sympathetic to those who complain that the class is too early or the roads are too crowded at certain times of the day. If you weren't in class, you'd likely be working, and your boss wouldn't tolerate your inability to show up, either. You are allowed three unexcused absences. I will deduct semester points for additional absences.

Tardiness:

When you make an appointment with a friend, you expect him or her to be on time. Your employer, too, depends on you to arrive promptly each day. Likewise, I plan to start class on time and expect that you will be there. Occasionally, you may find it necessary to be late. In that case, I would certainly prefer that you come after class has started rather than miss the entire hour. However, tardiness should never develop into a pattern.

Class Atmosphere: Any true discussion involves personal exposure and thus the taking of risks. Your ideas may not jibe with your neighbors'. Yet as long as your points are honest and supportable, they need to be respected by all of us in the classroom. Encouragement, questions, discussion, and laughter are a part of this class, but scoffing is never allowable, just as disruptive behavior is grounds for dismissal.

Required Text: John Smith and Jacqueline Schwartz, *Constitutional Law,* 3rd edition (New York: Legal Publishing, 1993).

Bookstore price: $78.95.

The Smith and Schwarz text is challenging and informative reading. As the authors state, this book has "never succumbed to the temptation of oversimplification" (p. xi). I chose this book because it is well organized and nicely combines text information with the actual cases. Former students have told me that they still use the book as a reference.

Supplementary Materials: Appropriate case studies and handouts will be used throughout the course. I also highly recommend a paperback law dictionary; several different ones are available at most bookstores. I prefer *Black's,* but any available law dictionary is probably fine.

Grading:	Requirements	Percentage of Course Mark
	Case Briefs	5%
	(Each Brief 1%)	
	Papers	35%
	(Paper 1 15%)	
	(Paper 2 20%)	
	Tests	30%
	(Test 1 10%)	
	(Test 2 10%)	
	(Test 3 10%)	
	Participation	5%
	Final Exam	25%

Grading Policies:

Case Briefs:	Case briefs on assigned cases must be submitted at the start of class on the dates stated on the assignment schedule. These briefs will be submitted on pre-printed forms that will be issued to you. They are graded on a pass/fail basis. Briefs may be up to one week late. Any brief more than one week late will not be credited. You will be assigned five briefs during the semester.
Papers:	Papers must be submitted at the start of class on the dates stated in the assignment schedule. No late papers will be accepted unless you and I have mutually agreed upon an extension before the paper is due. Let me tell you now that extensions are not often granted. Each paper will involve some research, should be thorough, thoughtful, and at least six pages long. The topics of the papers will be assigned later.
Tests and the Final Exam:	The tests and the final exam will each consist of objective questions (true/false and multiple choice), along with four short-answer questions and three essay questions. On the tests, you will be asked to select one of the essay questions; on the final exam, two. The final exam is cumulative.
Missed Tests:	There are no make-up tests. Generally, if a test is missed, the other two tests then become 15 percent of the final grade. But if you miss a test for a whimsical reason (I will define whimsy), I reserve the right to score that test as a zero. Zeros are tough to overcome.
Participation:	As a participant in this course, you are expected to contribute. This means being actively present in class—joining in discussions and raising questions. I will deduct a point for each unexcused absence beyond the allowable three. Should your course grade be on the cusp at the close of the semester, the fact that you have actively, appropriately, and consistently joined into class discussions will push your grade toward the higher mark.

But don't join in just for the points. Discussion is one of the best ways to clarify your understandings and to test your conclusions. After all, the framing of the Constitution owes much to debate.

Extra Credit: Completing all these requirements with distinction will keep you occupied. I do not give extra-credit assignments.

Plagiarism: Plagiarism is deliberately handing in another person's material as your own. It is stealing. It belittles you. Any evidence of plagiarism results in a double zero on that assignment (that is, an assignment that normally would count for 10 percent of the grade will be counted as 20 percent zero if plagiarized). Any evidence of repeated plagiarism will result in an *F* for the course.

Support Services: Free tutoring is available in the Writing Lab (Building 4) and from the Social Science Tutor in the Reading Lab (Building 5). The hours are posted each semester. There is no cost to the student. Do not hesitate to visit the labs if you have questions. The ability to write clearly and cogently is a skill that lies at the heart of being an educated man or woman. The ability to work easily within the text and assignments of this class is central to your success in the course. The writing and social science tutors are experts in helping you to achieve these goals. Give them a chance.

Course Outline and Assignments:

Date	Topic	Assignments
1/24	Introduction	None
1/26	Creation of the national government and the concept of federalism	Chap. 1
1/28	Creation of the national government and the concept of federalism (cont.)	Chap. 1
1/31	Speech, Press, Assembly **Hess** v. **Indiana**	Chap. 2
2/2	Speech, Press, Assembly (cont.)	Chap. 2

2/4	Speech, Press, Assembly (cont.)	Chap. 2
2/7	Speech, Press, Assembly (cont.)	Chap. 2
2/9	**Test 1**	
2/11	Authority to Detain and to Arrest	Chap. 3
2/14	Authority to Detain and to Arrest (cont.)	Chap. 3
2/16	Authority to Detain and to Arrest (cont.)	Chap. 3
2/18	Authority to Detain and to Arrest (cont.)	Chap. 3
2/21	*Presidents' Day (No class)*	
2/23	**Paper 1**	
	Search and Seizure	Chap. 4
2/25	Search and Seizure (cont.)	Chap. 4
2/28	Search and Seizure (cont.)	Chap. 4
3/2	Search and Seizure (cont.) ***Mapp* v. *Ohio***	Chap. 4
3/4	Search and Seizure (cont.)	Chap. 4
3/7	Electronic Surveillance	Chap. 5
3/9	Electronic Surveillance (cont.)	Chap. 5
3/11	**Test 2**	
3/14–3/18	*Spring Break*	
3/21	Interrogations and Confessions	Chap. 6
3/23	Interrogations and Confessions (cont.)	Chap. 6
3/25	Interrogations and Confessions (cont.)	Chap. 6
3/28	Self-Incrimination: Testimonial v. Non-Testimonial Evidence ***Schmerber* v. *California***	Chap. 7
3/30	Self-Incrimination: Testimonial v. Non-Testimonial Evidence (cont.)	Chap. 7
4/1	*Professional Day (No class)*	
4/4	Self-Incrimination (cont.)	Chap. 7
4/6	Self-Incrimination (cont.)	Chap. 7
4/8	Assistance of Counsel	Chap. 8
4/11	Assistance of Counsel (cont.) ***Edwards* v. *Arizona***	Chap. 8
4/13	Assistance of Counsel (cont.)	Chap. 8
4/15	Double Jeopardy	Chap. 9

4/18	*Patriot's Day (No class)*	
4/20	**Paper 2**	
	Double Jeopardy (cont.)	Chap. 9
4/22	Double Jeopardy (cont.)	Chap. 9
4/25	Double Jeopardy (cont.)	Chap. 9
4/27	**Test 3**	
4/29	Defining a Fair Trial	Chap. 10
5/2	Defining a Fair Trial (cont.)	Chap. 10
5/4	Prohibition of Cruel and Unusual Punishment ***Coker* v. *Georgia***	Chap. 11
5/6	Prohibition of Cruel and Unusual Punishment (cont.)	Chap. 11
5/9	Semester Review	
5/11	Final Debate	
5/16–5/19	**Final Exam (exact date and time to be announced)**	

Replay

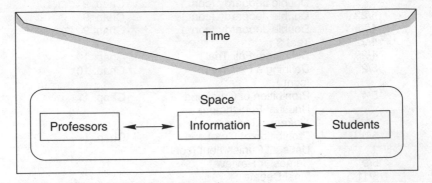

Time

Accurately reflected in the syllabus outline

Professors

Be aware of students' level of cognitive development

Consider the syllabus as a

- Learning tool
- Course contract

Design the syllabus as

- An enticer
- An organizer
- A sustainer
- A dignifier

Information

Meets diverse student needs

Models clear, concise, complete organization

Provides a road map for the entire semester

Serves as a reference and a review tool

Reflects the personality of the professor

Students

Read the syllabus to understand

- The nature of the course
- The overview of the course

Refer to the syllabus for

- Course approaches
- Course requirements
- Course policies

Return to the syllabus for

- Course directions
- Closure

4

$$\cdot \cdot \cdot \cdot \cdot \cdot \cdot \cdot \cdot \cdot \cdot \cdot \cdot \cdot \cdot \cdot \cdot \cdot \cdot \cdot \cdot \cdot \cdot \cdot \cdot \cdot \cdot \cdot \cdot \cdot \cdot \cdot \cdot \cdot \cdot \cdot \cdot$$

The Opening Weeks
Establishing Community

A bad beginning makes a bad ending.
—*Euripedes, Aeolus*

Vignette: At five minutes of nine, Professor Simonds hurried into her advanced algebra class. She noticed that the students had left the first two rows empty and that they were still sitting as isolates, scattered around the room. No informal groups had formed. People were not chatting with each other as they usually did by this time in the semester.

Professor Simonds pulled a bunch of papers out of her briefcase and began reading off names from the tops of the sheets so that students could come up and get their graded quizzes. She was in a hurry; there was a lot to get done this period. Professor Simonds did not want to answer any questions, and so she didn't take time to look up at the students as they arrived. It had not been a good set of quizzes. It was just one of those quizzes, she reasoned. As she had planned her class last night, Professor Simonds had had a difficult time deciding the timing and the method of handing back the quizzes. She had vacillated between discussing the quizzes before she returned them or returning them first and discussing them later. She had also considered whether to wend her way around the classroom in order to pass out the papers separately or whether to ask the students to come up to the podium to get them. She realized that she didn't know the students' names. It would be awkward to circle around among the chairs. Professor Simonds opted for calling out the names before class.

Suspecting that the environment of the classroom was directly related to a student's ability to learn, Professor Simonds had thought about how best to create a learning community, but she had not yet found time to discuss the problem with the students or to ask for suggestions. Still, she worried that classes had been in session for over two weeks and that this math class, which should have come together by now, had not done so. She wondered why it had not.

Julia walked up to get her quiz, past two students she didn't know. She felt sure that she had aced this quiz. She had been afraid of math last semester, but her confidence had grown, she had finished the semester well, and now she almost looked forward to math class. Still, Professor Simonds did not seem to recognize her, even though she had volunteered in class. Perhaps she should stop talking and wait to be called on. She remembered that her previous math professor had known names by this time in the semester.

Felicia, on the other hand, was unhappy about leaving her seat to go to get her quiz. She was not as concerned about her grade as she was about having to walk by all those people. Even though on the first day of class she had looked around carefully and had selected a seat that seemed to be near a friendly group of students, she still hadn't found a way to meet anyone in the class. She wondered what they thought of her as she walked by. Should she have worn jeans today?

Juan was concerned that Professor Simonds did not speak to him directly as he came up to get his quiz, or even look up at him. Juan's family had moved to the United States from Puerto Rico two years ago, and Juan continued to be anxious about his accent. It made him nervous to raise his hand in class; he worried that people would comment. But Professor Simonds had encouraged them to ask questions, and he had. From his particular spot in the classroom, he had begun to feel a new connection with math. Now he was not so sure of that connection.

Sam was legally blind, but he could see large print and could get around fairly easily with his cane. He had asked Professor Simonds for permission to record the classes, and she had been comfortable with that, but he suspected the rest of the class found it a distraction. And now, would he knock his books off his desk as he went up to collect his quiz? Could a member of the class collect it for him?

Discussion

The vignette illustrates some of the issues that students must sort through as a semester begins. Professor Simonds understands that there may be tensions among the students and is concerned that the class is not yet a community, but she cannot analyze why. She has thought about the classroom environment and has pondered how to present the information and when to give back her tests. She has heard that the first few weeks are a honeymoon period, when energies are high and students open to new experiences; yet even so, her class has not come together—a challenge that many professors have faced. What is going on? What will help?

In order for professors to grasp what is going on in a classroom from the students' perspective, Kuh and Whitt (1988) suggest that it is important first that professors understand the culture unique to each college setting and then that they consider the subcultures that interact within the larger culture. They state that "instead of viewing colleges and universities as monolithic entities (Martin and Siehl, 1983), it is more realistic to analyze them as multicultural contexts (March and Simon, 1958; Van Maanen and Barley, 1984) that are host to numerous subgroups with different priorities, traditions, and values (Gregory, 1983)" (p. 11).

As members of the professorial subculture, complete with its tradition of head shaking, we, too, have certainly known classes like Professor Simonds'. We, too, have shaken our heads as we discussed similar opening days with our colleagues and agreed that days like that and classes like that "just happened." We have spent time trying to analyze the causes behind such openings. We have tried to consider the present student subculture, its priorities, traditions, and values, but we had been students at other institutions and in different decades. We could not accurately generalize. We were out of date.

In general, we needed to understand the classroom experience of a 1990s student and in particular the classroom experience of the culture unique to our college. And so, in the spring of 1990, each of us enrolled as a full-time student in one of the other's courses—courses we had not taken as undergraduates. In this way, we would truly be novice learners.

We managed to have Abnormal Psychology and Introduction to Poetry scheduled back to back, and as the semester progressed, we became adept at switching roles from student to professor or vice versa after each fifty-minute class. Because we attended all the classes (the attendance policy applied to us too) and did all the reading (we did not write the papers, but we took the quizzes, tests, and final exam), we had a chance to test some of our theories about the influences of time and space on the classroom community, and we became more sensitive to ways in which the rhythms of a whole semester affect the classroom environment.

Surprisingly, we gained significant insights into the subcultures not only of the students but also of the professors. We are not advocating that it is necessary to become a student in a colleague's class (although we vastly enjoyed it), but we are suggesting that our experience taught us much. True, our experience of trading roles in the classroom took place in a social science course and a humanities course at our particular college and therefore reflected the culture innate to our institution, but we felt that it was safe to extrapolate from these discoveries and apply the underlying themes to other divisions and to other institutions.

Before we began our stint as students, we talked together about how we would gather information and agreed upon both informal and formal methods. We also agreed to keep a journal. On the first day of classes, we introduced ourselves as professors of psychology or humanities, who for those particular courses had become students. We explained that it had been a while (a rather long while) since we had been undergraduates and that we were out of touch with that particular student experience, an experience that as teachers we felt was essential for us to understand. We added that like them, we were novice learners in the course—having never studied the material—and that we looked forward to joining them. As the semester progressed, we learned that the students respected our sometimes fumbling forays into the course materials and that they particularly valued the effort and the honesty of our comments and our struggles to keep abreast of the assignments. On the last day of class, we were each presented with a hand-drawn award for bravery in "surviving" a psychology or a poetry course.

We found that we gained many of our most important insights into the ups and downs of a course through three channels: first, the informal interchanges that took place before and after classes ("How's it going?" "Did you do all that homework?" "Do you think she'll ask us to discuss today?" "Could you understand what she meant by . . . ?" "This is too much. I have two other papers to do this week; doesn't she realize that?"); second, through our interactions with our fellow students during the classes (discussions, comments, disagreements, smiles, asides, and even notes (!) passed during class); and finally, through our dutiful completion of assigned homework and tests (which were a lot to do, we discovered).

We met weekly in serious but often amusing sessions to discuss how the week had gone and what we had learned. At the close of the semester, we turned from these informal and intuitive methods of information gathering to more formal and organized methods. We used two assessment tools: questionnaires and interviews. The student questionnaires were presented to forty-three students, while the interviews involved ten students in open-ended discussions of how it felt to have professors as fellow students.

Like Professor Simonds, we had seen fractured classrooms and had worried over what tensions were at work and what factors had gone unrecognized. We had suspected that harnessing the freshness and the less judgmental atmosphere of the first weeks in the semester was critical to the success of the classroom environment and that if a community was not created during this time period the community was just not going to happen.

Our supposition proved to be correct. During our time as students, we found that in order for the students to join together into a successful learning community in the opening days of the semester, a professor must meet not only individual student needs but also the needs of the larger group. The process of meeting these needs is complicated for the professor because many factors that are working simultaneously must be considered from the beginning. Professors struggling to set the tone are rather like jugglers as they try to keep many balls moving in the air without letting any one crash to the ground.

Figure 4.1 is a concept map that presents an overview of the answers we found to our question about the factors that affect the creation of a learning community in the classroom during the early weeks of the semester. A concept map is formed by placing the central question in the center of the space and then drawing arrows from this question to various containers, in this way linking the central question with possible answers. We found that the professor must consider the requirements not only of the students as individuals but also of the class as a whole.

Spitzberg and Thorndike (1992) have written that "the classroom is the most logical, most visible, most ubiquitous, and most neglected place for community on campus. It is a lost opportunity of the first order" (p. 116). If at the start of a semester, professors can successfully juggle the factors shown in Figure 4.1, they may well create a classroom community that will operate successfully throughout the semester. In the following discussion, we have integrated information from current research with insights gathered from our own recent experiences as students.

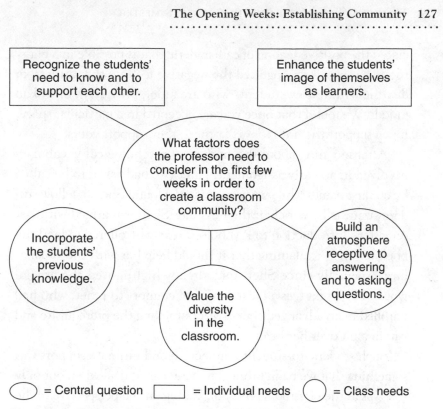

Figure 4.1. Concept Map: Factors That Create a Learning Community.

Recognize Students' Need to Know and to Support Each Other

As we began our stint as students, we were reminded that during the first few days of class students have a great many personal adjustments to make, and we realized that it takes time to find one's place. As we walked into the classroom, we found that we, too, had to worry about the personalities and the attitudes of our fellow students. Like Sam, we wondered what our student colleagues thought about us. Like Felicia, we thought about what to wear (we didn't wear jeans), and like them all, we had to figure out where we would sit in the classroom space (we both, quite independently of each other, opted for the middle, nearer the front than the back, one of us on the right, one on the left). We had to discern which students would be friendly and which would be supportive. We soon appre-

ciated the positive feeling of camaraderie that is possible in a classroom, but we also recognized the negative feelings that arise from
dealing with fellow students who are aloof, pressured, or in bad
moods. We found that once you are accepted in a particular space,
if you support the down days of others, they support yours.

After moaning about the amount of psychological vocabulary
involved in an early assignment, Janet (we had asked to be called
by our first names while we were students) found Sheri, a fellow student, waiting by her chair the next day. Sheri was armed with last
semester's Introduction to Psychology text. She offered to lend the
book to Janet, explaining that it should help her with the vocabulary, especially since Sheri had already highlighted the crucial
words. (The text *was* a great source of comfort to Janet, who had
enrolled in an advanced course without taking the prerequisite and
was in a bit over her head.)

Such student-to-student connection and ultimate support was
something that we hadn't thought about a great deal when our only
role was as the classroom professor. Taking on the perspective of the
student helped us to realize that in each semester and in each class,
students need to have opportunities to adjust to each other as well
as to their new instructor. Professor Simonds was concerned about
the creation of a learning community in her class, but she considered the creation of the community primarily from *her* perspective.
We found that in order to create an atmosphere conducive to discussion and later to group activities, it was essential that time be
made available during class for students to connect to each other at
the opening of the semester. If Professor Simonds had done this,
Julia and Felicia would then have known some of their fellow students, and a member of the class would have automatically picked
up Sam's paper for him, thus saving him the embarrassment of possibly knocking over his books.

Astin (1993, p. xiv) has pointed out that "the single most
important environmental influence on student development is the
peer group." By setting aside time for students to get to know each

other in the early weeks of the course, professors underscore the importance of the initial student-to-student interchanges, acknowledge the value of the student viewpoints and the contributions of each member of the class, and open the way for students to begin to value other students as resources—all qualities of a working community.

Certainly, Professor Simonds is not responsible for establishing friendships in her class, but she is responsible for setting up a learning environment. Julia, Felicia, Juan, and even Sam may not feel comfortable in sharing their questions with the entire class or revealing their ignorance to the professor, but they may be able to mention their concerns to a fellow student. If they have gotten to know their fellow students and are able are to turn to them for help, the classroom environment has moved one step closer to becoming the cohesive community of shared learning sought by Professor Simonds.

Enhance Students' Image of Themselves as Learners

Students enter a class with a particular image of themselves as learners. The attitude of the professor and of the other students in the class can either enhance or diminish this image. Brooks (1991), Bednar, Wells, and Peterson (1989), and Covington and Beery (1976) have investigated the links between self-esteem and risk-taking behavior. Learning equals risk taking. Learning involves exposure; it means searching for answers and perhaps making a mistake. If a student has a low self-image as a learner, he or she will be less willing to take such chances. Bednar, Wells, and Peterson (1989) state that "people fear and tend to avoid threatening situations they believe exceed their coping skills, whereas they get involved in activities and behave with assurance when they judge themselves capable of handling situations that would otherwise be intimidating" (p. 53).

In the early weeks of the semester, therefore, it is necessary for professors to create an environment in which not only do students know each other but in which mistakes are acceptable and students feel comfortable taking risks. Students need to feel either that their coping skills are adequate to handle the demands of the course or that they will be helped to build the skills that will enable them to handle the demands of the course. One day, before poetry class began, Donna turned to her fellow students, whom she had gotten to know pretty well by then, and feeling a bit old and inadequate, admitted that she was having trouble learning how to scan a line. They nodded and agreed that it was difficult and that others of them were struggling, too. Jack, who played the guitar, was able to show them some tricks that he had discovered from his knowledge of music notation, and during the ensuing class discussion, he elaborated on his techniques. At the close of class, Donna and others left feeling that they could cope.

In our vignette, Professor Simonds hands back quizzes and worries because the quizzes were not good. "Just one of those things," she reasons, and so she gives the quizzes back quickly without allowing time for questions, so that students can get over the shock of lower-than-expected grades before the beginning of class. What message was Professor Simonds giving to the class through her actions? The first evaluations in a course raise fears and anxieties for students and place the instructor in a position of control. Does Professor Simonds have any responsibility for the students' low grades? Did she write confusing questions or fail to explain a concept clearly?

If Professor Simonds had taken the time to present the low quiz grades as a problem for the whole class community to explore, she might well have helped the students to come together as a discussion team while they absorbed their individual low marks. She could have elicited oral feedback, or if she felt the students would not yet be comfortable with this kind of assessment, she could have asked them to write comments anonymously and hand them in, and then have discussed the comments in the next class.

It may be that her students simply did not prepare for the quiz, or it may be that her students misinterpreted some of the questions. Whatever the reason, by dealing with the low grades openly, Professor Simonds could have made clear that learning is a joint effort and that mistakes are part of the process of ultimate success. A tentative math student like Julia would then be better able to maintain her positive attitudes about herself as a learner, and she would be more likely to continue to see math as a subject she could enjoy.

Professor Simonds is aware that a student's ability to learn is influenced by the environment of the classroom, but she may have underestimated the importance of personal connections in creating an effective environment. "What's in a name?" Juliet queries. Recognition, self-image, confidence, one may answer. Being identified by name is a simple but a practical way to feel affirmed as an individual—an individual with an identity separate from that of the group. Knowing students' names does not ensure that a classroom will become a community, but it does set a tone of acceptance and friendliness. For hesitant math students Julia and Juan, Professor Simonds's failing to acknowledge them by name might well have rekindled some of their earlier insecurities as students and have forced them to question whether they could cope effectively in this setting.

Build an Atmosphere Receptive to Answering and to Asking Questions

At some point in the semester, we professors all, no matter what our teaching styles, turn to the students and ask a question that we either hope will be answered or expect will spark a discussion. Sometimes this is a successful technique, sometimes it results in what feels to be a terribly long and awkward silence. What can we do to avoid this experience? What steps can we take to create a classroom atmosphere in which students feel comfortable in problem solving and in jumping in both to answer and to ask questions?

Clearly, the way in which a professor may choose to respond to questions is critical, particularly early in the semester. A professor's tone of voice and body language are as important as the actual words used. Answers need to show students that their legitimate struggles to understand will not be belittled. Rather, they will be treated with respect. If, in addition to adopting a supportive posture, the professor calls on students by name for answers, the questions are somehow more legitimate, and the learning environment has become more comfortable. But that is not all, we discovered.

Janet raised her hand early in the semester in Abnormal Psychology to answer Professor Duffy's question about the symptoms of anxiety disorders. Professor Duffy called on her by name; so far so good. But Janet answered "hallucinations." Janet was just plain wrong. Oops. But Janet is an adult, if at that moment a blushing adult, and Professor Duffy let her down easily, so Janet didn't argue. Still, she burned. Later, in our weekly review session, we talked about this experience: about what Janet had felt as a student (puzzled, chagrined, but not defeated, for other students risked wrong answers, too) and about what she had learned as a professor.

What both of us learned as professors from this experience was important. As we discussed that class, Janet pointed out why one of her reactions had been to feel stung. She agreed that in her field of humanities there were also dead wrong answers, but she added that many answers were often negotiable. If you could support your answer, you could be right even though others disagreed with you. The poem "Stopping by Woods on a Snowy Evening" may be interpreted as imagery or as symbolism. Scholars disagree, but the point is arguable, and students in Introduction to Poetry who might answer one way or the other were not immediately wrong if they could support the answer they had chosen. This was not so in most cases in the field of abnormal psychology; there, you relied on research.

Janet pointed out that to her, it felt much less threatening to know she could raise her hand and attempt to answer a question when her answer might be arguable, especially if she was prepared to back it up, than it felt to raise her hand knowing that her answer would be simply right or wrong. She was not as comfortable when she had to stick to yes or no. Yet for some students in the dualist (Perry, 1970) or absolute knowing (Baxter Magolda, 1992) cognitive levels, it might feel safer to answer a question that could not be argued, that was simply right or wrong. Our discussion of Janet's experience helped us to rethink what it means to build a classroom community in which students feel comfortable both in answering questions posed to them and in framing their own questions. And it underscored what we already knew: it is no easy task to design a question that will result in learning.

We also realized that the nature of the risk taken in attacking a problem and in answering the resulting questions differs significantly with the subject matter being examined. Both Katz and Henry (1988) and Svinicki and Dixon (1987) discuss the distinct ways in which professors from particular disciplines approach problems and expect answers. A pure mathematician asks and answers questions quite differently from an applied physicist. A sociologist asks and answers questions quite differently from a psychologist. A historian will perceive and investigate a specific period in history rather differently from a literary scholar. Not only are the approaches different, but the nature of the expected answers is different. There are fields where there is one truth, and there are fields where there are many. There are fields, as Janet discovered in Abnormal Psychology, where the risk taken is clear—a 50 percent chance of being right and a similar chance of being wrong—and there are fields, as Donna found in Introduction to Poetry, where the chance of being wrong is reduced but only if you are prepared to argue your case. We realized that in the early days of the semester, students need to be taught the problem-solving methods specific to each course. They need to learn the nature of the questions that will be asked, the ways in which to frame the answers, and the risks involved in those answers. Only then, we discovered, is a classroom community created that becomes truly conducive to active participation in problem solving.

Not only did we learn more about the perils involved in answering questions and the skills needed to try it, we also learned more about what helps the members of the classroom community feel comfortable enough to ask questions. Students commented that having a professor enrolled as a student in the classroom "made a student and a teacher seem on the same wavelength [a phrase used by four students], more equal—like friends." Being on the same wavelength as students is a goal that the majority of professors would value at certain times, although encouraging students to view the professor as an "equal" or as a "friend" presents a challenge that for some professors is uncomfortable. Yet one of the students who attended both of our classes wrote that "at first it was tense [to have a professor who became a student in the class], but then it brought the professor down to the student level. As a student, she became a 'regular' person. This made it easier because you weren't talking to a professor, you were talking to a friend."

Friend, we discovered, could be translated as meaning a person who was not threatening, one who valued your input, one you could trust, one with whom you could risk speaking out in class. They were telling us not that professors needed to become students in the class but that students needed to feel that they were among friends before they felt able to take public risks.

We gained one further insight into what creates an atmosphere conducive to answering and to asking questions early in the semester. In their interviews, the students told us that by joining them in the classroom as learners, we clearly "cared." It is important to understand that the students' definition of *caring* included not only our concern for them as adult learners but, perhaps even more important, our concern for the experience of learning in the classroom—for them and for us. "It [the experience of having a professor as student in the classroom] sends a message to the other students that there is always more to be learned," said one student. Students' emphasis on the importance of dialogue between professors and students in a supportive, egalitarian classroom community is not a new idea. It is found in Shor and Freire's (1987) work on the pedagogy of liberation, in feminist approaches to education (Weiler, 1988), and in approaches focusing on classroom diversity (Adams, 1992; Fried, 1993). In our research, additional support for such a classroom community came from the students themselves.

Value Diversity in the Classroom

A successful classroom community must not only be receptive to asking and to answering content-related questions, it must also be proficient at listening for only then is real conversation possible. In order to engage in this conversation, the members of the community must value, or at least acknowledge, the importance of many perspectives. As Professor Simonds considers the environment of her classroom in the first few days and the learning community that she wants to establish, she is aware that students are not talking to each other. They are, therefore, certainly not listening to each other, yet she knows intuitively that there is a richness of experience among the students. She has read about the need to incorporate multicultural approaches within a classroom (Banks & Banks, 1989), she has heard about curricular transformation (Adams, 1992; Border & Chism, 1992), and she has been involved in informal discussions of the growing diversity in the classroom. Professor Simonds wonders whether dignifying the diversity in her classroom might help the members of her class more readily come together into a successful learning community.

The answer to her question is yes. Absolutely. But that answer is far more easily given than accomplished. Professor Simonds may then point out that she teaches Advanced Algebra. What has Advanced Algebra got to do, she asks, with multiculturalism? And what can she do to recognize and to teach to the diversity in her classroom? Professor Simonds has asked honest and legitimate questions. And she has asked two separate questions. She asks first how the content of her course can be changed to include multicultural approaches, and she asks second how the diversity of her students can be valued. The answer is that the inclusion of multicultural course content is only a part of the dignifying of diversity in the classroom.

Multicultural teaching is concerned primarily with curricular transformation. It focuses on weaving into a course materials and approaches that reflect differences in race, ethnicity, gender, and class. Researchers such as Schoem, Frankel, Zúñiga, and Lewis (1993) suggest four stages of strategies for the inclusion of multicultural materials into courses. The first and least intense stage involves presenting one lecture or section that includes multicultural content. The fourth and most intense stage provides for a "synthesis of understanding and analysis" (p. 4) throughout the course content. The fourth stage depicts the kind of classroom community hoped for by the students with whom we took our classes. Those students spoke of valuing "diversity" rather than "cultures." Yet, clearly, by diversity they meant the multicultural issues of differences in race, ethnicity, gender, and class. But they meant more. Within each of those cultures, there are other kinds of differences, equally important, that the students stressed and that needed to be recognized. These are differences in life choices, sexual orientation, life experiences, life responsibilities, life histories, traditions, practices, religions, jobs, learning styles, physical appearance, and physical ability. Students ask that all these differences, all these subcultures, be valued as a part of the greater diversity of the classroom community.

In Professor Simonds's class, Juan and Sam overtly represent two diversities: the cultures of the Spanish-speaking Puerto Rican and the physically challenged person. How many more subcultures might be represented just by these two students? Many. Juan may also be a visual learner and the fourth generation of a family of healers, or Sam may be a single parent and a born-again Christian. Not all courses lend themselves to discussions of diversity; not all courses can include material from many cultures—nor should they. But in every course, professors can value the diversity of the many subcultures in the classroom. They can work toward helping students to be open to differences and to learn to listen to each other.

The creation of a classroom community that respects the wisdom and experiences of many is not an easy task. The majority of professors are trained to work with intellectual content not emotional content. Discussions of diversity, however, involve emotion as well as intellect. They touch upon feelings as well as upon thinking and are, therefore, necessarily intense. Not all of us are comfortable with this kind of intensity. What, then, will help Professor Simonds?

The first step for us as professors is to confront ourselves. We need to consider both the intellectual components and the emotional components of dealing with diversity, to consider what we know about the many subcultures in our classes and the degree of comfort that we have with these subcultures. We need to read, to ponder, to ask questions, to listen, to discuss, to follow whatever is our own method of discovery. And then, we need to realize that all of us have areas where we tread with care and where we are not yet comfortable and that such uncertainty is all right as long as we continue to confront it.

It is important to realize that no matter what level of intellectual understanding you possess about a subculture, until you know how you stand on issues of diversity and until you are comfortable with your own emotions, you cannot effectively model respect for diversity in the classroom community, and you cannot successfully defuse the culturally based confrontations that increasingly arise in the classroom.

At the beginning of a session on sexual orientation, Janet and many of the other students heard a student mutter, "Why do these fags get all the attention? They're just perverts." Janet knew that Martha, who sat nearby, was a lesbian and that at least several other members of the class were gay. She felt Martha tense, the space around her contract. The class waited: some students turned toward those they suspected were gay, others looked down, still others stared at Professor Duffy. What would she do? Professor Duffy stopped the class, spoke about derogatory epithets, explained that such behavior was not allowable in her classes, and then went on to confront the fear behind the student's question. (The kind of action Professor Duffy chose to take is supported by Weinstein and Obear, 1992, who emphasize the importance of confronting possible triggers—such as words, phrases, or concepts that reflect an oppressive attitude toward a group—in the early part of a course.)

For Professor Duffy, this kind of discussion was perhaps easier than it would be for professors teaching other courses. The incident was directly relevant to the topic for the day, and the class was already used to discussions of differences. Professor Duffy knew the value of using conflict as a basis for change in the classroom (Schuster & Van Dyne, 1985) and was skilled in the handling of contention. Not all professors have had such training. Still, when similar incidents occur, something must be done. There are many ways of handling such a situation. The method chosen will depend on that self-searching that each of us as a professor needs to have begun. There is no one right way, but there is a wrong way, and that is to ignore the incident. Whatever your method, you must make clear to the class that a closed mind and a hostile attitude are not to be tolerated.

In their model for working with the increasing social and cultural diversity in college classrooms, Marchesani and Adams (1992) focus on four dimensions of teaching and learning. They emphasize the importance of professors' confronting their own perceptions, and they urge that professors study the variety of ways in which students perceive the classroom and thus are able to learn within it. They also urge professors to discover appropriate methods of including content that reflects diverse social and cultural perspectives.

It is essential that we all confront these challenges from the beginning of the semester, in our syllabi wherever appropriate, in an explanation of teaching philosophy, in a discussion of classroom atmosphere, in the goals and objectives, in the content of the course, and in the opening days through our modeling of awareness and appreciation. Without an atmosphere that respects individual differences, students like Sam, Juan, and Martha will withdraw into their own spaces. The sought-for learning community will not be possible, and all students will be diminished.

Incorporate Students' Previous Knowledge

Schuster and Van Dyne (1985) focus on four elements that help to create a classroom community that values diversity: attention to the learning process, recognition of how the macroculture is reproduced in the classroom, creative use of conflict for change, and incorporation of students' experience. We came to understand this last element quite clearly during our experience as students. As the semester progressed, we found ourselves somewhat hesitantly beginning to share personal episodes and previously gained understandings with the other students in our classes.

After an intense session on that oxymoron the poetry of war, the Introduction to Poetry class turned for a respite to Wendell Berry's "Peace of Wild Things." As the class discussed the poem, Donna began to talk about the last line, "I rest in the grace of the world and am free." She spoke of some of her experiences during her family's canoe trips, when she and her family came upon a loon or a moose and would enter together into the "peace of wild things." Other students nodded and joined in, volunteering stories of similar happenings on their camping trips—a bear glimpsed, a family of beavers observed. Through this sharing and valuing of personal past experiences, the meaning of "grace of the world" deepened and became a part of the present.

Students enter a class with years of background experience that are often discounted by professors. Our students commented frequently on the questionnaire and in the interviews that "it is good to know that just because someone is a professor, that does not mean that they know everything. By being able to explain skills and experiences to a professor, you feel that even though you do not have as much education, you can still teach someone else what you know." Baxter Magolda (1992) supports the students' point when she states that "the key to community building is connection. Connection in curricular life can be achieved through validating students' contributions to learning, situating learning in students' own experience, and defining learning as joint construction of meaning" (p. 391).

During our semester as students, we grew to understand the value of the classroom community. We came to agree that students often learn as much from the classroom processes as they do from the explicit content of the course (Gabelnick, MacGregor, Matthews, & Smith, 1990; Schneidewind, 1990). When we returned to our roles as professors, the challenge became how to foster the connections within the classroom that we knew to be essential to the community.

Application

We have suggested here a number of ways to begin the formation of a learning community.

Introductions

In the opening days, introductions are in order: introducing the students to the structure and the policies of the course, introducing the students to each other, introducing the students to the process of learning. True, your syllabus can describe and explain the structure and the policies of your course, but a syllabus is only one part of your introductions; it is not designed to cover the variety of introductions needed in the opening days.

If your style includes active, participatory learning, then try a technique suggested by a former participant in our Activating Learning in the Classroom seminars. Ask students to sign in on the board on the first day of class. Arm yourself with several pieces of chalk (colored if you like), and as students enter the room, hand each one a piece of chalk and ask him or her to write his or her name on the board before the start of class. This act of signing in accomplishes a number of things: students have to speak directly to you, the professor, rather than walking by like strangers; they have to find a place to put down their books (generally on their newly chosen chairs), walk back up to the front of the room, jostle fellow students aside to find space, interact, spell out their names, shake their heads in bemusement, and walk back to their own space through the space of others. In this way, they meet each other right away, if briefly; they take part in a community activity; and by writing on the board, often for the first time ever in a college class, they register their presence and assume a measure of responsibility. And they begin to share in the ownership of the classroom space.

Most students are surprised by this activity: some are intimidated, some embarrassed, some nonchalant. But we have found that eventually, nearly all students appreciate being asked to write their names, for they come to recognize the activity as the subtle gesture of empowerment that it is.

Names

All of us are listed in a multitude of files under our social security numbers. Those numbers label us. But unlike a social security number, our name is not a label; it is our identity. It connects us to who we were, who we are, and who we hope to become.

When you are asked to quote your social security number, you are depersonalized; you fit onto a form. When you are spoken to by name, you are recognized, and you enter into a conversation. Try to learn your students' names as soon as possible. One effective method is to arrive at class early during the first few weeks, position yourself near the door, and introduce yourself to the students as they come in. This welcoming gesture not only gives you a chance to connect names to individual faces (helpful for those of us who have trouble remembering names) but also fosters a feeling of community.

Try, also, to encourage students in the class to get to know each other's names. (Remember that during our stint as students, we learned that students wanted to know each other and thus be able to support each other. Remember, also, how many subcultures are present in a 1990s class and how much can be gained by breaking the ice.) There are a number of informal techniques for learning names on the first day. In some of the exercises, students stay in their seats and talk to their neighbors; in others, they get up and move around, talking to students across the room as well as to their neighbors. Which kind of exercise you decide to use depends upon several variables: the number of students in the class, the kind of space in the classroom, and your own teaching style.

Do you want students to move around? If not, and if the class is small, you can try a variation of the name game in which one student says her name and then the next student repeats that name and adds his own until the names of all students in the class have been heard. Or you can elaborate on this game by asking each student to talk to the student to his or her right. Allow a few minutes for students to gather information and to ask permission to use it and then start on one side of the room with the introductions. The first student introduces the student to his or her right: "This is Loretta Delaney, who has just completed her tenth sky dive." The next student repeats, "This is Loretta Delaney, who has just completed her tenth sky dive" and then introduces the next student by name and appropriate anecdote until the whole class has been introduced. This process is a little intimidating, especially for those near the end of the line, but it is nearly always an effective community builder, for the earlier members in the line begin to support and root for the later members.

The humanities half of us likes another twist on the name game. Professor Jones asks her students to introduce themselves with an alliterating adjective (anything to teach grammar and rhetoric). She has found this variation to be funny and surprisingly successful. The self-chosen alliterative name often becomes a sort of "in" nickname for that class. Throughout the semester, students continue to refer to their fellow classmates by their adjectives, saying, "Where is Marvelous Mary Beth?" or, "I haven't seen Perilous Paul."

If you have the space and are willing to ask students to move around, an interview approach is a good way to learn even more about students. In this exercise, a student interviews a partner and then introduces the partner to the class. The interview can be adapted so that students are given a card with a list of particular questions that require answers from a variety of people. The psychology half of us, Professor Duffy, has elaborated upon this approach. Each student finds a fellow student who is willing to respond to one of the listed questions. After the question is answered, the interviewing student then asks the other student to sign his or her name on the card next to that question. Students not only move around the room, but they also meet and chat with a number of fellow students.

Renner (1983) suggests an opening-day activity called "I Am . . ." Each student is given a sheet of paper with "I am" written at the top. The student then selects six (or fewer) different ways to complete the statement "I am" and lists them: "I am a mother, a camper, a person who likes to read magazines, able to speak some Italian, happy when the weekend comes, and a rock collector." Students then tape the sheets on themselves and walk around the room reading the sheets of other students. Talking is not allowed during this activity, so students have to figure out how to communicate in other ways. When students have had enough opportunity for interaction, the sheets are taped to a wall. This exercise is useful because it involves the whole group in small-group activities, thus opening the way to future small-group work. It also introduces the students to each other's names, interests, likenesses, and differences, laying the foundation for a community of acquaintances, not of strangers.

When students have been in class several days and gotten to know each other, you might suggest that they exchange names, addresses, and home or work telephone numbers (whichever is best) with one or two fellow students who will then be responsible to pick up handouts and get assignments in case one of the group has to be absent. This, too, is an act of support and an act of community that is not difficult, even in a large class.

Further Information

Are names all the information you need to know about your students? If not, on the day you suggest that students exchange contact information (perhaps right after the course add/drop period is over), why not ask them your own questions, too? Many of our colleagues hand out index cards and ask students to write down their names, addresses, telephone numbers, and other pieces of information such as work hours, reading backgrounds, or special interests related to the course. We have found that it is also helpful to ask students to list any further information they feel the professor should know. It is essential that it be made very clear that answering this question is entirely optional, for students have told us that if they have nothing to write down, they feel that perhaps they "should" make up something in order "not to let the professor down."

Some students, however, do have information that they would like us to know, but in the first few days, when they have not yet gotten to know the professors well, they feel more comfortable writing it down than explaining it face to face. One student wrote that she might be a little late at times because she had to drive her terminally ill husband to therapy. Another student explained her difficulty in leaving the house on schedule since she was responsible for taking care of a preschooler and two paralyzed grandparents. Still another described a learning difficulty with which he had had help. He had not declared his disability to the student services office, so his name would not appear on any list, and he felt that the disability no longer hampered his learning, but occasionally, he needed a little extra time on a test. In each case, a solution for a possibly difficult situation could be found.

If you are considering a teaching approach that requires you to shift the arrangement of the classroom, you may find it useful to ask students about their preferences for the design of the classroom space. Do they like rows? Circles? Groups? We have found this question an important one. From it, we have learned that students have definite feelings about rows versus circles (recently, many of our students have expressed preference for rows over circles, although the students are also comfortable with structured small groups) and that they appreciate being asked. Several students have taken time to thank us for asking, adding that they would like to be more actively involved in their own learning situations.

In a similar vein, you can ask students about their learning styles, but if you do, it is important to be specific (students are not always clear about what you may mean by "learning style"). You can ask if they find overheads, videos, music, or classroom activities helpful. Do they prefer lectures? How do they feel about small-group activities?

It is also useful at the beginning of the semester to get some idea of the students' comfort level with risk taking, particularly if yours is an interactive class. Try handing out a list of situations that are typical in your class, accompanied by a scale that allows students to rate their level of comfort in each situation from one to five. If you find that most of your students are uncomfortable with one of the situations (such as an oral presentation in front of the class), you then have sufficient time to help them develop coping strategies for this kind of risk taking.

Journals, too, are helpful not only in starting students to think about the course but also in providing another avenue for welcoming students to the content. Before they begin any reading for the course, ask students to write a journal entry explaining their experiences with or attitudes about the course topic. They can share their entries with each other in small groups, or you can jot brief replies in the margins, thus forging an early personal connection with your students, even in larger classes. If students are asked to hang on to these "before" comments, they can be compared with "after" journal entries at the end of the semester.

Classroom Assessment

How did it go? What worked? What didn't work? Do you have any suggestions? Many of us hand out an end-of-the-course questionnaire with these and similar questions in order to help us plan for the following semester. Consider handing out the same questionnaire near the beginning of the semester but worded in the present tense: How is it going? What works? An atmosphere open to questions is one of the qualities of a successful, working classroom community, and self-assessment is part of this questioning (Light 1990, 1992). A little daunting perhaps? Risk taking for the professor? Yes. But it is very, very helpful: sometimes wrenching, sometimes amusing, sometimes heart warming, often enriching. But if a questionnaire does not seem appropriate for your teaching style, there are many other ways of gathering early feedback on the success of the classroom environment.

Try an in-class suggestion folder, one that will not wander away easily and is somehow more scholarly than a box. Tack a folder to a wall at the side or back of the room (away from where you normally stand) so that students may drop in anonymous comments. Read the suggestions at the end of each class or at the end of the week and then take time to discuss the comments with the classroom community. Or eschew the folder in favor of a real person. Ask students chosen on a rotating basis to monitor a particular class meeting and then to provide feedback on their impressions of its pace, clarity, and interest level.

If yours is an interactive class and has begun to come together as a community, consider the Total Quality Management (TQM) teams of Project LEARN, discussed by Baugher (1993). According to Baugher, a quality team "uses the LEARN acronym to work through steps in a basic improvement model: Locate an opportunity for improvement; Establish a team to work on the process; Assess the current process; Research the root causes; and Nom-inate an improvement and enter the Plan-Do-Study-Act (PDSA) cycle (p. 3)."

If a professor decides to establish quality teams in a course, team members then continue to use the LEARN cycle throughout the semester. This is a sophisticated activity that needs to be carefully structured, but Baugher points out that students want to continue it in their other classes once they have tried it.

In their handbook of classroom assessment techniques, Angelo and Cross (1993) have organized a valuable compendium of assess-ment tools that may be used throughout the semester, including the Minute Paper, the Background Knowledge Probe, and the Pro and Con activity. Each tool furthers the integration of the critical think-ing skills that lie at the core of all learning. And each responds directly to at least one of the concerns that we found needed to be considered during the first few weeks.

Minute Paper

The Minute Paper is one of the simplest of Angelo and Cross's assessment tools and perhaps the most flexible. It takes just a few minutes and has many useful variations. In the Minute Paper, stu-dents are directed to think critically, to take a minute to review and evaluate a past learning experience. They are then asked to respond to two questions: first, what was the most important thing they learned in that experience and second, what question or questions remain. This is a technique that can be can be used at any point in a class: at the beginning as a tool to teach selection and categoriz-ing, as means of summarizing a homework assignment, or as a review of the previous class; in the middle to break the flow, refo-cus the information, or begin a discussion; or at the end to summa-rize what has been learned during the class period, to emphasize one particular bit of information, or to explore depth of understanding of a new technique.

The Minute Paper is especially helpful at the beginning of a course, for the responses to its two questions immediately focus both professors and students on ways to success in the class. In response to the question, "What is the most important thing you learned in Chapter One?" a student wrote, quite honestly: "The most important thing I learned is that from now on I'd better read the chapter." Such feedback may not be what the professor wanted or expected to hear, but it cuts to the heart of the matter.

Professor Simonds might well find the Minute Paper an effective way to get a "read" on class reaction to her quiz, without having to confront individual students. Through a Minute Paper, she could learn that the majority of the class felt uncomfortable with the quiz because they had not yet grasped the task at hand. Or through a more focused Minute Paper, one directed at particular quiz questions, Professor Simonds could learn that 35 percent of the students had a specific concern about the fifth example. She could then try to deal with the situation in a task-oriented way that would avoid raising feelings of failure in individual students. Such an approach would allow her to maintain a personal connection to students but still deal with the academic realities of the course. It would also help her to understand the nature of her classroom so that she could work more effectively at creating a community of successful learners.

Background Knowledge Probe

The Background Knowledge Probe might also have been useful to Professor Simonds in her search for better results on quizzes. It would certainly have made clear to her students that she respected their previous knowledge and experience and valued their potential as learners. In this activity, before students begin to study a new topic or work on a new task, they are asked to list for themselves, in small groups, or as a class, all they know about the anticipated topic or task. When they have written down what they know, what they think they know, and what they have heard, their background knowledge (both real and apocryphal) can be shared, sorted, organized, discussed, and recorded and can then serve as a foundation for the work ahead (see Professor O'Reilly's use of the Background Knowledge Probe in the vignette that opens Chapter One).

There are at least four powerful results of the Background Knowledge Probe. First, students practice the basic critical thinking tasks of listing, sorting, and organizing—no small feat. Second, they come to realize that they already know something about the topic or task at hand and are, therefore, more confident in tackling what may initially have appeared daunting. Third, they learn that their knowledge is valued by the classroom community and important to the understanding of the new material. Fourth, they build a shared body of community knowledge. Thus, in Professor Simonds's class, the skills needed to learn the new tasks covered on her quiz could have been rediscovered and any latent fears dispelled.

Pro and Con

Pro and Con is an assessment technique that not only expands the platform of community knowledge by emphasizing the necessity of viewing a topic from many angles, it also underscores the value of diversity of experience and of conflicting opinions, one of the factors that we found essential to the forging of community.

Unlike the Minute Paper and the Background Knowledge Probe, this technique can take a full class period. Students are directed to think clearly and equably. They are asked to consider a given topic and then to write their own list of pros and cons—positive and negative aspects—for that topic (the positive and negative aspects of using flextime in a large business for instance). The lists are shared and analyzed by pairs, groups, or the whole class. Clearly, a classroom environment open to controversy is essential to this activity. Pro and con discussions may lead to the framing of a majority opinion or they may terminate in a decision to agree to disagree. Whichever the result, it is important to reach some kind of closure during the class, one that is predicated on a thoughtful discussion of many points of view.

Pro and Con is a helpful critical thinking tool, particularly for students like Felicia who are at the first stages of cognitive development. Each student creates a tangible list that initially states the kinds of right and wrong answers that absolute knowers like to have at hand. As they discuss lists with their classmates and as they discover together that the right and wrong answers are not the same for everyone, students begin to learn to work with uncertainties. They start to develop the critical thinking skills necessary to move them toward the next stage of cognitive development. And they grow in their awareness that diversity of experience and opinion is one of the strengths of a learning community.

Pro and Con can be used at any point in a semester: before a topic is discussed (when Pro and Con is a kind of background probe), while the topic is being explored (Bredehoft, 1991), or at the end of the section of study as a review or as a grist for a final community discussion. Students can be asked to list reasons for or against a wide range of issues, from the mundane to the scientific to the social and political. In English 101, students can be asked to list the reasons for and against studying grammar. In a nutrition class, students can be directed to list the reasons for or against taking megavitamins. In a sociology course, students can be told to consider the reasons for and against housing the homeless. The possibilities are endless, but you must be ready for debate and be sure to be able to allow enough time for the students to hear all sides before reaching a conclusion.

Cooperative Learning Groups

Cooperative learning groups are small classroom groups that work toward a common goal. These groups emphasize positive interdependence, individual accountability, social skills, face-to-face interaction, and understanding of group processes (Johnson, Johnson, & Smith, 1991a). In the early weeks of the semester, these groups are particularly helpful for students who are still uncomfortable speaking out in a large-group setting. The small-group setting gives students a less risky atmosphere in which to interact and to discuss specific course material in depth and in which to become comfortable with working as a community. There are infinite configurations for cooperative learning groups. They may be informally gathered by seating or number of participants, or they may be more formally gathered by assignment. They may be loosely formed, or they may be carefully constructed. They may last for one day, several weeks, or the whole semester. Whatever the arrangement, the value of cooperative learning for building community is thoroughly documented in numerous books and articles (Goodsell, Maher, Tinto, & Associates, 1992; Johnson & Johnson, 1990; Johnson, Johnson, & Smith, 1991a, 1991b; Millis, 1990; Ventimiglia, 1994).

Informally gathered groups have no continuity; they are spontaneous and fluid. These qualities can be very useful, for informal learning groups can problem solve together, generate questions, or review material on the spur of the moment. If your students have raised a question or if the class needs to stop and ponder a problem, try restating the problem, asking the students to spend a few minutes writing a brief response, and then directing each student to pair-share responses with one neighbor or to form a group with three or four students in neighboring chairs.

A pair is useful for a quick in-depth discussion; a group of three guarantees a tie-breaking member in a dispute; a group of four or larger may need more structure. Whatever the number you designate (and you do need to designate a number), you will find that informal group work breaks the pace, gives students an opportunity to meet each other, and builds students' confidence in themselves as learners—all requisites of a successful classroom community.

Formally gathered groups are prearranged, made up of students who will work together for completion of one or more projects throughout a semester. These formal groups allow for consistency; they may also mirror more accurately the working groups that exist in employment settings. Separating larger classes into such fixed learning groups has a number of advantages. Professors can use the groups in a wide variety of ways and can encourage group members to study together and support each other throughout the semester, thus fulfilling one of the needs of a classroom community. Students such as Sam and Juan, who may feel out of place in the larger class setting, can establish connections within a smaller group. Groups members can develop a feeling of camaraderie, and friendly competitions among groups can generate energy and enthusiasm in the class as a whole.

While activities such as signing in on the board celebrate each individual in the class, the creation of groups underscores the necessity for individuals to work together. The process of assigning people to groups can become a festive occasion in the early weeks of the semester, allowing for movement around the classroom and giving students like Felicia the time they need to meet new people. Some professors hand out balloons of different colors, distinguishing group members through color coding. Others distribute puzzle pieces and ask students to find the students with the appropriate pieces to complete the puzzle. Still others hand out world maps with various countries colored in, asking students with the same colored-in country or contiguous countries to form a unit—thus sneaking in a little geography, especially if the students are then asked to name that country. The size of each group will depend to some extent on the class size and the professor's goals for group work. The smaller the group, the more opportunity each member will have to discuss ideas. Optimum group size ranges from three to five, for groups with over five members can become unwieldy.

Johnson, Johnson, and Smith (1991a, 1991b) suggest that heterogeneous groups are more productive in problem solving than homogeneous groups, yet in every community there are some individuals who have difficulty working together. A cooperative learning group is no exception. If a fixed group is malfunctioning, some professors encourage the students to learn the interpersonal skills for dealing with group interaction problems, while other professors are willing to rearrange the groups to restore harmony (see Tiberius, 1990, and Walvoord, 1986, for more discussion of managing small groups).

Whether the cooperative learning groups are formally or informally gathered, it is helpful for the professor to structure the groups so that they focus on task. A structure can be achieved by designating the roles to be played by each participant. However, once you designate the roles, Johnson, Johnson, and Smith (1991a, 1991b) recommend that instead of assigning them to individuals, you specify that roles are to be rotated among the group members at specific intervals. What are the roles that are useful? In a group of three students, one student can be the recorder (writes down information from the group discussion), another the timekeeper (keeps the group informed of time limits), and the third the checker of understanding (ensures that all group members can explain how the group arrived at an answer or conclusion and sees to it that group members sign off on assignments). Signing off is essential to a group project, according to Johnson, Johnson, and Smith (1991a, 1991b), for it commits each group member to the group activity. In a group of four, the fourth student can be the summarizer (restates the group's major conclusions), and in a group of five, the fifth student can be the encourager of participation (ensures that all members are contributing).

Should you decide that you want fixed learning groups that will remain the same over a period of time, you will find further organizing helpful. Hand out a list of general ground rules for group members at the first meeting. Include information on the expected behavior of members and suggestions for maintaining effective and positive group dynamics. Specify the structural roles that you want students to assume. Establish a recording format and a reporting scheme. One professor prepares a folder for each group and places a grid in the folder for group responses to projects. When a written group assignment is handed out, class members gather together in their fixed groups to respond to the problem. After they have discussed their responses, they enter them on the grid and hand the folder to the professor for commentary.

The professor has found that both the structuring of the assignment and the reporting process help to keep the students focused on the task at hand, as well as being quite effective in reducing student discussions of extracurricular activities. The mechanics of setting up groups may seem rather involved initially, but they are worth it, since once a pattern is established, group work can be integrated effortlessly into most class meetings.

There are many resources available for faculty who want to explore different ways to use cooperative learning in the classroom (Goodsell, Maher, Tinto, & Associates, 1992; Kadel & Keehner, 1994). The International Association for the Study of Cooperation in Education (IASCE) sponsors training and conferences as well as a magazine entitled *Cooperative Learning* (IASCE, Box 1582, Santa Cruz, CA 95061-1582; telephone: (408) 426-7926). In the fall of 1993, the *Cooperative Learning and College Teaching* newsletter began under the auspices of New Forums Press (P.O. Box 876, Stillwater, OK 74076; telephone: (405) 372-6158). The newsletter presents research and theory related to cooperative learning, with a strong emphasis on ways to implement cooperative learning approaches effectively in college classrooms.

Service Learning

As students come together into a classroom learning community, they bring with them their ties to multiple other communities: work-related, family, religious, political, social, recreational, and neighborhood communities, among others. As they enter the classroom, students generally submerge these essential connections in their lives, yet these communities are very much a part of the students' thinking and very much a part of their future. Might it be possible to continue connections to the outside community? Might not the community of the classroom be more vital if students did not put aside all their other communities when they entered the class? After all, students studying communications often volunteer at a television or radio station as a part of their coursework; students studying environmental science are frequently required to learn about conservation efforts; and students studying welfare need to have visited shelters for the homeless to know what it means to be homeless. Are there ways for students in these and other courses to receive course credit for volunteer work in the communities outside the college classroom? Perhaps not for all courses but for some, yes, there are.

To help students grasp the ways in which the material of the course will enrich their understanding of how the world works, professors from a variety of disciplines have recently included *service learning* (Harward & Albert, 1994; Campus Compact, 1993; Kendall, 1990) in their courses. Service learning requires that students volunteer in the community in class-related areas; they then receive class credit for their projects. Service projects are integrated into courses in a variety of ways. Sometimes a number of hours of service in the community is required for all students; often community service is an option for a paper, a lab, or a class project. Whatever the format of the community service, "the common denominator . . . is the deliberate linking of service, academic study, and structured reflection" (Harward & Albert, 1994, p. 11). And service learning has worked. To the doubting Thomases or Thomasinas, the course has become worthwhile. Students have been heard to admit that they now "understand" why an introductory course is required, a result devoutly to be wished.

Had Professor Simonds gathered information index cards at the start of her course, she might have discovered that several of her students were interested in teaching math or in discovering how math related to the business world. As an alternative to the required in-class math project, she could then have considered incorporating service learning into her course. She could have offered the students the option of volunteering in one of the local schools or at one of the local businesses. Clearly, such service learning projects are not for everyone. But they are an option, and if appropriate, students' reports of their firsthand experiences on such projects are one more way in which to enrich a classroom community.

Replay

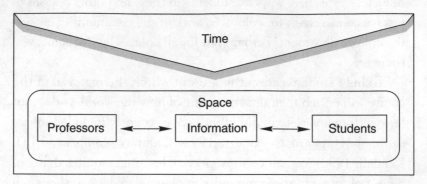

Time

The honeymoon period when energies are high and students are open to new approaches

The period when classroom community must be built

Space

Equally open to diverse subcultures

Used for a community of learners

Shared by professors and students

Focused on learning and questioning

Professors

Learn student names

Open atmosphere to

·   Learning
·   Questioning
·   Diversity·
·   Critical thinking

Organize

·   Introductions
·   Information exchanges

- Feedback channels
- Learning groups

Information

Is gathered through introductions

- Sign-in
- Learning names at door
- Name games
- Interviews
- "I am" exchanges

Is gathered through classroom assessment:

- Questionnaire
- TQM team
- Background Knowledge Probe
- Suggestion folder
- Minute Papers
- Pro and Con

Is gathered through

- Cooperative learning groups
- Service learning

Students

Become comfortable

- Meet each other
- Work with each other
- Rely on each other
- Respect diversity
- Build confidence as learners

5

The Interim Weeks
Beating the Doldrums

Day after day, day after day,
We stuck, nor breath nor motion;
As idle as a painted ship
Upon a painted ocean.
—Samuel Taylor Coleridge, "The Rime of the Ancient
Mariner"

Vignette: It was Wednesday, October 16, a few days after the
Columbus Day holiday. Faculty committees were pushing
toward November deadlines, the final interviews for a new dean of
administration were in progress, and exams and papers were
stacked high on professors' desks. Students were beginning to realize that the semester contained a lot of work—another set of tests,
final reports, exams, lots of reading to catch up on, and the big
game this weekend. The weather had held. Today was sunny, but
no one was out in the quadrangle throwing around Frisbees or
footballs.

Professor Abujian looked up at his architecture students as they
settled into their seats and shrugged off jackets. Sighing, he noticed
that the front rows were once again only sparsely filled, and today
even Robert and Asia, two of his best students, were missing. Without being aware of it, Professor Abujian grimaced, shifted his feet,
gripped the podium, and then leaned over to shuffle through his

briefcase. He realized that many of his students had probably not finished the text on Frank Lloyd Wright. It was infuriating; his lecture was not going to be comprehensible if they had not done the reading, but that was their responsibility. Professor Abujian had given this lecture a number of times before; he was comfortable with it, and he had not felt any incentive to reorganize it or to use slides to go with it. He preferred to rely on the photographs in the textbook. The semester was in full swing; the students should be able to read the textbook for themselves and then absorb his class lecture. Opening his folder, Professor Abujian took out his familiar notes and, feeling righteous, began to lecture.

Across the campus, Professor Cella was really tired. He had just had a cup of coffee with several colleagues, all of whom were griping about the poor quality of their last set of quizzes, drawings, or lab reports. One colleague commented that for the first time this semester, students were beginning to question her assignments. Professor Cella had listened and nodded, adding that he was also concerned about his students' creative energies; they were devoting effort, but it was difficult to ignite a spark.

Professor Cella taught physics. He was about to introduce the concept of the moment of inertia and had pondered the best way in which to involve his students. He had decided on an activity that directly engaged them in the moment of inertia, itself, and he hoped that his students would enjoy the activity as well as learn from it. Perhaps then that spark of creative energy might be reignited. Professor Cella planned to ask a volunteer to stand on a rotating platform that he had set up in the center of the room. He would then ask the other students to spin the platform around in time to music from a cassette provided by one of the students. When the students had gotten the rotation of the platform in sync with the music, Professor Cella would slow the music, ask the students to stop turning the platform, and direct the spinning student to put his arms out until his rotation matched the slower tempo of the new music. The exercise would illustrate how the moment of inertia affects the rotational speed, and Professor Cella hoped that the students might be able to discover this relationship. He planned to ask the students to break into four discussion groups and to ask each group to frame their discoveries in the form of a law.

Professor Kowalski had been teaching accounting for many years. She knew this was a low time in the semester. Actually, she realized, it was sometimes the second low period. Occasionally there was an earlier one, but this was the more challenging, and she had thought a great deal about how to handle it. Both she and her students needed a lift and a chance to laugh. At the end of the previous class, Professor Kowalski had handed out what she called a focus question. Unlike much else in accounting, focus questions have no one solution. They are interpretive questions that ask people to connect a common experience to a difficult skill or concept.

During the previous class, Professor Kowalski had begun to talk about methods of inventory. At the end of class, she had handed out a single assignment sheet covered with blank lines and brief, numbered directions. The assignment directed students to go home, open their top dresser drawers (or a similar small storage area) and after admiring the drawer, design a way to divide the contents into logical and separate categories. Once they had accomplished this, students were to calculate the percentages by volume of the objects in each category, not an easy task. Finally, they were to fill in the blank lines on the assignment sheet with their "inventory." Professor Kowalski hoped to begin the next class with a discussion not of the contents of the drawers, that would be invasive, but of design of a valid classification system. She had gathered together her own sample drawer of odds and ends for everyone to classify, and she planned to empty it onto the classroom table at the start of class. It should be a lively session.

Discussion

Professors Abujian, Cella, and Kowalski are mired in one of the most difficult points in the semester—a time when little seems to go forward, when energies falter, and when the community of the classroom appears to be disintegrating. Though the effect is not the same in each course (it varies with the subject being presented, the individuals in the classroom, and the flow of that particular semester), these days happen as Professor Kowalski observed, near midsemester, after a vacation or a long weekend, or just before or following hour tests. When they happen, they plunge both students and professors alike into what we have called the doldrums, a period, says *The American Heritage Dictionary*, "of stagnation or of unhappy listlessness."

For students, the doldrums often follow the semester pattern presented by Mann and others (1970). The honeymoon period is over. The reality of papers, projects, and exams seems to color every course. Grades begin to influence students' moods, often leading to criticism of the professor. More students are absent from classes, and those who are in class frequently appear distracted or overwhelmed. During our semester as students, we recall wondering if we would have enough energy to get through the low period and survive to the end of the course. Our journal entries dropped off at this time, and homework assignments were completed in a less thorough manner. Routine tasks became a challenge. For professors, the doldrums often follow the semester pattern depicted in the article "Will the School Year Ever End?" (1989): "Tasks that seemed routine, almost welcome in September now loom large, unrelenting and . . . worst of all . . . uninspiring. The motivation to teach has reached its lowest point" (p. 6).

During a class period, professors and students interact intellectually and emotionally; they rely on each other for the stimulation to move the course forward. From an emotional point of view, the responses of students can influence a professor both positively or negatively. Students who are attentive and focused in class provide the necessary spark for a professor who is feeling tired or discouraged, and a student with a good sense of humor can shift the mood of a class, redirecting potentially negative feelings into positive interactions. This synergy from attentive students is one of the most powerful rewards for professors. In contrast, the apathy of inattentive students is one of the greatest challenges. The ways in which professors acknowledge the doldrums and the techniques that they use to cope with them are critical, for it is often professors' responses that will determine whether the semester ends with a bang or with a whimper.

In our vignette, Professor Abujian is encountering the challenge of the doldrums. Students are missing from class, and Professor Abujian is beginning to take these absences personally. He assumes that his students did not complete the required reading and then feels angry about their lack of responsibility. His class is plagued by both his and his students' listlessness, but he rationalizes that this slow period is not his problem. He reassures himself that he has given this particular lecture before and was comfortable with it. He sighs and feels defensive. One gets the distinct impression that magical moments will be missing as he begins his class presentation. An adversarial mood is forming in the classroom space and may escalate unless some type of intervention takes place. What can be done to improve this situation? Need we professors confront such periods of low motivation? Yes, we must, for it is these flagging energies and this failing motivation that feed the doldrums. And it is at this period that a number of students drop out of classes.

Wlodkowski (1985) in his Time Continuum Model of Motivation (Figure 5.1) broke the learning sequence into beginning, middle, and ending periods and suggested factors that affect a learner's motivation during each period. Wlodkowski states that during each of these time periods, there are "two major factors of motivation that serve as categories for strategies that can be applied with maximum impact" (p. 61). During the beginning of a learning sequence, the pivotal factors for motivation are, first, the learner's attitudes (toward the learning environment, instructor, subject matter, and self), and second, the basic needs that exist within the learner as he or she begins to learn. We have addressed these initial aspects of the learning sequence by focusing on ways to create a syllabus that will

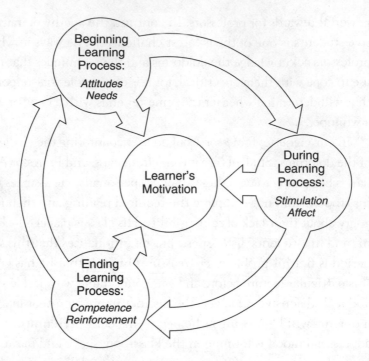

Figure 5.1. Time Continuum Model of Motivation.
   Source: Wlodkowski, 1985, p. 61. Reprinted by permission.

foster a positive learning environment (Chapter Three) and by discussing approaches for creating an effective classroom community (Chapter Four).

During the middle period, stimulation and emotion are the key factors affecting motivation for learning. Wlodkowski suggests that while planning this middle phase, instructors should consider two basic questions: first, "What about this learning sequence will continuously stimulate my learners?" and second, "How is the affective experience and the emotional climate for this learning sequence positive for learners?" (p. 67). In planning to use the turntable experiment, Professor Cella has begun to address these very questions. He has acknowledged the fatigue at this time of the semester and has recognized that other colleagues are also experiencing this low period. He does not feel he is totally responsible for the unhappy listlessness that is consuming the environment of his classroom, but he does want to wipe it out and to reignite students' creative energies, and so he begins to think about what he has done in past semesters when something did not work. He has come to the conclusion that his students need a new approach to help them and to help him (that is equally important) regain momentum. As Professor Cella begins to revise his plan for his upcoming class on the moment of inertia, he recalls a recent faculty forum on Howard Gardner's frames of mind and decides that he will follow Gardner's dictums. He will experiment with sending out different signals to reach the variety of receivers (learners) in his class; he will develop and use new approaches.

Howard Gardner (1983) proposes that intellectual ability is defined too narrowly in our society. He argues that it is more realistic to think of multiple intelligences rather than the usual verbal and performance abilities measured in standard intelligence tests. Gardner believes that there are seven types of intelligence: linguistic, musical, logical-mathematical, spatial, bodily-kinesthetic, and personal (which includes both intrapersonal and interpersonal). In educational settings, particularly at the postsecondary level, most instruction is focused on the linguistic and the logical-mathematical approaches. In a typical classroom, students who excel in one of the five other types of intelligences may not receive the stimulation best suited to their abilities or to their ways of learning.

When Professor Cella began thinking about new approaches to his material and consulted a list of Gardner's seven types of intelligences, he realized with a shock that in his course he concentrated almost exclusively on only one of the frames of mind—the logical-mathematical. He was therefore pitching his class to one way of learning and one kind of critical thinking. He encouraged students to reason, to use logic in solving problems, and to use mathematics to find solutions. Yes, he did incorporate the use of linguistic intelligence by requiring students to explain their experiments through lab reports, but he tended to be more concerned about their math and their logic than about their writing style when he graded the reports. Since he was taking the time to rethink his presentations for the next few classes, and because he enjoyed setting out plans (to him it was rather like setting up equations), Professor Cella decided to see how many of Gardner's intelligences he could successfully include in his next classes without changing the focus of the topic. Perhaps this way he could break the grip of the doldrums.

Professor Cella stared at Gardner's list. He decided that if he tried a bodily-kinesthetic approach, he would get students moving around. That would certainly attack the lethargy. Just yesterday, Professor Cella had seen the students playing Hacky Sac and Frisbee in the courtyard before class; in fact, he had joined in an impromptu Frisbee game for a few minutes. He really had never thought about incorporating this kind of movement and laughter into his class, but why not? It made sense for him to consider the physical self and the control of bodily movements to explore the concept of the moment of inertia. He realized that including a physical exercise might result in a fairly rowdy class, but he was certain that he could restore a modicum of decorum before the class ended, and he reasoned that the action and laughter were important. Besides, he expected to enjoy it, too. After all, the doldrums affected them all.

Professor Cella also knew that his students liked music; in fact, some of them seemed to have Walkmans attached to their ears as permanent fixtures. Why not bring music into his class? Perhaps the students would perk up and put away the Walkmans less grudgingly. Music would be an excellent way to regulate the speed of the spinning student. Professor Cella then decided to involve the students in the selection of the music—a wise decision, for his choice of music might well not mean much to them. He asked them to bring in tapes that they thought would be helpful in an experiment having to do with tempo. With this request, Professor Cella had both stimulated his learners and intuitively addressed the affective needs of students, the two critical aspects that Wlodkowsi emphasizes as crucial in this middle phase of the learning sequence.

On the day of the turntable experiment, Professor Cella rediscovered how much his students enjoyed collaboration and interpersonal interaction; they were still arguing as they filed off to their next classes. The doldrums were beginning to lose their hold on the classroom community. Professor Cella's own motivation for teaching increased after he saw the enthusiasm engendered by his experiment—his interpersonal intelligence had been touched, too. He went back to Gardner's list. He realized that spatial intelligence (the ability to deal with aspects of the visual and spatial world) is used effectively in many of the computer simulation programs he had been considering. A number of his students were computer junkies and had shown real spatial understanding in their drawings. Professor Cella decided to tap into these strengths and to purchase a computer simulation program depicting the conservation of momentum in the collision of two vehicles.

The final intelligence in Gardner's list, the intrapersonal intelligence of knowing oneself, was more challenging for Professor Cella. He himself valued that intelligence highly. For him, the laws of physics were one of the avenues for self-discovery. Yet he had not considered including this intelligence in his physics class. He decided to ask students to keep a personal journal in which to reflect on what they did and did not find stimulating about the study of physics. And he planned that he would review the journals in order to figure out whether he was on track with his approaches. Professor Cella began to feel that the period of unhappy listlessness in his classroom was starting to come under his control. He realized that he might not reach everyone in his class, but at least he was not giving up on the learning process.

Refusing to let lethargy envelop you is a first step in confronting the doldrums. The next step is to figure out a plan for revitalizing and redirecting the learning energies in the classroom. Professor Cella accomplished this task through designing approaches to appeal to the different types of intelligences present in his classroom. Professor Kowalski, on the other hand, came up with the idea of inventorying a dresser drawer as a way to move through the various phases of the learning cycle. Professor Kowalski was a proponent of Kolb's model of experiential learning (Kolb, 1984). She felt strongly that it is critical for students to act on information in different ways if they are to maximize their learning experience. She had read Svinicki and Dixon's (1987) suggestions for ways to modify Kolb's model for the college classroom and had been experimenting for several semesters with adapting Kolb's learning cycle to her course in accounting.

According to Kolb (1984), a learning cycle involves four processes: concrete experience, reflective observation, abstract conceptualization, and active experimentation. In Kolb's view, students who move through the activities of all four phases of the learning cycle will both learn and retain information more effectively than if they concentrate on only one or two of the phases. The initial phase, concrete experience, requires students' personal involvement in an activity in order to understand it firsthand. In Professor Kowalski's class, students encounter this experience by taking an inventory of their dresser drawers, sorting through disorganized materials, and then figuring out their own systems for dividing drawer contents into logical and separate categories.

The next phase, reflective observation, encourages learners first to examine the problem and then to reflect on it from a variety of perspectives. Professor Kowalski's students were asked to calculate the percentages by volume of each category and to respond to thought questions from the assignment sheet. They were directed to assess the drawer contents as impartially as possible and then to answer open-ended focus questions.

In the third phase, abstract conceptualization, students are asked to figure out some logical method of integrating their experiences during the activity with their reflective observations. In their efforts to explain their discoveries, they may form analogies or create models or hypotheses, or they may apply other theoretical viewpoints. After Professor Kowalski discussed the inventory of her own dresser drawer, she planned to present several different theoretical frameworks to her accounting class. Students would select one of these frameworks to gain more understanding of the inventory process.

Finally, in the active experimentation phase, students apply their explanations or theoretical frameworks to other situations. Professor Kowalski's next class session was to involve a case study dealing with large-scale inventories. Students would apply to a business setting what they had learned through their own experience, observation, and conceptualization.

Svinicki and Dixon (1987) suggest "designating the four activities [of the Kolb learning cycle] with action verbs that describe the activity of the learner at each step. Thus, concrete experience becomes experiencing; reflective observation becomes examining; abstract conceptualization becomes explaining; and active experimentation becomes applying" (p. 144). This cycle of learning is not a panacea, but Professor Kowalski reasoned that students who are experiencing, examining, explaining, and applying information in class are going to be more involved in the learning process, value the classroom experience more, and be less likely to cut classes. Both Professor Cella and Professor Kowalski also recognized that beating the doldrums required not only considering *what* they would teach next, but also contemplating *how* they would teach it. Intuitively, they realized that they must move away from their own learning approaches (for we professors tend to teach in ways consistent with our personal learning styles) and instead, inject materials into their classes that recognized other styles of learning.

Gardner and Kolb are but two of the researchers who present insights into the ways of learning. Claxton and Murrell (1987) go further in their analysis of learning styles and suggest that a student's learning style can be defined according to the four dimensions of personality, information processing, social interaction, and instructional preference. In order to illustrate their findings, Claxton and Murrell adopt Curry's figure (1983), which depicts the progression of various learning styles by comparing them to the layers of an onion (see Figure 5.2). In Curry's figure, the outer layers of the onion represent areas that are easiest to alter, while the inner layers represent those that are more difficult to alter. Each is subscribed to by several theorists, and each can be measured by some type of instrument, whether the Myers-Briggs Type Indicator, which is widely used in academic settings, or others that are used primarily for research.

The inner layer of the onion, the personality models, are represented by the research of Chess and Thomas (1986) on temperament, by the types of the Myers-Briggs Type Indicator (Myers & Myers, 1980), and by the longitudinal studies of Katz and Henry (1988) using the Omnibus Personality Inventory. Kolb's model fits into the next layer of the onion, information processing, as does research by Pask (1976), Gregorc (1979), and Schmeck (1983). Studies by Mann and others in 1970 were the first attempts to look at the role of social interaction in the classroom. They paved the way for the next layer of social interaction models, which are best represented by the work of Reichmann and Grasha (1974). The outer layer of the onion, instructional preference, incorporates many components of learning styles: conditions students prefer for learning, areas of interest, and preferred modes of learning. The models of Hill and Nunnery (1973), Dunn and Dunn (1978), and Canfield (1980) fit into this category.

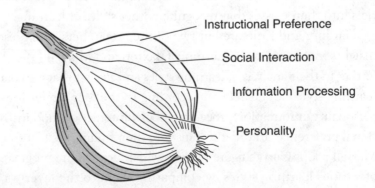

Figure 5.2. A Framework for Learning Style Models.
Source: Claxton & Murrell, 1987, p. 7; adapted from Curry, 1983.

Two basic tenets of all these learning style models are that a student's learning style remains stable over time and that whatever the style, it is not under the student's individual control. However, Pintrich and Johnson (1990) question these assumptions. Their research is not into learning *styles* (the ways in which we learn), but rather into learning *strategies* (the methods through which we learn). They claim that learning strategies, unlike learning styles, can be controlled by the learner and can change under certain situational demands. The learning strategy approach focuses strongly on assessment, emphasizing the need to measure students' motivation for learning as well as their ability to adapt to different learning situations.

Pintrich and Johnson (1990) suggest two instruments for measuring students' learning strategies: the Learning and Study Strategies Inventory (LASSI) developed by Claire Weinstein and her colleagues (Weinstein, Goetz, & Alexander, 1988; Weinstein, Schulte, & Palmer, 1987; Weinstein, Zimmerman, & Palmer, 1988) and the Motivated Strategies for Learning Questionnaire (MSLQ) developed under the leadership of Pintrich (Pintrich, McKeachie, & Smith, 1989). Both instruments are self-report questionnaires that take approximately twenty minutes to complete. From these instruments, a professor can gain insight into how students' motivation and learning are operating in a specific course, and students can obtain valuable information regarding their areas of strength and the areas in which they need improvement.

Professors may not want to invest the time required to uncover each student's learning style or learning strategy. Nor is it necessary that a professor's teaching style match perfectly with the styles of his or her students (Grasha, 1984). It is valuable, however, for instructors to realize that such assessment instruments are available and that they can be used to provide a more detailed picture of the ways in which one's students learn. To manage a period of the doldrums when nothing seems to work, instructors might consider exploring one of these models, for "variety is the salt of the classroom earth. If students learn in documentably different ways,

instructors need to use different instructional strategies and provide students opportunities to demonstrate their mastery of the content through various vehicles" ("How Students Learn," 1989, p. 4).

Application

The doldrums present an emotional as well as a cognitive challenge for both professors and students. Even while they worry over the dwindling numbers in their classes and struggle with how to re-stimulate the thinking of their students after the novelty of the early weeks has faded, professors must deal with both the sagging spirits of the class and their own waning energies. The three faculty members described in our vignette go about this task in different ways and with varying degrees of enthusiasm. Professor Abujian does not see a low period as a normal part of the rhythm of the semester: he sees the students' drop in motivation as their fault and their responsibility. He feels angry. Professor Abujian's frustration will almost certainly lead to greater negativism in the classroom atmosphere. It will also erode his confidence in himself as a teacher as well as his enthusiasm in teaching.

Professor Cella, on the other hand, recognizes the existence of the doldrums. He talks about it with other faculty members, sharing in their frustrations and arriving at the realization that he is not the only professor struggling with classroom lethargy. He realizes that it is up to him to design a plan to combat ebbing energies. Deciding that it is important to involve his students, he works out an interactive class activity that presents information in a new way. His activity is a success, and Professor Cella's physics class comes alive once again.

Professor Kowalski has looked at the rhythm of her class for several years and now recognizes the doldrums pattern. She not only talks to other faculty members about the doldrums, she also talks with her students. She brings in props. She connects new concepts directly and concretely to the experiences of her students. She schedules creative and humorous activities into her classes. Professor Kowalski is successful in banning the blues not only for her students but also for herself. Her students are renewed, their enthusiasm restored.

We have observed that there is a direct relationship between recognition of the doldrums, action to combat the doldrums, and eventual success. Professor Abujian's situation underscores the significance of recognizing that low points in the semester do exist for everyone and that these low points must not be personalized but, instead, actively confronted. It is essential that Professor Abujian realize that he must not let low attendance, incomplete assignments, and flagging energies eat at him; he must try (and it is difficult, sometimes) to maintain an emotional distance from such manifestations of the doldrums. If he can reframe the challenges of the doldrums in a way that does not lead him to feel antagonism or anger toward the class, he is on his way to success.

Professor Cella's actions reinforce the value of professors' sharing their experiences with each other, particularly during this time, in order to gain support and to come up with practical solutions. Yes, it is a risk to talk about the apathy in your class with your colleagues, but it is also the first step in gaining more insight into the reasons behind the low motivation and in discovering renewed enthusiasm for combating it. Professor Kowalski accepts the probability of the doldrums appearing during any semester and has come up with a workable solution. She has kept track of the low points in her classes for several semesters and has noted a particular pattern over time. She anticipates a low period and has prepared herself and her students to navigate the doldrums with a minimum of distress. By turning the doldrums into a challenge for the classroom community, Professor Kowalski has dignified the existence of down periods as an integral part of the semester. She has enriched her classroom and given her students a sense of control over their learning experience.

The basic nature of college teaching makes it difficult for some faculty members to confront the doldrums. College teaching, in many respects, is a private exchange taking place behind closed doors. Professors value the freedom and autonomy of this arrangement, but they often miss out on the support and encouragement other faculty members can offer. It is helpful to compare experiences with other professors in order to get a sense of overall energy levels at an institution. In our seminars over the past five years, we have noted the relief among our colleagues when a professor shares an episode from a low point in the semester and then hears several other professors echo similar experiences.

Being open with students also has real merit and appears to reunite the classroom community. Students are likely to feel overwhelmed at various points during a semester. Learning that they are not alone in these feelings helps them decide to stay with the tasks at hand. During the past few semesters, we have experimented with confronting down periods in our own classes when they begin to manifest themselves. We have talked about these periods with the students, acknowledging the stresses and pressures that contribute to the feeling. At the end of such discussions, students inevitably come up and say something like: "I thought that I was the only one going crazy. It really helps me to hear that this is a difficult time of the semester for lots of people."

In the same vein, should you choose to apply Gardner's or Kolb's approaches as doldrums busters and as potential retention devices, it is helpful to explain the philosophy behind the chosen approach to your students and then to ask the students to monitor whether their motivation or thinking changes when different teaching and learning techniques are used. In this way, students become licensed partners in the learning processes of the classroom community. What they may have intuitively known—that learning is not accomplished through one avenue or in one step—is illustrated with their involvement and reinforced through their practice.

Applying Gardner's Perspectives

Gardner emphasizes the importance of understanding information from more than one perspective and states that "the adoption of a family of stances toward a phenomenon encourages the student to come to know that phenomenon in more than one way, to develop multiple representations and seek to relate these representations to one another" (Gardner, 1991, pp. 246–247). Although much of the research into the application of his theories has been at the K–12 level (Gardner 1983, 1991, 1993; Armstrong, 1987, 1993; Campbell, Campbell, & Dickinson, 1992), we have found his ideas extremely helpful at the college level, both throughout the semester as course enrichers and at specific intervals as doldrums busters. In our ALC seminars, we have illustrated how the seven multiple intelligences, or frames of mind, that Gardner has delineated can be integrated throughout the subject matter of an entire course or into the discussion of a single topic.

In the vignette at the start of Chapter One, Professors Capriani, Freneau, O'Reilly, and Nordstrom had each chosen to discuss Robert Frost's poetry near the beginning of their literature courses. But assume that another professor, Professor Nady, had arrived at her discussion of Robert Frost near the middle of the semester and that her class had been stuck in the doldrums as she prepared to teach "Stopping by Woods on a Snowy Evening." Knowing that the poem was familiar to many of her students and that some were less than excited about discussing it again, she had turned to Gardner's *Frames of Mind* (1983), and partially as a reenergizer for herself, she had decided to find a way to appeal to each of Gardner's seven intelligences as she taught the poem.

Professor Nady had noticed a number of her students doodling, even drawing their notes. What if she could harness this talent from the start? As a part of their assignment for the upcoming class, she asked students to sketch or to create a model of the journey described in the poem. She did not collect the drawings or the models nor judge them for artistic quality. Instead, she used them as references during the class discussion. Professor Nady discovered that by requiring students to depict the narrative of the poem visually and spatially, instead of verbally, she assisted them to gain new insight into its imagery and its direction. (Think about it. Are the woods on the right or the left? Are the woods small or immense? Which way is the wind blowing?) The ensuing discussion, she found, was more animated than it had been in many of her previous classes.

Bowing to the dominant teaching approach in her course, linguistic intelligence, Professor Nady read the poem aloud at the beginning of her class, paused, and then, before the discussion of the content, turned to an explanation of scansion. A challenging task, but easier, Professor Nady reasoned, through math, music, and bodily-kinesthetic approaches than solely through a linguistic approach. She asked the students to number each of the syllables in two lines of the poem and then went on to explain the notation and the divisions involved in meter. She illustrated these concepts on the board and then told the students to write out the probable scansion of one of the chosen lines as a sort of an equation.

This technique worked well for those of her students who thought in mathematical sequences and for those who heard the music of words. It did not work as well for others. Even so, several of the students who had not previously been much interested in the poetry section of the course seemed to perk up. Professor Nady turned next to a bodily-kinesthetic approach and asked the students, as she read aloud, to beat out the stresses of the lines on their desks, on the floor, on the wall, even on their friends' heads. At least the class laughed and began to move.

When the class turned to a discussion of the content of the poem, Professor Nady asked her students to look at their drawings or models and to imagine themselves "between the woods and frozen lake," to picture it, even to drive the horse—a blending of the spatial and bodily-kinesthetic intelligences—and then to talk in small groups about their ideas for the interpretation of the final two lines of the poem. The latter step was a use of interpersonal intelligence and one that her students were very familiar with from previous classes.

Professor Nady planned to ask the students to connect the message of the poem as they saw it to some piece of their own experience (a use of intrapersonal intelligence) and to write about that connection as a part of the assignment for the next class. But she had one last trick up her sleeve, her final bow to the musical intelligences in her class. At the end of the class, Professor Nady played a few verses of "Hernando's Hideaway" from the musical *Pajama Game*, asking students to beat out the rhythm on their desks. Then, she asked students to read, or even to sing, the first verse of "Stopping by Woods" as she replayed the song. The class went out singing, with apologies to Robert Frost (who had once had the same verse sung to him by his students at the Bread Loaf School) and perhaps with a better grasp on scansion—certainly with spirits emerging from the doldrums.

It is not necessary, or even possible, to connect to each of Gardner's seven frames of mind in every presentation. It is important, however, particularly during the doldrums, to consider enriching your course with new ways of using the dominant mode of your particular teaching style and with new approaches that you incorporate less dominant modes.

Linguistic

Most of us were ourselves taught through the linguistic mode; many of us continue to rely heavily upon it. After all, it is the method of communication for the majority of the world. How can we inject new energy into this mode? You can use writing in different ways. You can assign personal narratives that connect students' experiences to the course content, as Professor Nady planned to do. You can use *free writing*. Free writing, whether the topic is assigned and is therefore focused free writing or unassigned and therefore *free* free writing, is quite different from the writing usually assigned in a class. It is personal, and often it is not collected. If it is collected, it is not corrected for spelling or punctuation, nor is it graded. You can begin a class with free writing in order to center the upcoming discussion.

You can stop the class for a brief period of focused free writing on the topic just discussed. You can close the class with free writing to help students make connections.

You can assign focus questions. Professor Kowalski used focus questions in her accounting class. Focus questions are not graded and there is no one correct answer to them—the responses differ with the experiences of each responder. Focus questions require thought about rather than assimilation of the material just studied; they require students to pause, to search their personal knowledge, and then to apply that knowledge. Biology students about to begin their first dissections might be asked to describe how they cut up their fish or meat or how they make carrot sticks. History students about to study South Africa might be asked to list the five most important facts that they know about the Boers or to describe their vision of the land around Johannesburg. Sociology students might be asked to describe the television commercial that they feel is most destructive to the family. Focus questions are as inventive as the professor designing them wants them to be. They are exploratory questions that spade the way for the learning of new information or the building of new understandings.

Just as you can use writing in new ways, you can use conversation in new ways. You can ask students to share personal histories relating to the topic at hand. You can ask them to create dialogues between two or more leaders just studied or conversations between authors just read. You can make use of the vocabulary of controversy and conflict, asking students to present two sides of a question: two theories about vitamin E, two ways to construct a bridge, two visions of the legalities of civil disobedience. Each of these activities changes the rhythms of the class—one excellent way to combat the doldrums.

Musical

Students know music, many kinds of music. They listen to it, daydream to it, study to it, dance to it, sing it, play it, watch it, write it, and generally relate to it. Music is a conduit of their thought and an expression of their emotions, yet music is not often incorporated into college classrooms. Connecting coursework to the musical intelligence is always helpful, but it is especially useful during the dulled and weary times of the doldrums.

There are innumerable ways to include music in your classes. It can be woven directly into the content of the material. Professors of history can incorporate music into a class in order to set the stage for a discussion of specific historical events. Tchaikovsky's *1812 Overture* certainly opens the door to a discussion of the brutalities of that war and of Napoleon's overweening pride. In our ALC seminars, professors of English as a second language and professors of foreign languages have demonstrated how they have used popular songs as a way to make translating come alive. In our vignette, we showed Professor Cella effectively incorporating music into his teaching of the moment of inertia, involving his students both in the music itself and in the selection of it. Professors of philosophy have used student-selected music to generate a discussion of images of death. Professors of nursing have enriched a presentation on stress management techniques with the use of music. And professors interested in incorporating information from other cultures into their classes have found music an effective tool for beginning a discussion of attitudes, values, and societies.

Music can be used simply as a way to change moods. Students often comment that music helps them to relax and to escape from a negative day. This coping technique can be adapted effectively to the classroom by a professor who recognizes a low-energy period and begins class by playing music aimed at stress reduction. The music provides a segue into a discussion of the tensions of the time period and sets the stage for a dialogue about how to survive effectively. Different types of music can ease anxiety on difficult days during the semester (days following an exam, days when papers are due) and can help students to focus more positively on the opportunities that lie ahead. In the same way, there is nothing like a drum roll to announce a deadline.

Music can be used as a mnemonic, a review technique, and a

reminder. Students have created rap songs to review basic information in science, logic, and math courses; musicians have brought in instruments to reinforce concepts such as different rhythms in poetry. In a child education course, a student played Harry Chapin's "Flowers Are Red" to demonstrate how a teacher can crush a child's enthusiasm and creativity by demanding that all students conform to a standard way of doing things—drawing flowers red and leaves green.

Logical-Mathematical

The logical-mathematical intelligence is the other of the two most commonly used intelligences. It is interwoven with the linguistic intelligence and closely relates to the musical intelligence. It is the language of logic and of many approaches to critical thinking. Gardner (1983) points out that this is the form of thought that "can be traced to a confrontation with the world of objects" (p. 129) and that "moves toward increasingly abstract formal systems" (p. 135). How can this intelligence be interwoven into the presentations of professors accustomed to linguistic methods or be used in new ways in quantitative courses?

The logical-mathematical intelligence is the intelligence of counting, enumerating, listing, bulleting, dividing, sorting, categorizing, and sequencing. It can be the intelligence that understands cause and effect, that will find progressions in history and the law, that will grasp proportions, numbers, and divisions into columns. It is the intelligence that will be intrigued by organizing thought and discovering patterns. Harness the logical-mathematical intelligence by using one of these approaches in new ways in your courses.

Present ideas as a linear progression (taxation + underrepresentation = tea dumped in the Boston Harbor). Point out repetition in material and ask students to find a pattern—numerical or sequential. Ask students to sequence the development of an idea (such as people's yearning to fly: Icarus, balloons, biplanes, single-wing propeller planes, jet aircraft, SSTs, solid-fuel rockets) or the steps needed to acquire a particular skill. In a sociology course, ask students to illustrate a social situation in a diagram of cause. In a composition class struggling with style, ask students to use symbols to show the patterns of sentences (N [noun] + V [verb] + CC [coordinating conjunction] + N + V = compound sentence). In a history class, ask students to depict the progression of an event numerically, or in a science class, ask students to categorize by progressive clusters and then to recategorize numerically.

Spatial

Spatial intelligence is the intelligence that allows one "to perceive a form or object" (Gardner, 1983, p. 174). This does not necessarily mean that one can draw that form or even optically see it (a blind person can have a strong spatial intelligence); rather, it means that one can visualize the dimensions of that form and can manipulate the form and the space around it. The spatial intelligence is often a dominant intelligence in engineers, artists, illustrators, packers, athletes, architects, surgeons, dancers, and navigators.

Many professors already incorporate the spatial dimension into their classes, using overhead projectors, films, videocassettes and videodiscs, or CD-ROMs. Photographs, paintings, maps, models, various objects and reproductions also relate to the visual and spatial intelligence. Reproductions of Mondrian's paintings can bring new understanding to a music class, and regional sculptures can enrich a study of history. Examples of coffee pots can clarify concepts of the evolution of automation for a mechanics class. Pictures of Giacometti's figures can excite new understanding of isolation. An exhibition of Ansel Adams's photographs can enrich an environmental studies class, or a collection of Annie Liebowitz's photography a sociology class. A world map posted on the wall of classrooms becomes a drawing card for many of our amateur geography students. Try taking the use of the map one step further and post questions next to it: Where is Iraq, Cambodia, Nigeria, or Bali? Can you locate Los Angeles, Budapest, Tokyo, or Sydney? The possibilities are as great as the energies of the professor.

It is also possible to harness the energies of students. Try asking students to search for advertisements that typify an new ethic in society or illustrate an emerging trend in business. Or direct students to collect political cartoons as the basis for a class discussion in a history or government class. Set up a flip chart for posting additional resources or references for the topic of the day. Use the flip chart for announcements of class assignments and deadlines, or reserve a section of the chart for congratulations to students and reminders of course-related upcoming campus and local events.

During the doldrums, ask students or student groups to contribute an idea, a list of questions, or an article to the flip chart. Or consider the use of collages, murals, and posters. Groups of students can work together to create murals depicting a timeline in history, a process in the sciences, a life cycle in the social sciences, or a specific concept in other disciplines. An Ishikawa Diagram or fishbone diagram (Chapter Two) can be tacked up on the wall or drawn on the board and used as the focus for class or small-group discussions. Or the professor can begin class by handing out blank fishbone diagrams which each student then completes with information from that day's class discussion.

Although spatial intelligence does not necessarily imply the ability to draw, it does imply a propensity to relate through pictures. For students who prefer to organize information in a visual, spatial dimension, concept maps are invaluable. In a concept map, the main idea is placed in the center of a page and then related ideas and concepts are connected by lines or arrows (see Figure 4.1). A student in a composition class who learned that it was "all right" to *draw* an outline for a paper that she would translate into words later, overcame her fear of outlining and moved her course marks from C's to A's. Spatial intelligence is clearly her dominant frame of mind. She now draws her review notes for all of her classes.

Professors have used concept maps to summarize chapters, to clarify procedures for medical assistants, to outline papers in economics classes, to brainstorm in music classes, or to serve as an alternate way for taking notes in all subjects. Students can create maps to depict a particular process or idea and then compare maps to see where their thinking is similar and where it is different. A faculty member in biology asks students to create maps on file folders using Post-Its to represent different ideas and concepts. When the students compare their maps, they can move the Post-Its to arrive at new configurations. Through computer software programs (for example, *Inspiration* for Macintosh or *Visio* for IBM), professors can experiment with using concept maps to illustrate their course outlines or their reading lists.

Bodily-Kinesthetic

The bodily-kinesthetic intelligence is closely related to spatial intelligence. It involves two capacities: "control of one's bodily motions and [the] capacity to handle objects skillfully" (Gardner, 1983, p. 206). It is one of the primary intelligences of athletes, dancers, and actors. It is also one of the intelligences central to the skills of typists, carpenters, musicians, inventors, surgeons, typesetters, and machinists.

At first blush, the use of the body may seem far removed from the college classroom. Incorporating this intelligence, even to alleviate the low moments of the doldrums, may appear an intrusion into the business at hand, getting on with the teaching of content. But paradoxically, the bodily-kinesthetic intelligence is often one of a professor's strong intelligences. In fact, it is one of our primary teaching tools. "All the world's a stage," and certainly, the classroom is the stage where we professors perform. We use the bodily-kinesthetic intelligence in our dialogue with students far more than we may have realized. We pace behind the lectern, wave our hands to illustrate a point, lean forward to emphasize the importance of our words, walk back and forth from the blackboard. Some move about the room. This is a generation of students that has grown up in front of television sets. Anyone who gets up in front of them is often expected to be an entertainer. Although professors must divert students' customary expectations that they will be spoonfed, professors ought not to deny students' expectations of entertainment when times are tough.

How can professors harness the bodily-kinesthetic intelligence in new ways? One way to include more kinesthetic and tactile processing in a class is to incorporate manipulative materials into presentations. Professors of science, mechanics, and nursing have given out colored modeling clay to their students and suggested that they sculpt their own models of the topic at hand. Professors of psychology, literature, and humanities have asked students to give form in clay to new and difficult concepts. How would you shape fear or hope or beauty? Professor Abujian, the tired professor of architecture, might have passed around examples of building materials in order to spark his lecture on Frank Lloyd Wright. On a really stagnant doldrums day, in the midst of a lifeless discussion, try posing a question and then yanking out a Koosh Ball and tossing it to the students. The fortunate student who catches it (clearly a student strong in the bodily-kinesthetic domain) responds to the question, asks a new topic–related question, and tosses the ball to someone else. And on goes the action.

Models, games, and simulations all make use of the bodily-kinesthetic intelligence and bring new enthusiasm to a classroom stuck in the doldrums. Somers and Holt (1993) discuss the effectiveness of games in a graduate education course. They also review approaches for evaluating the games. They recommend Greenblat's (1988) handbook *Designing Games and Simulations* as a valuable resource for game developers. In social science courses, students have designed games for stress management; in economics classes, students have designed games to clarify the theories behind the stock market. In child psychology, in lieu of an hour test, students have been asked to design a game, a toy, or a book appropriate for different stages of cognitive development, test it out on a child of the corresponding age, write a paper explaining why it was stimulating for that age level, then share the results with their classmates.

These are all good approaches to try out when the doldrums strike and to integrate more fully into the classroom.

Like models and games, simulations allow for a different way of knowing and for many students, a more effective way of learning (Jones, 1993, is a source book of simulation activities). These activities call upon students to become actors and thus to control their bodily movements and to manipulate objects, the two capacities of the bodily-kinesthetic intelligence. Should you decide to include simulations in your course, it is important to allow time for thorough preparation before the activity as well as for discussion after the activity (Dorn, 1989; Shannon, 1986). A professor of criminal justice effectively used a simulation activity as the culminating event for a unit on evidence. Students began by answering a series of questions on the textbook chapter on evidence. They considered cases involving confusing pieces of evidence and other complicating factors and began slowly to appreciate the problems, but they still maintained a rather cocky attitude about their abilities to solve crimes. In the simulation activity, they were divided into small groups and were handed a description of a hypothetical situation involving drugs. The situation required them to search the offices of several (pre-enlisted) faculty members for evidence of illegal drugs. (It was simply an exercise. No drugs were planted in the offices.) In the process of the investigation, students learned the relevance of the information they had read in their textbooks, experienced firsthand the complexities of interpreting clues, developed a more cautious attitude about making judgments, and perhaps most important of all, busted the doldrums (for them and perhaps also for the enlisted professors) as they endeavored to bring "a wayward professor" to justice.

Personal

The intrapersonal and interpersonal intelligences involve the ability to know oneself and the ability to distinguish among and relate to other selves. Intrapersonal intelligence is often highly developed in poets, philosophers, leaders and followers of religious groups, therapists, novelists, and playwrights. Interpersonal intelligence is often a strong domain in successful politicians, salespersons, restaurateurs, clowns, interviewers, therapists, cartoonists, comedians, parents, and teachers.

Intrapersonal.   Research on students' cognitive development in college (Perry, 1970; Belenky, Clinchy, Goldberger, & Tarule, 1986; Baxter Magolda, 1992) stresses the importance of students' learning how to reconcile their own viewpoints with the multiple new perspectives presented in their courses. Students need opportunities to reflect upon and sort out the confusion that results when they are exposed to new ways of thinking. Keeping a journal in any course provides a way for students to become more conscious of their personal connection to course material and to document their cognitive growth. A student may be in a quandary about the notion of hypothesis testing in statistics because he or she has difficulty in formulating the null hypothesis. By writing about this problem in a journal, the student will be helped to accept the fact that confusion is sometimes inevitable in the process of learning and that not everything is learned by magic in a flash; some things require perspiration and even plodding.

Writing journals during the doldrums not only helps students restore flagging energies and sort out confusion; it also helps professors break the stagnation. Professors who collect the journals, not for grading but for insights, can gain feedback on individual students and on the overall pattern of class concerns. After reviewing class journals, professors may decide to talk about their own struggles with learning as one way to generate a discussion of approaches for dealing with the discomfort that sometimes accompanies the integration of new knowledge.

The biggest intrapersonal obstacle for students during the doldrums is often negative evaluations of self. Most students are disappointed when they do poorly on a paper or an exam; several disappointments can lead to negative self-talk: "I'll never make it through!" "Why am I so dense?" "This is a lost cause." Work in cognitive therapy (Burns, 1980, 1990) supports the view that negative thoughts and attitudes lead to negative feelings, which in turn lead to more pessimistic ways of looking at the world. A Pollyanna outlook on life is not a requirement for learning in a classroom, but recurring negative thinking and moods are sure to limit one's receptivity to new ideas and experiences, a crucial factor in successful learning.

In his book *Learned Optimism* (1990), Martin Seligman (along with colleagues Steven Hollon and Arthur Freeman) adapts Albert Ellis's ABC model into a concrete approach for dealing with pessimistic beliefs. Seligman's ABCDE model can be introduced during the doldrums as a way for students to gain more control over negative thinking. In this approach, students think about an Adversity (A), describe their Beliefs about the situation (B), consider the Consequences of their beliefs (C), Dispute these beliefs (D), and then become Energized by the new outcome (E). Seligman presents the example of a student named Judy who used the ABCDE approach to change her despair over low grades into a more hopeful attitude. Here is a shortened version of Judy's thoughts in each step of the procedure.

> *Adversity.* "I recently started taking night classes after work for a master's degree. I got my first set of exams back and I didn't do nearly as well as I wanted."
>
> *Belief.* "What awful grades, Judy. I no doubt did the worst in the class. I'm just stupid. That's all. I might as well face facts. I'm also just too old to be competing with these kids."
>
> *Consequences.* "I felt totally dejected and useless. I was embarrassed I even gave it a try, and decided that I should withdraw from my courses and be satisfied with the job I have."

Disputation. "I'm blowing things out of proportion. I hoped to get all A's, but I got a B, a B+, and a B-. Those aren't awful grades. I may not have done the best in the class, but I didn't do the worst in the class either. . . . The reason that I didn't do as well as I hoped isn't because of my age. The fact that I am forty doesn't make me any less intelligent than anyone else in the class. One reason that I may not have done as well is because I have a lot of other things going on in my life that take time away from my studies."

Energization. "I felt much better about myself and my exams. I'm not going to withdraw from my courses, and I am not going to let my age stand in the way of getting what I want" (pp. 218–219).

Introducing students to the ABCDE approach does not guarantee a classroom filled with smiling faces, but it may help some students gain more control over maladaptive thinking patterns. Increasing numbers of students have had negative experiences with learning throughout their academic careers; their low opinions of themselves as learners are often automatic reactions and can distort situations out of proportion. During the doldrums, when negative thinking may be pervasive, Seligman's approach to help students learn optimism can be an essential lesson both for students and for faculty.

Interpersonal.   Clearly, the interpersonal intelligence is one that needs to be considered a part of the purview of higher education. Many life situations after college involve interpersonal skills: the workplace, job interviews, volunteer activities, meetings, organizational activities, political gatherings, and all of an individual's social and family activities. Interpersonal settings are one of the universal avenues of communication.

We have already discussed the use of collaborative learning

groups, which are one way to build interpersonal skills and one method of building community (Chapter Four). Group work can also be effective in combating the doldrums (Bergquist & Philips, 1975). Try the Jigsaw for instance (Aronson, 1978). In this strategy, students are asked to tackle new material as a team, rather than trying to master all the information on their own. The professor divides the new material into four, five, or six segments, and then creates collaborative groups with the same number of participants as the number of segments. Each student in a group is assigned a piece of the new information. It is then the student's job to research and to explain his or her assigned piece to the other students in the group. In this way, the pieces are fitted together, and the puzzle begins to form.

The division of material into these jigsaw pieces pushes each student into taking an active role in the learning environment of the classroom, first as researcher, then as teacher. The team approach decreases the amount of information each student must cover outside of class.

The jigsaw strategy can be varied in a number of ways. Ask entire groups, rather than individual group members, to be responsible for a segment of a topic. Each group must then organize its own system for group members to work together to research and then to teach information to the classroom community. Students could cover a challenging textbook chapter or summarize areas having many categories. For a chapter on addiction, a professor of nursing poses three questions pertaining to drugs: effects, treatments, and critical questions about the drugs. Each of the six groups in the class is assigned a different drug and is asked to respond to the three questions. Group members discuss the questions among themselves and arrive at answers. Each group then enters its results in a row of a matrix drawn on the board. At the end of class, students are able to copy the matrix and refer to it for review.

If collaborative learning is a regular part of the teaching approaches in a class, it is important to dignify the group process and to allow time for students to evaluate its success. Johnson and Johnson (1991) suggest encouraging students to analyze their methods of sending and receiving messages in a group setting in order to gain more insight into their interpersonal styles. To guide group members as they analyze their group process, give each group a question sheet, including questions about whether individuals feel comfortable expressing their views in a group situation, about the number of times the group process is interrupted, about the ability of the group to focus on the task, and about problems in following assigned group roles (Angelo, 1994). Then, discuss the answers in the individual groups or with the class as a whole to celebrate the total process.

Debating is a more formal approach to using and developing interpersonal skills. You can select the topic for debate yourself, or you can encourage the students to suggest a topic by polling the class. Student teams then research various aspects of the issue and organize information in written notes. The teams also decide on the time frame, format, and speakers for the debate. On the day of the debate, the teams take over the classroom and rearrange the space. The excitement and the change of pace captured in a lively debate is certainly an effective antidote for the doldrums.

In classes that have incorporated service learning into the curriculum, the doldrums are an ideal time for students to share and to synthesize their experiences with their classmates. Students who have been volunteering from the beginning of the semester will have made connections with clients and with staff members by this time, and it is likely that a number of interpersonal dilemmas will have surfaced. These situations need to be worked out. A brainstorming session with the whole class will not only help individual students reach solutions to their dilemmas, it will also unite the classroom community in the joint effort of searching for answers that are immediately relevant. The class discussion will help to rebuild low self-images, as the students see that they are able to support each other and to apply their problem-solving skills to a very real situation.

Like simulations and like service projects, cases studies also involve the classroom community in the solution of a relevant problem. Cases are a familiar tool to many professors of psychology, education, business, and law, where they have traditionally been a part of the curriculum, but they are equally useful in other classes. A class-period case is essentially a brief (one or two pages) written scenario relevant to the skills, concepts, or information being discussed in that course. At the beginning of class, the case is handed out to the students, who read it over several times to discover the major issues involved. The professor then begins a discussion with an open-ended question that encourages students to consider the case from a number of different perspectives and eventually to come to an understanding of the complexities of the situation presented in the case if not a solution for it. The discussion is led by the professor, but the answers are discovered by the students. Experts in the area of teaching with case studies (Christensen, Garvin, & Sweet, 1991; Christensen & Hansen, 1987) suggest using several different types of questions to guide and to maintain the discussions. Questions can be open-ended, diagnostic, information seeking, or hypothetical; they can be built on challenges, predictions, generalizations, or priority and sequence; they can be action questions or questions of extension (Christensen, 1991, pp. 159–160).

For a Spanish class mired in the doldrums, a case depicting a bumbling traveler in Madrid confronting new customs and trying to settle into a hotel would certainly highlight the need to learn the ways of the country as well as its language. For a calculus class that is tearing its collective hair out trying to understand integration over a surface, a case that portrays a hypothetical but typical student working out a similar problem might enable the whole class to learn the correct method. For an ethics class, a case that describes three reactions to a cry for help might initiate a heated discussion on responsibility.

You can decide to use predesigned cases in your classes, or you can create your own. It takes time to write a case, but because the case will then reflect the particular questions and subtle nuances that you want to raise in your class, it is often worth finding the time to write your own. Besides, many professors find it energizing and intriguing to design cases. Keep the narrative brief, direct, and accurate and try to use material that connects to the experiences of your students. The more relevant the case, the more successful the integration of learning.

Applying Kolb

As we discussed earlier in this chapter, Kolb's model of learning emphasizes the dynamic nature of learning. The learner is in process on a learning cycle and must interact with information in a variety of ways in order for comprehensive learning to occur. This active approach to learning goes beyond the concept of learning as merely taking in information on the spot. The Chinese express the verb "to learn" in two ideographs: one means to study and the other means to practice constantly. One cannot, therefore, consider learning without thinking both of studying and of practicing. During the doldrums, students often feel overwhelmed—there is so much to be taken in: how can I learn it all before the end of the semester? Suggesting that they think of learning as the Chinese do—an ongoing process of studying and of practicing—may help to remove the urgency students feel of needing to know it all *now*.

In our example, Professor Kowalski used Kolb's model as a guide for designing assignments and activities that would teach concepts about inventory in a way that would also generate renewed enthusiasm and motivation during the doldrums. Enns (1993) suggests that Kolb's experiential learning model can also provide an effective framework for integrating separate and connected knowing into the processes of learning. Enns goes on to point out that "diversity is acknowledged and appreciated when the model is implemented in a manner that values different learning styles as well as gender, race, and class variables. As a result, this model will help instructors to establish a multifocal, gender-balanced, inclusive approach to teaching psychology" (p. 12). A multifocal, gender-balanced, inclusive approach is valuable for the teaching of all subjects, not only for the teaching of psychology.

Consider the example of Professor Medeiros, a professor in the mechanical engineering department, who has heard about Kolb's model and has become intrigued with figuring out how to adapt the model to the topic of fluid mechanics. Typically, most of the laws of engineering are simply presented to the students. Professors do not generally encourage the students to try to discover the laws through their own experimentation. Having been a proponent of this teaching approach himself, Professor Medeiros now considers whether Kolb's experiential learning could be adapted to his engineering courses. He decides to try to structure a unit that teaches the relationship of drag force on a body to the air velocity and shape of the body. He pulls out a copy of Kolb's learning cycle (Figure 5.3) and studies it intently.

Professor Medeiros wants students to discover the laws regarding drag and to apply them to something practical, such as the design of an outside rearview mirror on an automobile. As he prepares his class, he jots down the following notes:

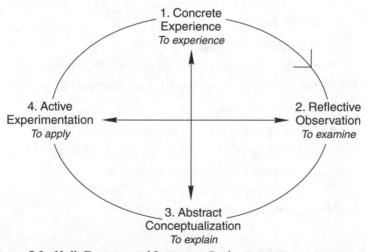

Figure 5.3. Kolb Experiential Learning Cycle.
Source: Adapted from Svinicki and Dixon, 1987, pp. 142.

1. Concrete Experience:
    - Students perform a series of experiments in a small wind tunnel.
    - Provide objects with three different shapes that can be used for rearview mirrors.
    - Change air velocity in wind tunnel for each shape and ask students to measure the drag force.

2. Reflective Observation:
    - Examine data by plotting drag force vs. air velocity for the three different shapes.
    - Use collaborative groups for students to discuss their findings.
    - Groups report on results to class.

3. Abstract Conceptualization:
    - Groups infer a mathematical model from the graphs.
    - They should discover that the drag varies with the square of the airspeed.
    - Cover this in a lecture and assign readings to clarify this law.

4. Active Experimentation:
    - Assign collaborative groups to work together to design a rearview mirror for a car that will minimize drag.
    - Ask students to survey rearview mirrors of cars and trucks in their neighborhoods as assignment for next class and to apply their mathematical models to estimate the drag on these mirrors at different auto speeds.

Professor Medeiros is on his way to formulating an approach that allows for many different ways of learning about the laws and the practical applications pertaining to drag. Instead of his usual approach of lecturing about the laws and then assigning homework, he is trying to get students more involved in the process of discovery. Rather than asking students to compete individually, he is incorporating cooperative groups for discussing and analyzing information. Professor Medeiros knows that it may take some time for him and his students to get accustomed to using this new approach. He is excited about the active experimentation phase of the learning cycle and is curious to see what students will create.

Replay

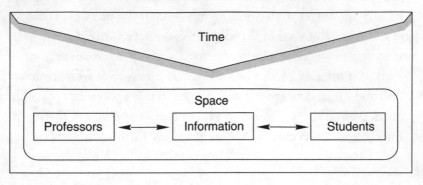

Time

A stagnant tempo of

- Low energy
- Low motivation
- Low humor
- Low self-esteem
- Possible attrition

Space

Appears to be

- Unwelcoming
- Unconnected

Needs to be

- Revitalized
- Restructured
- Redirected

Professors

Cope with feeling

- Angry
- Defensive
- Deflated

Fight the doldrums by

- Accepting
- Discussing
- Taking action

Reconsider learning styles and learning cycles:

- Gardner's seven intelligences
- Kolb's learning cycle

Information

Provides

- Stimulation
- Positive emotional climate

Uses new approaches:

- Free writing
- Focus questions
- Histories
- Dialogues
- Conflict
- Musical supports
- Rap reviews
- Equations
- Audiovisual materials
- Flip charts
- Murals
- Fishbone diagrams
- Koosh Balls
- Games
- Journals
- Groups
- Debates
- Cases
- Reproductions
- Maps

- Concept maps
- Clay models
- Models
- Simulations
- ABCDE
- Jigsaw
- Service
- Learning cycles

Students

Cope with feeling

- Overworked
- Unmotivated
- Enervated

Accept the doldrums as integral to the learning process

- Realize that they're not alone

- Build self-confidence

- Discover personal avenues of learning and strategies of attack

The Final Weeks

Achieving Closure

It is a rough road that leads to the heights of greatness.
—*Seneca, Epistles*

Vignette: The final two weeks of the semester had arrived. Professor Bronfman's students were settling wearily into their seats. Putting down their books and backpacks, they opened their notebooks, and turned to talk to each other while they waited for Professor Bronfman to return last week's hour test. The talk was dominated by discussions of the work ahead in all their classes—so much to do, so little time. Professor Bronfman's students were, of course, concerned about the results of their tests, but they were also worried that there were still a number of assignments due in his class before the semester ended, and they were anxious to learn how the pieces would come together. When the tests were handed back, the students filed them in the personal portfolios suggested by Professor Bronfman. The students were beginning to realize that these portfolios would be very helpful in reviewing for the final.

Shelley reached up to take her graded bluebook from Professor Bronfman as he walked around the room. Shelley was a good student, but she had been nervous about this test. In fact, she was always nervous about a test. She liked to get settled in her place well before class, lay out her extra pens, her Lifesavers, and a soda or juice—if allowed—wait quietly, and then begin the test promptly.

She did not like to be interrupted; she liked to get on with it. Shelley really hated it when the professor talked on and on before the test. Professor Bronfman's last hour test had been a challenging test and a long one. Shelley remembered that Chris and Melissa had clutched and had walked out after only fifteen minutes. Almost everyone else had stayed, working on their tests until the next class arrived. Lynda, who had a reading disability, had not finished, and Professor Bronfman had sent her to the reading lab to complete the test.

Shelley was thankful that she had not drawn a blank on one of the multiple-choice questions as she had on the first two of Professor Bronfman's tests. Perhaps she was getting better at them after all. She had always been comfortable with the true/false questions, although her close friend Keith was not, but for her true/false questions were easy—you were either right or wrong. She could also readily answer the fill-in-the-blanks section. But multiple-choice questions were difficult for her—too many uncertainties, she felt. Still, she had been able to answer all of them this time.

Shelley wondered whether she might have preferred to have an essay question included in the test, one that was clearly worded so that she understood both the question and what was expected in the answer. Then she could have discussed rather than merely indicated what she knew and could have applied her knowledge to show how much she had learned this semester. Perhaps Professor Bronfman would include essay questions on the final. He hadn't talked about the final yet, and there was no discussion of the final in the syllabus. Shelley had checked the syllabus because there were just two weeks left in the semester, and she needed to plan ahead. She had so many outside responsibilities that it sometimes was difficult to find enough time to study. Still, she and several other students had formed a study group which was proving to be a great help and a good time, too. They sometimes met in the Caf, just to socialize.

Shelley has enjoyed this class. She knows that she has gained insight into how to use her new knowledge and skills after the course is over, and she has appreciated Professor Bronfman's habit of presenting topics that expand into parallel themes. Because of this method of teaching, she reasons, there have been some wonderful moments when suddenly she knew how the topic being discussed enriched her understanding of the world. And there have been times when the class came together to explore differences of opinions. Those discussions were sometimes heated, and Shelley was not always comfortable with the ideas and perceptions expressed, but she has learned to listen, and she is pleased with that. There have also been times when they all have laughed.

Shelley wonders how Professor Bronfman will bring the class to a close. There is still some material to cover and some questions to be answered. As she opens her bluebook, Shelley hopes that she has done well on this test.

Discussion

What has happened since the time of the doldrums? Lowman (1984) has stated that approximately the last half of the semester provides "the optimal work atmosphere, in which students more readily participate in discussion and show independent thinking and work outside of class . . . [a time that] according to Mann's thinking could not occur without the emotional crisis that precedes it" (p. 43). Professor Bronfman and his students appear to have successfully navigated the emotional crisis of the doldrums and to have capitalized on the period of high productivity that follows. As they approach the final week, attendance has remained high. Professor Bronfman's students are in class, at ease with the atmosphere and with each other. They slump into their seats comfortably, if wearily, and readily talk with each other. They are involved in the classroom environment and look forward to the action of the final two weeks.

A learning community has been formed in this classroom. Professor Bronfman has emphasized understanding in depth, rather

202 TEACHING WITHIN THE RHYTHMS OF THE SEMESTER

than in breadth, and students have interacted successfully with the information of the course. According to Shelley's musings, they have progressed from merely reiterating the course information to being able to test their newly formed concepts in heated classroom discussions. To make this progress possible, Professor Bronfman has built some important approaches into his course. He has moved away from a content-intensive course toward a concept- and process-oriented approach, thus encouraging the discussions that Shelley has valued.

Langer (1989, 1993), Perkins (1992), Gardner (1991), and Bloom (1956) each discuss the phenomenon of acquiring knowledge. They approach the process from different angles and with somewhat different emphases, but they all agree on the necessity of considering any problem from several perspectives in order to reach genuine understanding. Langer (1993) encourages a practice of "mindfulness," explaining mindfulness as "an open, creative, probabilistic state of mind in which the individual might be led to finding differences among things thought similar and similarities among things thought different . . . a process in which one views the same situation from several perspectives. Rather than rushing headlong from questions to answers, we seek out other vantage points when we are mindful. An answer from one perspective may raise questions from another" (p. 44).

Perkins (1992) calls the ideas that spawn this process of discovering new correspondences "generative topics." Generative topics "invite understanding performances of diverse kinds" (p. 92) and are not only central to the subject but also provide for richness of connection and extrapolation. These topics encourage exploration and therefore appeal to a variety of learning styles. They expand to foster the understandings of parallel and repetitive patterns that Shelley found exciting and that Langer suggests will raise new questions. For example, in mathematics, Perkins suggests that a discussion of probability and prediction will highlight "the ubiquitous need for simple probabilistic reasoning in everyday life" (p. 94); in literature, a comparison of classical and modern allegory and fable will foster an understanding of recurrent themes and forms; in social studies, an exploration of the origins of government will provide insight into the progression and contradictions of ruling systems; in the natural sciences, a study of evolution and the process of natural selection will serve as a catalyst for the discovery of parallels in other settings—in fashion, in music, in invention (Perkins, 1992, p. 93–94).

Perkins stresses that there is a vast difference between *knowing* and *understanding*. He explains that teachers can "easily check whether learners possess the knowledge that they are supposed to. But understanding somehow goes beyond possession" (p. 76). A generative topic encourages students to do just this—to go beyond comprehension and application toward understanding.

It also speaks to Gardner's concern (1994) that "the greatest enemy of understanding is coverage." (Project 2061 members presented similar concerns about science, technological, mathematics, and social science K–12 curricula in their two reports: *Science for All Americans*, American Association for the Advancement of Science, 1989, and *Social and Behavioral Sciences*, Appley & Maher, 1989.) Gardner defines genuine understanding as the capacity to take information and concepts and to apply them to new situations for which that knowledge is appropriate. He maintains that much of the learning in educational institutions is superficial and encourages teachers to consider covering less content while focusing on true understanding. He states that rather than have a surface grasp of many things, it is far more important that students truly understand a few things (Gardner, 1991). The use throughout the semester of a few carefully selected generative topics that culminate in a complex product such as an essay, a project, or the solution to a practical problem accomplishes what Perkins and Gardner propose and moves the students through the processes of learning.

It is helpful to consider Bloom's Taxonomy of Educational Objectives (Bloom, 1956) as one designs a generative topic. This taxonomy organizes six levels of instruction into a hierarchy: knowledge, comprehension, application, analysis, synthesis, and evaluation. Students need to learn information (knowledge) before they can grasp the meaning of that information (comprehension). When they comprehend the meaning, they can apply knowledge to situations (application), break down ideas into smaller parts and find how these parts are organized (analysis), and rearrange the resulting ideas into a new whole (synthesis). Finally, they can make judgments based on specific criteria (evaluation). Professor Bronfman's students appear to be progressing through this hierarchy, for at the close of the semester, they are less concerned about the results of a specific hour test than they are about the ways in which the course topics will come together into a new whole, and they worry that some questions might remain unanswered.

Professor Bronfman has used another technique besides generative topics to help his students navigate the semester. He has also suggested that each of his students keep a personal portfolio. A personal portfolio generally contains work collected by a student over a specific time—for several weeks, for the first half of the course from beginning until midterm exams, or for an entire semester. Portfolios can be comprehensive, including all of a student's work in a course (Schilling & Schilling, 1993), or they can be student selected, allowing a student to choose his or her best material.

In the past, student portfolios have been most frequently used in writing and in art courses, but because their makeup is so flexible, they can be useful in any content area. Crouch and Fontaine (1994) suggest that no matter what the course, student-selected portfolios share four important features: they illustrate the development of a student's learning over a period of time; they can provide a grace period during which an underprepared student can catch up; they emphasize rethinking, reworking, and revising; and they encourage students to work from an apprentice skill level toward an expert skill level in the course material.

Portfolios can be used by the professor as part of a student's evaluation, or they can be used by the students as a way to monitor their own growth throughout a course. Suggesting the use of portfolios to students early in the semester communicates several fundamental messages: it encourages students to take responsibility for their own learning; it helps students realize that learning is a process that requires rethinking and revising; and it opens the way for students to begin to see how assignments in the course can relate to life beyond the classroom.

Professor Bronfman had suggested that students keep portfolios for their own use. He suggested that they put their tests, their papers (all drafts), their journals, and any commentary (theirs and his) into their portfolios. Not only will the resulting portfolios be helpful for review, as the students are now realizing, but they will also be records of personal progress through the course. The students can turn to their portfolios to track their individual journeys toward understanding and to discover some of the answers for themselves.

The generative topics and the personal portfolios have proved to be successful techniques for Professor Bronfman as he has moved his students through the processes of gaining understanding and discovering connections, but what of the final two weeks ahead? What are the characteristics of this closing period? This is the period of the last chance: when perfectionists must let go; when procrastinators must buckle down; when professors behind in their courses must wrap it all up; when everyone must meet final deadlines. Unfortunately, this is also a period of isolation: everyone is focused on making his or her own way through the last challenges and has little time or energy to bolster fellow travelers. It is a time when fatigue is a way of life and bodily reserves are stretched by skipped meals and no time for exercise. Professors and students alike talk about "getting through."

In addition to the general feeling of stress, this is the time when a life is coming to an end; the community of a particular class is about to dissolve. Lowman (1984) has noted that "for groups having a limited life, such as college classes, a period of heightened emotionality always occurs at the end. Sadness is common as members withdraw their emotional investment in the leader and in each other" (p. 40). The question, then, is how does one reduce the inevitable stress reflected in the students' concern over so much to do and so little time left? How does one capitalize on the period of high productivity now winding down and cope with the sadness of an ending? How does one achieve closure?

It is important to consider the sources as well as the nature of end-of-the-semester stress, and then, as is always true with stress, to consider the ways in which to cope. Three factors are critical: the first, and most important of all, is to recognize that stress is manageable: ways to deal with it can be found; the end of the semester need not be fraught with all-encompassing tensions. The second factor is to realize that stress is rather like the yeast in bread dough: some is helpful, too much is explosive. Whitman, Spendlove, and Clark (1986) point out that "the goal is not to *eliminate* stress but to *moderate* it. Some stress is motivating. It makes students just anxious enough to study for tests and prepare assignments, thereby challenging them to reach their potential. This 'good stress' correlates with maximum learning, while no stress or extreme stress correlates with little or no learning" (p. 53).

The third factor is that if one discovers the sources—physical, environmental, cognitive—of end-of-semester stress, then one knows the enemy and can devise ways to cope. According to Whitman, Spendlove, and Clark's (1986) explanation of Lazarus's view (1966), "what makes a situation stressful is largely the degree to which it is perceived as such" (p. 11). Or as Pogo said, "We have met the enemy and he is us" (Kelly, 1970). Neither professors nor students cope well with uncertainty at this point in the semester. In order to cope, we all need to know the nature of what is ahead; we need to know as much as possible about what to expect. Only then are we no longer our own enemy.

It is true that we professors have little control over the physical and environmental stress at the close of the semester. Meetings seem somehow to multiply, deadlines pile up, colleagues are pressured. No matter how much we've organized, the semester has been demanding and exhausting. People will therefore be tired and cranky. No question about that. So what do we do? This is the time for Gmelch's high payoff activities (see Chapter Two), for invention, for humor, for new approaches, and even for cookies. In a social science course, when the professor took time out to ask students for suggestions for dealing with stress—a good student-involving coping technique in itself—one student volunteered that he always baked cookies when he was stressed. At the beginning of the next class, he shared his personal coping technique; he arrived with a bowl of homemade cookies—nothing like homemade double chocolate chip cookies to relieve stress.

One might also hope for some sort of cognitive vaccine that, like a flu vaccine, would lessen the impact of the affliction and render it manageable. Meichenbaum (1977, 1985) and Janis (1982) have introduced just such a technique. They label it "stress inoculation." According to Whitman, Spendlove, and Clark (1986), the "primary concept associated with stress inoculation appears to be giving people information or educating them as to what is stressful, what to expect and how best to cope" (p. 63). We know what is stressful—those final responsibilities: assignments, papers, projects, exams, and committee meetings. But students often do not know what to expect. Shelley and her classmates worry about the nature of the final. They are concerned about how the class will come together. In order to cope effectively, they need that "inoculation." They need as much tangible, specific information about what is ahead as possible.

As you approach the rush of the final two weeks, try handing out a brief, clearly constructed, and quickly scannable reminder sheet of what lies ahead—with page numbers of assignments, dates of papers, projects, review sessions, and the time and place of the final exam. Students have repeatedly asked us not to schedule review sessions for the final day. They want to begin reviewing sooner, or at least they want to relieve their stress by having the option to start before the last moment. It may well be difficult for a professor to begin reviewing before all the course material is covered, but you can refer students to the course outline in the syllabus and highlight what portions of that outline will be covered in the final. It is also possible to discuss the nature of the final exam before the last days of class, to hand out examples of previous exams, to discuss how to answer specific questions, and to explain what you will be looking for.

Still, some students continue to feel overwhelmed even though they have been given a clearer idea of what to expect and an indication of some ways to proceed. These students may be limited by negative thinking, which can lead to such maladaptive strategies as procrastination, panic, or just plain giving up and quitting the class. Another stress inoculation technique suggests that individuals learn to combat stress with an internal monologue of positive coping statements. You begin by analyzing how your self-talk is influencing your performance, then move on to practicing more positive self-statements, and finally to applying the coping statements in actual situations.

Professors who decide to use this technique need to encourage their students to examine and to monitor their own negative self-statements and then to replace these statements with positive coping statements. Students often exaggerate situations in gripe sessions; stress inoculation recommends reframing the gripes into something more positive. Professors can begin a class by asking students to write down their worries and then breaking the class into small groups where the concerns are read aloud, thus engendering a sort of legitimate and organized gripe session within the classroom environment. The groups are then directed to find ways to reframe the gripes. The statement, "It's no use, I'll never get it all done," can be replaced with, "I'll just take things one step at a time. I'll manage." The familiar cry that "I have to get an A in this course" can be countered with "I'll do my best" or "I'll do my best on that final—I bet I'll get through it okay."

Certainly, the final exam is one of the primary sources of stress. Unfortunately, it is also the last act of the course. Shelley, reflecting on Professor Bronfman's last test, thinks about what evaluation means to her and to her classmates. She looks back on her progress with pride. She has moved from the first level of cognitive development, in which the right or wrong true/false question seems preferable, to a level of comfort with the multiplicity and transitional knowing required to answer multiple-choice questions. She wonders if an essay question would give her an opportunity to apply her knowledge. She would like to prove to herself and to Professor Bronfman that she can analyze and that she can synthesize.

Both Gardner and Perkins recommend the use of authentic assessment—assessment that is open-ended, that requires an understanding of meaning, and that involves the use of several different perspectives. Gardner (1991) explains that "if you answer a question on a multiple-choice test in a certain way, or carry out a problem set in a specified manner, you will be credited with understanding. No one ever asks the further question 'But do you *really* understand?' because that would violate an unwritten agreement: A certain kind of performance shall be accepted as adequate for this particular instructional context. The gap between what passes for understanding and genuine understanding remains great" (p. 6). Unwittingly, Shelley reflects Gardner's concern. As the end of the semester approaches, she feels a need for closure that makes clear to Professor Bronfman and to herself that she can use her new skills—in essence, that she now makes connections. It is this feeling that she remembers as she looks back on those "moments in the course when suddenly she knew how the topic being discussed enriched her understanding of the world."

Professor Bronfman is faced with how to accomplish this closure, both in the last days of the course and in the final exam. He wants closure with dignity, closure that underscores the information and skills absorbed and opens the doors to future connections. Above all, he wants to obviate another vaccination theory, this time from Postman and Weingartner (1969): "once students have taken a course and passed the test, they are 'immune' and will never again have to demonstrate any real learning in that subject" (McCutcheon, 1985, p. 96). How does one juggle these needs? A final review of the course syllabus is a good way to start.

Each time Professor Bronfman had completed a section of his course, taught a new skill, or introduced a new concept, he had asked his students to pull out the syllabus and to revisit the list of course objectives. Together, they had checked off those objectives that had been accomplished. Not only did this review allow Professor Bronfman a chance to point out to his students, who were often feeling burdened or confused, how much they had learned and how far along in the journey of the class they had come, it also gave him the opportunity to discuss what lay ahead. The list of the course objectives became a familiar road map that the students were able to navigate increasingly successfully as the class progressed.

Now, as the semester moved toward closure, Professor Bronfman returned once again to his syllabus and reviewed its pieces with his students. Try it. The course outline provides an excellent tool for review; the explanation of policies, a succinct reminder of expectations; the description of teaching procedures and educational philosophy, a catalyst for a final discussion; and the listing of the educational goals and objectives, a framework for the course.

Turning from the list of measurable knowledge acquired in his course (the objectives) to a review of the unmeasurable knowledge (the goals), Professor Bronfman sets the stage for a discussion of how his students' new understandings might become a part of their future. As he talks about the course goals and the concepts that the students have mastered, he begins the process of closure. Reaffirming his belief in the students' new competence, he dignifies their individual journeys.

It still remains for him to place the course into the students' ongoing process of learning and to point the way to future connections. When Professor Bronfman had first written his course goals, he had asked himself what he wanted his students to remember from his course in five years. That had been a valuable question for him. It had helped him to cull the relatively unimportant from the important and to chart a new direction for his course. He now asks his students to ponder the same question, but from a slightly different angle: he asks them to consider how they think the course will serve them in their future careers. By shifting their focus to a broader time frame, Professor Bronfman and his students are able to put the immediate course information in a context of future understandings and to bring closure to the course.

Applications

We look at applications in three main areas: closure, stress, and the final exam.

Closure

Consider the medicine wheel, the ordered tree, and the guided design.

Medicine Wheel

The medicine wheel (Figure 6.1), an ancient and sacred symbol of the North American Indians, pictures life as a circle that is divided into four quadrants corresponding to the directions of north, south, east, and west. Viewing the world from a point inside the wheel, celebrants are able to gain a sense of their relationship to the physical universe, to celebrate the equinoxes, and to study the stars. Each direction has its own meaning and its own gifts; each represents different aspects of ourselves. Simply put, the south symbolizes our feelings, emotions, and reactions. The north represents reason, intellect, and wisdom. The west encompasses the physical: death of form and matter and its transformation. The east embodies evolution, illumination, and eternity. The total image of the wheel, depicts the interconnectedness of various aspects of life and "represents a holistic approach to four dimensions of learning: mental, emotional, physical, and spiritual" (Frederick, 1991, p. 202).

Just as Kolb's learning cycle and Gardner's seven frames of mind

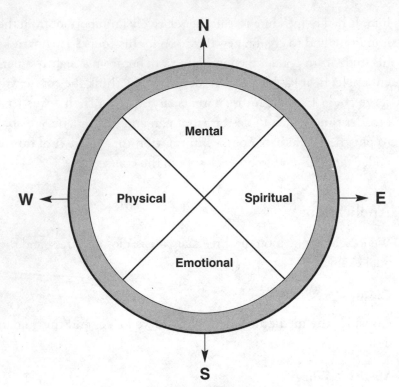

Figure 6.1. A Model of the Medicine Wheel.
Source: Adapted from Frederick, 1991, p. 203, by permission.

approach learning and ultimately understanding from a number of angles, the medicine wheel also stresses that knowledge is reached through many avenues. It reflects the Lakota (and Confucian) saying about how a student learns.

Tell me, and I'll listen
Show me, and I'll understand
Involve me, and I'll learn [Frederick, 1991, p. 202].

Because it underscores the need for a holistic understanding, the medicine wheel is an ideal teaching tool to use in the final weeks of the semester, when professors are faced with the paradoxical task of bringing closure while new opening connections. After all, the line of the circle does just that—it draws a closed form but is a never-ending line.

During the semester, it may well have been necessary to teach primarily within the area of one of the quadrants represented in the medicine wheel: for example, the physical quadrant, which would encompass the pieces of the text in sociology, the materials of the lab in biology, the minutiae of directions in computer technology, and the complexities of equations in statistics; or the mental quadrant, which would include the explanation of events in history, the interpretation of solutions in mathematics, the application of theories in business, and the discovery of themes and patterns in art and in literature. Yet the final weeks of the semester are a period of "heightened emotionality" (Lowman, 1984, p. 40) and of increased stress. If we do not include the other two quadrants of learning, it will be difficult to be effective in bringing closure, for it is in the emotional quadrant that the process of selecting and transforming information into genuine understanding often begins, and it is in the spiritual quadrant that many connections and genuine understandings are reached.

There are many ways to adapt the medicine wheel to a course. Frederick (1991) suggests that you begin by introducing the students to the medicine wheel and then "suggest that they keep the four dimensions in mind as they read a text, confront a problem, or are introduced to a new concept or skill" (p. 204). In Technology and Human Values, as the class approaches a study of nuclear power—certainly a complex problem needing to be studied from many angles—students can be given a medicine wheel diagram and introduced to its four quadrants, then asked to consider not only the design of the nuclear plant (the mental quadrant) and the construction of the plant (the physical quadrant), but also the community reaction (the emotional quadrant) and the ethical issues surrounding disclosure of risks as well as advantages (the spiritual quadrant) as they read the text. During the closing days of his class, Professor Bronfman might choose to discuss his final topic through the use of a medicine wheel, thus confronting some of Shelley's questions, while at the same time reinforcing her confidence in her ability to reach independent solutions.

Twotrees (1994) proposes that teachers arrange a classroom as a medicine wheel, with students grouped at each of the four directions. The instructor then poses a question, going around the circle four times for answers so that the students respond from the viewpoint of each quadrant. Or as an alternative, once students are familiar with the technique, Twotrees suggests that the instructor present a problem and then direct each student to move to the quadrant that best fits with his or her personal interpretation. As the discussion continues, students can move to different quadrants to reinterpret the issue from varying perspectives.

You can initiate a discussion from any quadrant in the circle, but often it is helpful to begin in the south, the emotional quadrant, by asking students what connections they see to their own experience; then move to the west and the physical tools of texts, directions, experiments; next, to the north to engage in the mental exercises of discovering issues, patterns, and themes; and finally, to the east to discover what unifying and transforming connections can be made. The creativity and the flexibility of the medicine wheel make it a splendid tool for meeting the challenges of the final weeks, whether you use it for a final unit of the semester, or whether you use it to discuss the central theme of the course. It is, however, only one way to reach a satisfactory closure.

Ordered Tree

The ordered tree technique, based on the work of Reitman and Reuter (1980), is another way. It connects to many of the multiple intelligences presented in Gardner's theory, for not only does it appeal to the dominant linguistic and logical-mathematical teaching modalities, it also appeals to the spatial and personal intelligences. But unlike the medicine wheel or Kolb's learning cycle, the ordered tree does not ask students to progress through a series of approaches; instead, it requires one demanding step that involves the upper levels of Bloom's taxonomy: selecting, linking, and ordering (analysis and synthesis).

The ordered tree pictures a course as a tree, or a fan. Initially, as you identify primary concepts of the course, they are pictured as branches that spread out singly and randomly from the course base. As the semester progresses and students become more familiar with the course content, you can ask them to consider new patterns and to draw a tree that shows the branches emerging in a more ordered manner, coming together into clusters and subdivisions. As the course ends, you can direct students to picture the course as a whole and to draw a final tree that reflects the logic of the completed course.

Figure 6.2 illustrates an ordered tree for a course on aging that the professor initially divided into fourteen primary topics and only two linked topics, or subtopics (retrieval and midlife crisis). By the end of the course, the students had reduced the primary concepts to six and had linked the remaining ten topics to the primary topics in complex subdivisions.

If you decide to try an ordered tree, you can use it at many points throughout the semester. You can hand it out at the start of your course as a visual introduction or include it in your syllabus; you can use it every time you introduce a new concept or turn to it when you finish a section; you can distribute it just before a test as a review tool. Or, as in the example in Figure 6.2, you can hand out the original tree at the end of the course and ask your students to reorder a new one.

Guided Design

Guided design provides a third approach to consolidating learning. It represents a systematic approach to decision making and to problem solving. Like the medicine wheel and the ordered tree, a guided-design structure can be used at any point in the semester, and like them both, it is also a particularly valuable tool for closure.

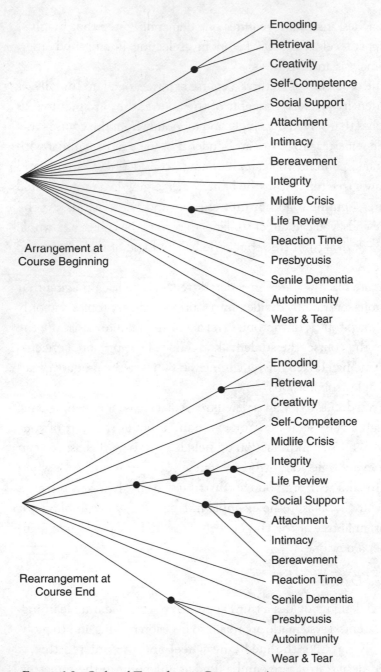

Figure 6.2. Ordered Trees from a Course on Aging.

Source: National Center for Research to Improve Postsecondary Teaching and Learning, 1990, p. 3. Reprinted by permission.

A guided-design project begins with an unknown, sets a goal, and then follows a structure that leads systematically to a resolution. The structure consists of several steps (Wales and Nardi, 1982) that encourage students to work in a logical and incremental progression from a stated problem and a probable goal to the discovery of possible solutions, to the selection of a workable solution, and ultimately to recommendations for a course of action.

The final weeks of Professor Jansen's adult development class have arrived, and she is about to end the course with a study of Alzheimer's disease. Professor Jansen is proud of this class. It began in disarray with students who were timid and unsure, but they have made significant progress. Still, many of them remain uncertain of their capabilities. Professor Jansen wants to make it clear to her students that they have learned a great deal and have developed the ability not only to apply but also to analyze, to synthesize, and even to evaluate. For her final activity, she therefore turns to the guided-design technique, following this format:

Steps of Guided Design	Student Discoveries and Procedures
1. *Identify situation:*	As people age, they often exhibit behaviors such as forgetfulness, disorientation, and lack of judgment. They may then be misdiagnosed as having Alzheimer's disease.
2. *Set a goal:*	Design an approach to clarify the diagnosis of Alzheimer's disease.
3. *Gather relevant information:* (consider other reasons for symptoms)	Decreases in sensory abilities, communication problems, nutritional deficiencies, self-

	medication, drug interactions, confusion, depression, anxiety.
4. *Generate possible solutions:*	Detailed interview of patient, observations in a variety of settings, hearing and vision checks, physical exam, interview with family.
5. *List constraints:*	Ageism, lack of time to form a relationship with patient, lack of cooperation from patient and family, dysfunctional family dynamics.
6. *Choose a solution:*	Work out a list of possible techniques to obtain necessary information easily and select best approaches.
7. *Analyze factors:*	Find an appropriate sample of people. Figure out an effective approach for physical evaluation, interview, and observation.
8. *Synthesize a detailed solution:*	Design a study to pilot the diagnostic tools in a clinical setting.
9. *Evaluate the solution:*	Determine how easily these tools can be adapted to a clinical setting.
10. *Recommend a course of action:*	Create a checklist that can alert the public to possible misdiagnoses.

As Professor Jansen's students work through this final task, they begin to integrate the techniques, the skills, and the compassion that they have learned throughout the semester. Professor Jansen is confident that this exercise will bring closure to the course, and underscore the students' belief in the importance of their new knowledge. Further examples of the use of the guided-design approach can be found in Coscarelli and White (1986) and in Wales, Nardi, and Stager (1987).

Stress

In a tale by Dr. Seuss, the unnamed protagonist, who faces "so many problems, I just can't think," much like our students at the end of a semester, sets off for Solla Sollew where he has heard that no problems exist (*I Had Trouble in Getting to Solla Sollew*, 1965). Along the way, he encounters many obstacles and ultimately finds that the gate to Solla Sollew is locked and he has no key. He cannot gain entrance to a space where there are no problems. But along the way, he discovers that he has tools of his own with which to conquer his problems, and so he returns home armed with his own "big bats." As the students face the snowballing challenges of the final days of the semester, they, too, need to discover their big bats. In particular, they need to learn ways in which to manage their time and to control their anxiety over the final exam.

Ways to Manage Time

Time is precious, and it is running out. Deadlines are rapidly approaching. There are many commitments and a lot to finish. Final marks loom ahead. How does one cope? Research by Britton & Tesser (1991) has suggested that students can improve their academic performance through effective time management. They need to find ways in which to organize their time so that tasks can be completed with the least amount of stress possible.

The student who proclaims that "I never begin studying until the night before the exam," or that "I begin writing review cards at least two weeks before the final; then I have time to sort them, put them on different colored cards, and rewrite them," falls at the extreme ends of the time-management continuum. Such students are procrastinators and perfectionists, both of whom present special challenges at the end of the semester. Burns (1990) has devised a number of cognitive techniques that procrastinators and perfectionists can use to modify their maladaptive behavior. The techniques are easy to adopt and are a practical resource for both students and faculty.

Then there are those who are not dedicated procrastinators nor are they absolute perfectionists, yet they too are not managing their time as effectively as possible. These individuals also fall into two groups: the last-minuters, who may try to plan ahead, but who do not complete projects until just before they are due, and the worriers, who rush to complete a task well before it is due. Professor Bronfman appears to be a last-minuter while Shelley is more of a worrier.

A number of researchers have made suggestions for time management (Lakein, 1974; Bliss, 1976; Winston, 1978). We have incorporated many of their suggestions in the list below. You may want to hand out a similar list to your students or post it on your own bulletin board.

- Adapt to the shortage of time.

    Use your best time of day for tackling the most pressing problems.

    Learn to recognize when you need to take a break and do so.

    Compile a list of short tasks (for example, reviewing notes) that you can complete while you are waiting for other appointments.

    Set aside extra time for the inevitable interruptions and unexpected problems that happen at the end of the semester.

    Schedule in time for unwinding.

- Prioritize your obligations

  Create a to-do list for the remaining weeks, then separate tasks into to-do lists for each day.

  Develop a "Sorry, but" response that you can use automatically to control distractions, interruptions, and requests that take you away from your to-do lists.

  Minimize outside responsibilities (get take-out food, overlook clutter, cut back on meetings, delegate household chores).

  Reward yourself when you complete tasks on time.

- Question yourself. Ask:

  "'Is this a piano?'" (Ellis, 1991, p. 55). Ellis explains that carpenters building rough frames ask themselves this question when they wonder if they have made a mistake. Realize that some errors are acceptable for certain tasks, and do not waste time on perfection when it is not necessary.

  "'Would I pay myself for what I'm doing now?'" (p. 56).

  "Can I complete one more task?"

  "Is worrying interfering with my productivity?" If so, Borkovec (1985) recommends that you put aside a half hour each day to be a worrying period and postpone your worrying until then.

Ways to Deal with Test Anxiety

All of our students have had the experience of dreading a test; some have been able to develop ways to help themselves make it through the test, but most of our students will benefit from learning new techniques. In a society where exams are often the final hurdle to acceptance (Hanson, 1993), test anxiety is a very real phenomenon. We have all had the experience of having a student who just never took the final. Sadly, this student is often a student who has been doing well. Perhaps there was an emergency, but then there is a scheduled time for make-up exams, and the student does not turn up there, either. We wonder why. Most likely, test anxiety has crippled the student to the point that he or she is unable to walk into the exam room. We have known students so hampered by test anxiety that they get to the steps leading up to the building where the exam is to be given and then turn around. They can not go in. They fail the exam, risk failing the course, and thus end up reconfirming their feelings of total inadequacy.

Test anxiety is the result of two factors: heightened physiological arousal and excessive worry. Everyone is familiar with the physiological symptoms—tension, pounding heart, perhaps sweating or clamminess. But when these symptoms intensify beyond a mild reaction, they interact with worrying and result in a rush of negative thoughts.

Students may begin by worrying whether they will forget everything and go blank during a test. They go on to question whether they can pass the exam, and then progress to worrying about whether they will pass the course. As their anxiety escalates, they start to lose sight of reality and begin to exaggerate the possibilities. They wonder whether they should remain in college and worry about how they will survive without a degree. They envision themselves rejected by their families and friends, penniless and pathetic on a street corner. Extreme thoughts and feelings, perhaps, but they can seem very real when anxiety begins to spiral, and they certainly are not conducive to an effective performance on a final exam. It is our responsibility to teach and thus to make it possible for students to learn. Test anxiety clearly negates the process of learning. We professors must, therefore, try to confront the specter of test anxiety. But how?

There are several avenues you can follow to help your students navigate the rigors of test anxiety. You can begin by acknowledging the prevalence of test anxiety and ease its impact on your students by discussing its existence. (You may find that sharing a time when you clutched before or during an exam will help students realize that they are not alone in fearing tests and that people do survive and do go on to successful careers.) You can incorporate review sessions into your classes and encourage your students to begin reviewing. You can clarify your procedures for test taking (perhaps referring back to an explanation in your syllabus) and relieve student uncertainty about what to expect and what is allowable. You can discuss ways to reframe negative thinking as the students approach the final weeks, and you can introduce relaxation techniques as the students prepare to face the final exam.

Most students who struggle with test anxiety have developed their negative thoughts and feelings about testing from a number of experiences throughout their academic careers. It is important to acknowledge and certainly not to scoff at this past baggage, but it is also equally important to help students look at their anxiety as nonproductive and to encourage them to reframe the way in which they view tests. They can try to see tests as an opportunity to succeed (be sure to encourage the idea that they can succeed). Help them to see tests as a way to confirm their newly constructed expertise and to prove their newly cemented knowledge rather than as a chance to fail. It is useful, also, to put the exam into perspective. Remind your students that the exam is only one of the ways they demonstrate mastery in your course. If you return to a final discussion of your syllabus, the listed requirements for the course will serve as a concrete reinforcement of this point.

The syllabus is also a good place to begin a discussion of review. Some students feel that if they begin studying early, they are overdoing it. They are somehow being too organized, not casual enough. But you can stress that it is not being a perfectionist to begin studying a week or so ahead of the exam, but that it *is* being a procrastinator to begin studying the day before the exam. If students can begin diligent preparation ahead of time for an exam, they are far more likely to feel in control and thus to stifle those ugly, upsetting thoughts and feelings.

As for your part in the review process, remember that many students would like a review session before the final classes and remember that many students, like Shelley, need to plan ahead. Try handing out review sheets a couple of weeks before the close of the semester, or try creating a review game to lighten the tensions of the final days. Consider asking one cogent review question at the start of each of the final several classes and reserve the opening five or ten minutes for a discussion of the answer.

Early, organized, and calm review reinforces students' sense of control over the content of the exam, just as a discussion of your procedures for the exam itself relieves students' uncertainty about your rules for that final day. Explain whether you allow snacks and if so, what kinds. Many students find Lifesavers and a soda helpful during the exam period, just as Shelley did. Discuss whether you will allow students to stand up next to their seats and stretch for a moment in order to release tensions. Clarify whether you encourage students to come early so that they can collect themselves. Specify how much time you expect the exam to take, and make clear whether students like Lynda, who may need extra time, are able to stay late. Be as specific as you can and then let it rest. Dwelling too much on the technicalities of the exam can also increase tensions.

Remind your students that not only will positive coping statements help them to deal with the stress of the final weeks, such statements will also help them to wend their way through the morass of exam doubts. Some professors suggest that students make a list of the self-defeating thoughts that distract them on an exam, then share these worries in small groups. Students find to their relief that a majority of their fellow classmates share the same fears. You can ask groups to devise ways to reframe their worries and to share them with the class, either through a class discussion or through handouts. Each student will then be free to select a personal coping statement to use before and during the exam. If students preparing for exams repeat the statement, "Nobody's perfect. I'll just do my best. My best has worked in other situations," the statement will soon become a familiar personal coping technique and a sort of reassuring old friend to be called upon during the tension of an exam session.

There are two components in the equation of test anxiety: excessive worry (which you have helped alleviate in several ways—with review sessions, explanations of exam day procedures, and coping statements) and that other bugaboo, physiological arousal, the butterflies in the stomach. Relaxation techniques can help with the butterflies. *The Relaxation & Stress Reduction Workbook* (Davis, Eshelman, & McKay, 1988) presents a wide variety of techniques that can be adapted for a classroom setting. Tubesing and Tubesing's four volumes on *Structured Exercises for Stress Management* (1994) provide exercises designed for group work. And work by Ottens (1984) suggests approaches for coping with academic anxiety for individual students.

One simple relaxation technique is to close your eyes for a few moments and then concentrate on your breathing until you feel the tension fade and the butterflies recede. This exercise is quick and easy to use in many situations. Another, somewhat more complex approach incorporates the use of images and touches upon the sensory ways of knowing. In the Sandbag Technique (Wexler, 1991), you imagine yourself in a hot air balloon that is resting on the ground, waiting to take off. The bags of sand that keep the balloon from taking off are filled with your anxieties and worries. As you toss the bags out of the basket of the balloon, you begin to float free of your worries, and as you physically eject your worries, you start to regain a sense of control.

Fenker (1981) suggests a different guided-imagery exercise, one that can be modified for a variety of settings. After sitting quietly, closing your eyes, and taking deep breaths, visualize a place that is very special to you. "It should be a place that is calm, restful and feels very pleasant. Explore this place in your mind. Examine your surroundings. Study their colors, shapes and textures. If it is outside, feel the warmth of the sun and the light breeze. Notice the smells and sounds. You may want to visit this special place many times in the future. Visualize yourself coming to this place to rest, to work on problems or to practice other exercises" (p. 142). Once students have practiced this exercise in moments of tension, they will find that in the future merely closing their eyes and naming the place will bring about a sense of calm and will help them to recharge their energies for tackling the next challenge—certainly a useful resource during a surge of test anxiety.

Final Exam

The final exam is the closing scene of the course. It can include convergent questions, low-level questions intended to verify what students know, or divergent questions, open, high-level questions that ask students to apply what they know, or it can combine both kinds of questions. Shelley hopes for both. Whatever the nature of the final, professors are faced with a triple challenge in designing it: first, it must present a cogent and challenging test while enabling tense students to perform to the best of their abilities; second, it must dignify the classroom community experience, even though the class members work on the exam in isolation at their desks and then file by singly to hand in their bluebooks; and third, it must test specific information while encouraging students to demonstrate genuine understanding. Creating a final exam is not an easy task, especially when humor and energies are low. But the exam is the finale, and it is as important to plan the design as to grade the performance (see Jacobs & Chase, 1992; and Davis, 1993, for a discussion of test construction).

Exam Design

Shelley wonders whether she might have welcomed an essay question on the last hour test; she hopes that there will be one on the final. This is significant progress for Shelley. Professor Bronfman has opened the way for Shelley and for her fellow students to move

beyond Bloom's first levels of cognition (knowledge and comprehension), into the more advanced levels of application, analysis,
perhaps synthesis and evaluation. As she has witnessed her own success on assignments, papers, and tests and recorded them in her
portfolio, Shelley has gained the confidence to want to test these
new skills. She looks forward to success. This chance to prove her
new mastery is one of Shelley's personal techniques for closure and
connection. It is up to her professors to make such closure and connection possible.

Whether you decide to include essay questions or whether they
are not appropriate for your course or for the numbers of students
in your class, there are ways to dignify Shelley's and her classmates'
journeys. Think carefully, extremely carefully, about exam questions:
the layout, the levels of cognitive sophistication, the wording.

Should you decide on true/false or multiple-choice questions,
consider the spacing and consider the arrangement of choices. Students with perceptual difficulties need extra space between questions—space that is greater than the space the question itself takes
up. In addition, these students are more successful with multiple-
choice questions that are presented vertically, rather than horizon-
tally. Scheiber and Talpers (1987) and Brinckerhoff, Shaw, and
McGuire (1993) provide more detailed information about ways to
meet the needs of college students with learning disabilities.

Duch and Norton (1992–1993) point out that even in multiple-
choice machine-graded tests, you can shift the focus from questions
that meet the absolute knower's, or dualist's, preference for situations
in which he or she can select one right answer toward questions that
require more sophisticated knowing in the form of "arguments and
evidence by adding short answer questions or by having students
offer reasons for some of their answers" (p. 2). Duch and Norton go
on to state that "true/false tests can ask students to write correct
answers to the questions they marked false or can include choices
like 'true with the exception of . . .'" (p. 2). Kee (1994) elaborates
on the idea that students be given some control in how the ques-

tions are answered. She suggests that students be given the chance to alter one multiple-choice question that they find confusing or misleading, either by changing the stem of the question or by rewriting one of the answer choices. Should these sorts of additions be included in Professor Bronfman's final, Shelley will feel that her understanding of the course material has been more fully tested.

If you decide to elaborate on true/false or multiple-choice questions or if you decide to include questions that require longer answers, you face the challenge of wording the questions. Questions are very difficult to frame. Shelley is concerned about the nature of a longer question. She wants a question that is "clearly worded so that she can understand both the question and what is expected in the answer." We, the framers, understand the question; we know what we expect in the answer; we are sure that the directions are clear. In fact, yes indeed, it is a splendid question, certain to elicit astounding insights from the students.

Yet how many times have you crafted just such a question, only to be faced with a pile of confused and garbled answers? Perhaps you are too close to the question. Can you stand back and scrutinize each one for direction, clarity, specificity, and brevity. Is it written so it cannot possibly be misunderstood?

There are certain typical pitfalls to avoid.

- Omission of the cue word

- Unclear cue word

- Embedded questioning

- Unclear sequencing

- Overloading

In every directed task, there are words that indicate what you are to do. These are the cue words. Sometimes they are found at the opening of the directions (the clearest method of including them); sometimes they are hidden within the directions (a less clear method). The most directive and therefore the most effective cue words are imperative verbs, such as those listed here.

Delimited	More Open	Even More Open
Categorize	Define	Agree
Compare	Explain	Disagree
Contrast	Identify	Analyze
Divide	Sort	Characterize
List	Arrange	Describe
Name	State	Discuss
Paraphrase	Illustrate	Summarize

It is possible to use adverbs and interrogative pronouns to give instructions, but they are less directive than imperative verbs:

Delimited	More Open
What	How
Where	Why
When	
Which	
Who	

We professors must consider these cue words from a number of angles, starting with degree of specificity. Should you frame the question so that it asks for small, separate, and definite tasks, or should you frame it so that it asks a student to explore? Are the students able to discover the steps required for the answer by themselves, or do the students need the steps delineated?

What is the process of the question (does it ask for division into categories, definition, or discussion)? What sort of answer are you expecting, and therefore how much direction must you provide? Do you want to ask for a simple response of concrete material? You might be directive and specific, choosing such cue words as *divide*, *list*, and *name*, or you might be less directive, using the interrogative pronoun, *who*.

Where are your students in their cognitive development? Are they ready for you to ask for comprehension or application in a short answer? If so, you must still be directive, but you can be less specific by using such cue words as *explain* or *state*, or by asking *which*. Are students ready to be asked for analysis, synthesis, or evaluation in a longer essay? You are then at liberty to choose the cue words *analyze*, *discuss*, or even *why*.

It is these cue words that will guide the student to provide the kind of response you want. Do not omit them: they need to be there in a prominent position, generally at the beginning of the question, and they need to be appropriate to the task and the cognitive sophistication of your students. If they are not, you will be inundated with muddy answers. A final exam question without a prominent cue word or with an unclear cue word will not dignify the journey, nor will it bring satisfactory closure for you or for your students.

Once the cue word is in place, we professors face another challenge: the ordering of the question itself. Beware the embedded question: two or more questions somehow tangled together into a single question. Such a question can confuse a student in several ways: first, the nature of the requested content (indicated by cue words) is unclear, and second, the way in which to organize the answer (indicated by such processing words as *first*, *second*, *then*, and *next*) is garbled. Consider the following relatively undemanding question:

> In the final section of the story, what is revealed about
> Jeb and Althea and about the identity of the searchers?

Not only is the cue word ambiguous (what do you mean by *what?*), but also two separate questions have been mixed together into one. Such a question is likely to result in a confused and unsatisfactory answer. Try:

In the final section of the story we learn a good deal about Jeb and Althea.

1. List (very specific), or explain (not so specific), or discuss (least specific) what is revealed about Jeb and Althea.

2. Name (more specific than "give the identity of") or name and list two physical characteristics of (still specific and requiring more information about "revealed") each of the three searchers for Jeb and Althea.

By breaking the longer question into two sections, you have clarified your expectations. Still, you have divided the question into two parts. What if that is not your intent? Perhaps you want only one longer question, involving several steps. Consider this question:

Mitosis and meiosis are different types of cell reproduction. How are they similar and dissimilar? Why is each type important?

Ouch! This is an embedded question with two traps: the cue words are vague, and the sequencing is unclear. You might try this revision:

Mitosis and meiosis are different types of cell reproduction. First, define each method of reproduction. Next, explain their similarities and then their differences. Finally, state why each of the two types of cell reproduction is important.

Now the cue words (*define, explain, state*) are definite, the question is not embedded, and the sequence (*first, next, then, finally*) is both clear and logical. True, it is a long question, but a possible one, and by its specificity and clarity, it avoids the final pitfall—overloading a question.

Beware the whole-world question, the overloaded question:

> Discuss the causes and the results of the American Civil
> War, and be sure to include in your answer whether you
> think that another such war is likely.

This is an impossible question. Is the whole exam on the American Civil War? If so, you may decide on two separate questions: one question on the causes of the Civil War—stating the number of causes that are to be listed or discussed and clarifying how significant the causes are to be—and a second and separate question on the results of the Civil War. Perhaps you want a discussion of the two most significant results of the Civil War, and you want your students to include why they feel that these results were the most significant. Such a question would allow Shelley to demonstrate her specific knowledge and then to move through the last three stages of Bloom's taxonomy: analysis, synthesis, and evaluation. It would be a worthy challenge and a connective closure. However, you would need to be sure to separate and to sequence the parts of that question with care.

The Day of the Exam

No one really enjoys the day of the final exam, but there are tools to make that experience more relaxed and thus more effective. Two of the tools involve the design of the exam, itself. First, you can ask the students to submit their own questions for the final and then you can weave one or two into the exam (Brown, 1991). By including these questions and labeling them as student questions, you have welcomed your students into the teaching and learning of the class and once again recognized their journey. Second, you can include humor. Try a cartoon. A cartoon can be the basis of an identification question, a short-answer question, or a comparative question. It could even supply the central image for an essay. Whatever the purpose of the cartoon, its visual humor will change the modality of the written exam as well as altering the pace. It will connect the information to an outside and generally familiar source, and allow students to relax for a moment. We have heard students chuckle, or even look up and laugh, when they arrive at a cartoon.

Consider, also, your use of the space of the exam room. Putting a smiley face on the board may not be your style; however, we have found that simply moving into the students' space in front of the podium just before handing out the exams; directing the students to think of one thing that they know they do well and that they feel good about; and then asking that they remember that thing as they work through the exam works wonders. So does encouraging students to organize their own private space before the exam, as Shelley does with her pens, Lifesavers, and juice. Finally, students have consistently commented on the questionnaires from our classes that they find chatter before a test extremely disconcerting. Begin on time, without much preamble.

A bowl of wrapped candy or dried fruit is a splendid calming device and a recognition of community and closure. At midpoint or at any point in the exam, you can walk about with your bowl of goodies, speak quietly to students like Chris and Melissa who are clutching, monitor students who are going too fast, and distribute quick energy to those who want it. We have found lollipops (search for those that stay stuck to their sticks) particularly successful—they come in a variety of flavors, and they provide a laugh. Look around a room of grown women and men, bent over bluebooks, lollipop sticks bobbing as they write; you are bound to smile and to relax, if only for a moment.

Shelley left Professor Bronfman's exam exhausted, but pleased. Once again, it had been a long test and a difficult one. There had been the usual multiple-choice questions and short-answer questions. However, this time Professor Bronfman had also included two essay questions, asking students to choose one to answer. Yes, the essay question had given her a chance to demonstrate her mastery and to apply her understanding, but so had the questions on some of the other sections. In fact, it had been a good exam. She had laughed at his wry humor in Section II, struggled to organize Section IV, and enjoyed the cartoon at the end.

Shelley had particularly appreciated the final question that asked students to explain how they felt their new knowledge would be helpful in the future. The question had been carefully worded so that students could choose to list their ideas or to present them in a map, a flowchart, or a paragraph, as long as the ideas were ordered in some way. That question had counted for only five points, and Professor Bronfman had noted that he was more interested in the connections made than in the specific content, a comment that made sense to Shelley since there was no one right way to answer such a question. Shelley had found that final question helpful: it had successfully closed the course, but it also had opened up the meaning of the course content and had enabled her to leave the final exam without that vague feeling of loss she had felt so often after other exams.

Professor Bronfman stood up from the table where he had been sitting during the exam, gathered up the pile of bluebooks that the students had handed him, and walked to the door of his classroom. He had taken a number of risks this semester: he had tried new approaches and new methods; he had modified his teaching style. From the beginning, he had made an effort to create a community of learners and had tried to make clear the direction of the content. He had initially been concerned about the time taken away from lecturing in order to involve the students more directly in the process of learning, but in the end, he had realized that he had covered the same material as in previous semesters. In fact, he had enjoyed organizing his course to reach a variety of learners, and he had found it renewing to place the content in perspective with other avenues of learning.

Professor Bronfman had been pleased to see his students smile at the humor in the exam and at the final cartoon, and he had appreciated their comments as they left the classroom. But there was still more to do with this course. Professor Bronfman had read McKeachie's statement that perhaps the reason that "teachers continue to be fascinated by teaching is that the rewards are never certain and the task of teaching continues to reveal unsolved problems" (McKeachie, 1982, p. 11).

As he turned off the light and walked out of his classroom, Professor Bronfman noticed Shelley greeting a young man with orange-tipped hair and a young woman in a neat blue uniform. Professor Bronfman thought: "Yes, next semester."

Replay

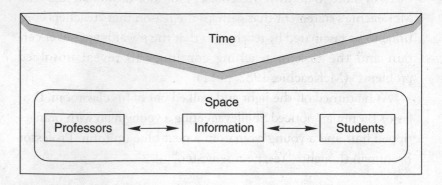

Time

Rapidly running out

Punctuated by deadlines

Characterized by feelings of last chance

Closed with the final exam

Opened to future

Space

Constricted by

- Stress
- High emotion

Needs

- Lessening of tension
- Tumbling of walls
- Celebration of journey

Professors

Recognize stress

Use new approaches

Use humor

Try stress inoculation

Return to syllabus

- · For closure
- · For connection

Acknowledge test anxiety through

- · Review techniques
- · Testing procedures
- · Reframing
- · Imaging

Information

Reflects Bloom's Taxonomy

Contributes to closure through

- · Generative topics
- · Student portfolios
- · The medicine wheel
- · The ordered tree
- · Guided design
- · The final exam

Reflects clear

- · Structure
- · Content
- · Presentation

Students

Recognize

- · Symptoms of stress:
  Procrastination
  Perfectionism
- · Need for
  Structure
  Review

Deal with test anxiety through

- Relaxation techniques
- Time management
- Coping statements
- Mapping

References

Adams, J. L. (1986). *Conceptual blockbusting*. Reading, MA: Addison-Wesley.

Adams, M. (Ed.). (1992). *Promoting diversity in college classrooms: Innovative responses for the curriculum, faculty, and institutions* (New Directions for Teaching and Learning, no. 52). San Francisco: Jossey-Bass.

Altman, H. B. (1989, May). Syllabus shares what the teacher wants. *The Teaching Professor*, pp. 1–2.

American Association for the Advancement of Science. (1989). *Science for all Americans*. Washington, DC: Author.

American Association for Higher Education Continuous Quality Improvement Project. (1994). *CQI: A first reader for higher education*. Washington, DC: American Association for Higher Education.

American Psychological Association. (1993). *Learner-centered psychological principles: Guidelines for school redesign and reform*. Washington, DC: Author.

Anderson, J. R., Eisenberg, N., Holland, J., Wiener, H. S., & Rivera-Kron, C. (1983). *Integrated skills reinforcement*. White Plains, NY: Longman.

Angelo, T. A. (1993). A "teacher's dozen": Fourteen general, research-based principles for improving higher learning in our classrooms. *American Association for Higher Education Bulletin, 45*(8), 3–7.

Angelo, T. A. (1994). Using assessment to improve cooperative learning. *Cooperative Learning and College Teaching Newsletter, 4*(3), 5–7.

Angelo, T. A., & Cross, K. P. (1993). *Classroom assessment techniques: A handbook for college teachers* (2nd ed.). San Francisco: Jossey-Bass.

Appley, M. H., & Maher, W. B. (1989). *Social and behavioral sciences* (Report of the Project 2061 Phase I Social and Behavioral Sciences Panel). Washington, DC: American Association for the Advancement of Science.

Armstrong, T. (1987). *In their own way*. Los Angeles: Jeremy P. Tarcher.

Armstrong, T. (1993). *Seven kinds of smart*. New York: Plume.

Aronson, E. (1978). *The jigsaw classroom*. Newbury Park, CA: Sage.

Association of American Colleges. (1985). *Integrity in the college curriculum: A report to the academic community* (Project on Redefining the Meaning and Purpose of Baccalaureate Degrees). Washington, DC: Author.

Association of American Colleges, Task Group on General Education. (1988). *A new vitality in general education*. Washington, DC: Association of American Colleges.

Astin, A. W. (1984). Student involvement: A developmental theory for higher education. *Journal of College Student Personnel, 25*(4), 297–308.

Astin, A. W. (1985). *Achieving educational excellence: A critical assessment of priorities and practices in higher education*. San Francisco: Jossey-Bass.

Astin, A. W. (1993). *What matters in college? Four critical years revisited*. San Francisco: Jossey-Bass.

Banks, J. A., & Banks, C.A.M. (Eds.). (1989). *Multicultural education: Issues and perspectives*. Needham Heights, MA: Allyn & Bacon.

Baugher, K. (1993, November). Using student teams to improve teaching and learning. *TQM in Higher Education*, pp. 2–3.

Baxter Magolda, M. B. (1992). *Knowing and reasoning in college: Gender-related patterns in students' intellectual development*. San Francisco: Jossey-Bass.

Bednar, R. L., Wells, M. G., & Peterson, S. R. (1989). *Self-esteem: Paradoxes and innovations in clinical theory and practice*. Washington, DC: American Psychological Association.

Belenky, M. F., Clinchy, B. M., Goldberger, N. R., & Tarule, J. M. (1986). *Women's ways of knowing*. New York: Basic Books.

Bennett, W. (1984). *To reclaim a legacy*. Washington, DC: National Endowment for the Humanities.

Bergquist, W. H., & Philips, S. R. (1975). *A handbook for faculty development*. Washington, DC: Council for the Advancement of Small Colleges.

Bliss, E. C. (1976). *Getting things done: The ABCs of time management*. New York: Bantam Books.

Bloom, B. S. (Ed.). (1956). *Taxonomy of educational objectives: Cognitive domain*. New York: Longmans, Green.

Boehrer, J. (1990–1991). Spectators and gladiators: Reconnecting the students with the problem. *Teaching Excellence, 7*, 1–2.

Bonwell, C. C., & Eison, J. A. (1991). *Active learning: Creating excitement in the classroom* (ASHE-ERIC Higher Education Report No. 1). Washington, DC: George Washington University, School of Education and Human Development.

Border, L.L.B., & Chism, N.V.N. (Eds.). (1992). *Teaching for diversity* (New Directions for Teaching and Learning, no. 49). San Francisco: Jossey-Bass.

Borkovec, T. D. (1985, December). What's the use of worrying? *Psychology Today*, pp. 59–64.

Boyer, E. L. (1987). *College: The undergraduate experience in America*. New York: HarperCollins.

Boyer, E. L. (1990). *Scholarship reconsidered: Priorities of the professoriate*. Princeton, NJ: Carnegie Foundation for the Advancement of Teaching.

Bredehoft, D. J. (1991). Cooperative controversies in the classroom. *College Teaching*, 39(3), 122–125.

Brinckerhoff, L. C., Shaw, S., & McGuire, J. (1993). *Promoting postsecondary education for students with learning disabilities: A handbook for practitioners*. Austin, TX: Pro-ed.

Britton, B. K., & Tesser, A. (1991). Effects of time-management practices on college grades. *Journal of Educational Psychology*, 83(3), 405–410.

Brookfield, S. D. (1990). *The skillful teacher: On technique, trust, and responsiveness in the classroom*. San Francisco: Jossey-Bass.

Brooks, R. (1991). *The self-esteem teacher*. Circle Pines, MN: American Guidance Service.

Brown, I. W. (1991). To learn is to teach is to create the final exam. *College Teaching*, 39(4), 150–153.

Burns, D. D. (1980). *Feeling good*. New York: Signet.

Burns, D. D. (1990). *The feeling good handbook*. New York: Plume.

Buscaglia, L. (1982). *Living, loving & learning*. Troy, MO: Holt, Rinehart & Winston.

Campbell, L., Campbell, B., & Dickinson, D. (1992). *Teaching and learning through multiple intelligences*. Stanwood, WA: New Horizons for Learning.

Campus Compact. (1993). *Rethinking tradition: Integrating service with academic study on college campuses* (T. Y. Kupiec, Ed.). Denver, CO: Education Commission of the States.

Canfield, A. (1980). *Learning styles inventory manual*. Ann Arbor, MI: Humanics Media.

Cantor, N. (1953). *The teaching-learning process*. Troy, MO: Holt, Rinehart & Winston.

Chess, S., & Thomas, A. (1986). *Temperament in clinical practice*. New York: Guilford Press.

Chickering, A. W., & Gamson, Z. F. (1987). Seven principles for good practice in undergraduate education. *American Association of Higher Education Bulletin*, 45(8), 3–7.

Christensen, C. R. (1991). The discussion leader in action: Questioning, listening, and response. In C. R. Christensen, D. A. Garvin, & A. Sweet (Eds.), *Education for judgment* (pp. 153–172). Boston: Harvard Business School Press.

Christensen, C. R., Garvin, D. A., & Sweet, A. (Eds.). (1991). *Education for judgment*. Boston: Harvard Business School Press.

Christensen, C. R., & Hansen, A. J. (1987). *Teaching and the case method*. Boston: Harvard Business School Press.

Civikly, J. M. (1986). Humor and the enjoyment of college teaching. In J. M. Civikly (Ed.), *Communicating in college classrooms* (New Directions for Teaching and Learning, no. 26, pp. 61–70). San Francisco: Jossey-Bass.

Clarke, E. (1985). Grading seminar performance. *College Teaching, 33*(3), 129–133.

Claxton, C. S., & Murrell, P. H. (1987). *Learning styles: Implications for improving educational practices* (ASHE-ERIC Higher Education Report No. 4). Washington, DC: Association for the Study of Higher Education.

Cohen, A. M., & Brawer, F. B. (1989). *The American community college* (2nd ed.). San Francisco: Jossey-Bass.

Coles, R. (1989). *The call of stories: Teaching and the moral imagination*. Boston: Houghton Mifflin.

Cornesky, R. (1993). *The quality professor: Implementing TQM in the classroom*. Madison, WI: Magna.

Coscarelli, W. C., & White, G. P. (1986). *The guided design guidebook: Patterns in implementation*. Morgantown, WV: National Center for Guided Design.

Covington, M. V., & Beery, R. G. (1976). *Self-worth and school learning*. Troy, MO: Holt, Rinehart & Winston.

Creed, T. (1993). "The" seven principles . . . NOT! *American Association of Higher Education Bulletin, 45*(8), 8–9.

Cross, K. P. (1986). A proposal to improve teaching. *American Association of Higher Education Bulletin, 39*(1), 9–14.

Cross, K. P. (1988). In search of zippers. *American Association of Higher Education Bulletin, 40*(10), 3–7.

Cross, K. P. (1990, June). *Introduction to classroom research*. Paper presented at the Second Annual University of California, Berkeley, Faculty Development Institute Workshop on Classroom Research, Berkeley, CA.

Crouch, M. K., & Fontaine, S. I. (1994). Student portfolios as an assessment tool. In D. F. Halpern & Associates (Eds.), *Changing college classrooms: New teaching and learning strategies for an increasingly complex world* (pp. 306–328). San Francisco: Jossey-Bass.

Csikszentmihalyi, M. (1990). *Flow: The psychology of optimal experience*. New York: HarperCollins.

Curry, L. (1983, April). *An organization of learning styles theory and constructs*. Paper presented at the annual meeting of the American Educational Research Association, Montreal, Quebec. (ERIC Document Reproduction Service No. ED 235 185)

Davis, B. G. (1993). *Tools for teaching*. San Francisco: Jossey- Bass.

Davis, M., Eshelman, E. R., & McKay, M. (1988). *The relaxation & stress reduction workbook* (3rd ed.). Oakland, CA: New Harbinger.

deBono, E. *deBono's thinking course*. (1985). New York: Facts on File.

De Felice, L. (1989, April). The bibbidibobbidiboo factor in teaching. *Phi Delta Kappan*, pp. 639–641.

Dorn, D. S. (1989). Simulation games: One more tool on the pedagogical shelf. *Teaching Sociology, 17*, 1–18.

Duch, B. J., & Norton, M. K. (1992–1993). Teaching for cognitive growth. *Teaching Excellence, 4*(8), 1–2.

Duffy, D. K., & Jones, J. W. (1991). ALC: Activating learning in the classroom. *Innovation Abstracts, 13*(27).

Dunn, R., & Dunn, K. (1978). *Teaching students through their individual learning styles: A practical approach*. Englewood Cliffs, NJ: Prentice Hall.

Eble, K. E. (1976). *The craft of teaching: A guide to mastering the professor's art*. San Francisco: Jossey-Bass.

Edgerton, R. (1993, July/August). The tasks faculty perform. *Change*, pp. 4–6.

Edgerton, R., Hutchings, P., & Quinlan, K. (1991). *The teaching portfolio: Capturing the scholarship in teaching*. Washington, DC: American Association of Higher Education.

Edwards, C. M., & Gibboney, E. R. (1992, February). *The power of humor in the college classroom*. Paper presented at the annual meeting of the Western States Communication Association, Boise, ID. (ERIC Document Reproduction Service No. ED 346 535)

Ellis, D. B. (1991). *Becoming a master student* (6th ed.). Rapid City, SD: College Survival.

Enns, C. Z. (1993). Integrating separate and connected knowing: The experiential learning model. *Teaching of Psychology, 20*(1), 7–13.

Fenker, R. (1981). *Stop studying, start learning: Or how to jump start your brain*. Fort Worth, TX: Tangram.

Fideler, E. (1991). Inquiry-based faculty development. *The Journal of Staff, Program, & Organization Development, 9*(4), 197–203.

Fox, D. (1983). Personal theories of teaching. *Studies in Higher Education, 8*(2), 151–163.

Frederick, P. J. (1990). The power of story. *American Association of Higher Education Bulletin, 3,* 5–8.

Frederick, P. J. (1991). The medicine wheel: Emotions and connections in the classroom. *To Improve the Academy, 10,* 197–214.

Fried, J. (1993). Bridging emotion and intellect: Classroom diversity in process. *College Teaching, 41*(4), 123–128.

Fuhrmann, B. S., & Grasha, A. F. (1983). *A practical handbook for college teachers.* Boston: Little, Brown.

Gabelnick, F., MacGregor, J., Matthews, R. S., & Smith, B. L. (1990). *Learning communities: Creating connections among students, faculty, and disciplines* (New Directions for Teaching and Learning, no. 41). San Francisco: Jossey-Bass.

Gabennesch, H. (1992). The enriched syllabus: To convey a larger vision. *The National Teaching and Learning Forum, 1*(4), 4.

Gardner, H. (1983). *Frames of mind.* New York: Basic Books.

Gardner, H. (1991). *The unschooled mind.* New York: Basic Books.

Gardner, H. (1993). *Multiple intelligences.* New York: Basic Books.

Gardner, H. (1994, June). *Assessing understanding within and across the disciplines.* Closing plenary session at the 9th annual conference of the American Association for Higher Education Assessment & Quality, Washington, DC.

Garvin, D. A. (1991). Barriers and gateways to learning. In C. R. Christensen, D. A. Garvin, & A. Sweet (Eds.), *Education for judgment* (pp. 3–13). Boston: Harvard Business School Press.

Gmelch, W. H. (1987). What colleges and universities can do about faculty stressors. In P. Seldin (Ed.), *Coping with faculty stress* (New Directions for Teaching and Learning, no. 29, pp. 23–31). San Francisco: Jossey-Bass.

Gmelch, W. H. (1993). *Coping with faculty stress.* Newbury Park, CA: Sage.

Goodman, J. (1992, November 2). The laughing/learning link. *New York Teacher,* p. 20.

Goodsell, A., Maher, M., Tinto, V., & Associates (Eds.). (1992). *Collaborative learning: A sourcebook for higher education.* University Park, PA: National Center on Postsecondary Teaching, Learning, and Assessment, Pennsylvania State University.

Grasha, A. F. (1984). Learning styles: The journey from Greenwich laboratory (1796) to the college classroom (1984). *Improving College & University Teaching, 32*(1), 46–53.

Greenberg, J. S. (1987). *Comprehensive stress management* (2nd ed.). Dubuque, IA: William C. Brown.

Greenblat, C. S. (1988). *Designing games and simulations: An illustrated handbook*. Newbury Park, CA: Sage.

Gregorc, A. R. (1979). Learning/teaching styles: Their nature and effects. In J. W. Keefe (Ed.), *Student learning styles: Diagnosing and prescribing programs* (pp. 19–26). Reston, VA: National Association of Secondary School Principals.

Gregory, K. (1983). Native-view paradigms: Multiple culture and culture conflicts in organizations, *Administrative Science Quarterly, 28*, 359–376.

Hanson, F. A. (1993). *Testing testing*. Berkeley: University of California Press.

Harvard Committee. (1945). *General education in a free society*. Cambridge, MA: Harvard University Press.

Harward, B. M., & Albert, L. S. (1994). Service and service learning. *American Association of Higher Education Bulletin, 46*(6), 10–12.

Hill, J. E., & Nunnery, D. N. (1973). *The educational sciences*. Bloomfield, MI: Oakland Community College Press.

How students learn: A question of style. (1989, February). *The Teaching Professor*, pp. 3–4.

Ishikawa, K. (1976). *Guide to quality control*. Tokyo: Asian Productivity Organization.

Jacobs, L. C., & Chase, C. I. (1992). *Developing and using tests effectively: A guide for faculty*. San Francisco: Jossey-Bass.

Janis, I. J. (1982). *Stress, attitudes, and decisions: Selected papers*. New York: Praeger.

Jensen, E. P. (1988). *Superteaching*. Del Mar, CA: Turning Point for Teachers.

Johnson, D. W., & Johnson, F. P. (1991). *Joining together* (4th ed.). Englewood Cliffs, NJ: Prentice Hall.

Johnson, D. W., & Johnson, R. T. (1990). *Cooperation and competition: Theory and research*. Edina, MN: Interaction Book Company.

Johnson, D. W., Johnson, R. T., & Smith, K. A. (1991a). *Active learning: Cooperation in the college classroom*. Edina, MN: Interaction Book Company.

Johnson, D. W., Johnson, R. T., & Smith, K. A. (1991b). *Cooperative learning: Increasing college faculty instructional productivity* (ASHE-ERIC Higher Education Report No. 4). Washington, DC: George Washington University, School of Education and Human Development.

Jones, J. W., & Duffy, D. K. (1991). Activating learning in the classroom: Challenge, collaborate, celebrate. *The Journal of Staff, Program, & Organization Development, 9*(4), 231–237.

Jones, K. (1993). *Imaginative events for training*. New York: McGraw-Hill.

Jordan, J. V., Kaplan, A. G., Miller, J. B., Stiver, I. P., & Surrey, J. L. (1991). *Women's growth in connection*. New York: Guilford Press.

Kadel, S., & Keehner, J. A. (Eds.). (1994). *Collaborative learning: A sourcebook for higher education* (Vol. 2). University Park, PA: National Center on Postsecondary Teaching, Learning, and Assessment, Pennsylvania State University.

Katz, J., & Henry, M. (1988). *Turning professors into teachers*. New York: Macmillan.

Kee, C. C. (1994, June/July). Multiple choice questions: A new twist for an old standard. *The Teaching Professor*, p. 6.

Kelly, W. (1970). *Pogo*. (Comic strip)

Kendall, J. (1990). *Combining service and learning* (2 Vols). Raleigh, NC: National Society for Internships and Experiential Education.

Klein, A. (1989). *The healing power of humor*. Los Angeles: Jeremy P. Tarcher.

Kolb, D. (1984). *Experiential learning: Experience as the source of learning and development*. Englewood Cliffs, NJ: Prentice Hall.

Kuh, G. D., Schuh, J. H., Whitt, E. J., & Associates. (1991). *Involving colleges: Successful approaches to fostering student learning and development outside the classroom*. San Francisco: Jossey-Bass.

Kuh, G. D., & Whitt, E. J. (1988). *The invisible tapestry: Culture in American colleges and universities* (ASHE-ERIC Higher Education Report No. 1). Washington, DC: Association for the Study of Higher Education.

Lakein, A. (1974). *How to get control of your time and your life*. New York: New American Library.

Langer, E. J. (1989). *Mindfulness*. Reading, MA: Addison-Wesley.

Langer, E. J. (1993). A mindful education. *Educational Psychologist, 28*(1), 43–50.

Lazarus, R. S. (1966). *Psychological stress and the coping process*. New York: McGraw-Hill.

Leff, H. L. (1985). *Playful perception*. Burlington, VT: Waterfront Books.

Levine, A. (1993, September/October). Student expectations of college. *Change*, p. 4.

Light, R. J. (1990). *The Harvard assessment seminars* (First Report). Cambridge, MA: Harvard University Graduate School of Education and Kennedy School of Government.

Light, R. J. (1992). *The Harvard assessment seminars* (Second Report). Cambridge, MA: Harvard University Graduate School of Education and Kennedy School of Government.

Loomans, D., & Kolberg, K. (1993). *The laughing classroom*. Tiburon, CA: H. J. Kramer.

Lowman, J. (1984). *Mastering the techniques of teaching*. San Francisco: Jossey-Bass.

Lyons, P. (1989). Assessing classroom participation. *College Teaching, 37*(1), 36–38.

McCutcheon, R. (1985). *Get off my brain*. Minneapolis, MN: Free Spirit Publishing.

McKeachie, W. J. (1982). The rewards of teaching. In J. L. Bess (Ed.), *Motivating professors to teach effectively* (New Directions for Teaching and Learning, no. 10, pp. 7–13). San Francisco: Jossey-Bass.

McKeachie, W. J. (1986). *Teaching tips: A guide for the beginning college teacher* (8th ed.). Lexington, MA: Heath.

Mann, R. D., Arnold, S. M., Binder, J., Cytrunbaum, S., Ringwald, J., & Rosenwein, R. (1970). *The college classroom: Conflict, change, and learning*. New York: Wiley.

March, J. G., & Simon, H. (1958). *Organizations*. New York: Wiley.

Marchesani, L. S., & Adams, M. (1992). Dynamics of diversity in the teaching-learning process: A faculty development model for analysis and action. In M. Adams (Ed.), *Promoting diversity in college classrooms: Innovative responses for the curriculum, faculty, and institutions* (New Directions for Teaching and Learning, no. 52, pp. 9–20). San Francisco: Jossey-Bass.

Marchese, T. (1993 May/June). TQM: A time for ideas. *Change*, pp. 10–13.

Martin, J., & Siehl, C. (1983). Organizational culture and counterculture: An uneasy symbiosis. *Organizational dynamics, 12*(2), 52–64.

Meichenbaum, D. (1977). *Cognitive behavior modification: An integrative approach*. New York: Plenum.

Meichenbaum, D. (1985). *Stress inoculation training*. New York: Pergamon.

Meyers, C., & Jones, T. B. (1993). *Promoting active learning*. San Francisco: Jossey-Bass.

Millis, B. J. (1990). Helping faculty build learning communities through cooperative groups. *To Improve the Academy, 10*, 43–58.

Milne, A. A. (1952). *When we were very young*. New York: Dell.

Milton, O., Pollio, H. R., & Eison, J. A. (1986). *Making sense of college grades: Why the grading system does not work and what can be done about it*. San Francisco: Jossey-Bass.

Myers, I. B., & Myers, D. B. (1980). *Gifts differing*. Palo Alto, CA: Consulting Psychologist Press.

Nash, L. L. (1991). Discovering the semester. In C. R. Christensen, D. A. Garvin, & A. Sweet (Eds.), *Education for judgment* (pp. 231–248). Boston: Harvard Business School Press.

National Center for Research to Improve Postsecondary Teaching and Learning. (1990, Spring). Figuring out how students organize information. *NCRIPTAL Update*, p. 3.

National Institute of Education Study Group. (1984). *Involvement in learning: Realizing the potential of American higher education*. Washington, DC: National Institute of Education.

Ottens, A. J. (1984). *Coping with academic anxiety*. New York: Rosen.

Palmer, P. J. (1983). *To know as we are known: A spirituality of education*. San Francisco: HarperCollins.

Pascarella, E. T., & Terenzini, P. T. (1991). *How college affects students: Findings and insights from twenty years of research*. San Francisco: Jossey-Bass.

Pask, G. (1976). Styles and strategies of learning. *British Journal of Educational Psychology, 46*, 128–148.

Perkins, D. (1992). *Smart schools: From training memories to educating minds*. New York: Free Press.

Perry, W. G. (1970). *Forms of intellectual and ethical development in the college years*. Troy, MO: Holt, Rinehart & Winston.

Pintrich, P. R., & Johnson, G. R. (1990). Assessing and improving students' learning strategies. In M. D. Svinicki (Ed.), *The changing face of college teaching* (New Directions for Teaching and Learning, no. 42, pp. 83–92). San Francisco: Jossey-Bass.

Pintrich, P. R., McKeachie, W. J., & Smith, D. (1989). *The motivated strategies for learning questionnaire*. Ann Arbor, MI: National Center for Research to Improve Postsecondary Teaching and Learning, University of Michigan.

Postman, N., & Weingartner, C. (1969). *Teaching as a subversive activity*. New York: Delacorte Press.

Reichmann, S., & Grasha, A. (1974). A rational approach to developing and assessing the construct validity of a student learning style scales instrument. *Journal of Psychology, 87*, 213–223.

Reinsmith, W. A. (1992). *Archetypal forms in teaching*. Westport, CT.: Greenwood Press.

Reitman, J. S., & Reuter, H. H. (1980). Organization revealed by recall orders and confirmed by pauses. *Cognitive Psychology, 12*, 554–581.

Renner, P. (1983). *The instructor's survival kit*. Vancouver, BC: Training Associates.

Rose, C. (1985). *Accelerated learning*. New York: Dell.

Rubin, S. (1985, August 7). Professors, students, and the syllabus. *The Chronicle of Higher Education*, p. 56.

Scheiber, B., & Talpers, J. (1987). *Unlocking potential: College and other choices for learning disabled people*. Bethesda, MD: Adler & Adler.

Schilling, K. M., & Schilling, K. L. (1993, March 24). Professors must respond to calls for accountability. *The Chronicle of Higher Education*, p. 4.

Schmeck, R. (1983). Learning styles of college students. In R. F. Dillon & R. R. Schmeck (Eds.), *Individual differences in cognition* (pp. 223–279). San Diego, CA: Academic Press.

Schneidewind, N. (1990). Feminist values: Guidelines for teaching methodology in women's studies. In S. O'Malley, R. Rosen, & L. Vogt (Eds.), *Politics of education: Essays from radical teachers* (pp. 11–21). Albany: State University of New York Press.

Schoem, D., Frankel, L., Zúñiga, X., & Lewis, E. A. (Eds.). (1993). *Multicultural teaching in the university*. Westport, CT: Praeger.

Schroeder, C. C. (1993, September/October). New students—New learning styles. *Change*, pp. 21–26.

Schuster, M. R., & Van Dyne, S. R. (1985). Feminist transformation of the curriculum. Wellesley, MA: Wellesley College Center for Research on Women.

Seldin, P. (1991). *The teaching portfolio*. Bolton, MA: Anker.

Seligman, M. E. (1990). *Learned optimism*. New York: Pocket Books.

Seuss, Dr. (1965). *I had trouble in getting to Solla Sollew*. New York: Random House.

Shannon, T. M. (1986). Introducing simulation and role play. In S. F. Schomberg (Ed.), *Strategies for active learning in university classrooms* (pp. 27–34). Minneapolis: University of Minnesota Press.

Shor, I., & Freire, P. A. (1987). *A pedagogy for liberation: Dialogues on transforming education*. South Hadley, MA: Bergin & Garvey.

Simpkinson, A. A. (1993, November/December). The instinctive life. *Common Boundary*, pp. 32–37.

Somers, J. A., & Holt, M. E. (1993). What's in a game? A study of games as an instructional method in an adult education class. *Innovative Higher Education, 17*(4), 243–257.

Sommer, R. (1969). *Personal space*. Englewood Cliffs, NJ: Prentice Hall.

Spitzberg, I. J., & Thorndike, V. V. (1992). *Creating community on college campuses*. Albany: State University of New York Press.

Stark, J. S., Shaw, K. M., & Lowther, M. A. (1989). *Student goals for college and courses* (ASHE-ERIC Higher Education Report No. 6). Washington, DC: George Washington University, School of Education and Human Development.

Steele, F. I. (1973). *Physical settings and organization development*. Reading, MA: Addison-Wesley.

Stull, R. S. (1992). Dusting off our personal teaching philosophies. *The National Teaching and Learning Forum*, 1(4), 11.

Svinicki, M. D., & Dixon, N. M. (1987). Kolb model modified for classroom activities. *College teaching*, 35(4), 141–146.

Sykes, C. J. (1988). *ProfScam: Professors and the demise of higher education*. New York: St. Martin's Press.

Tiberius, R. G. (1990). *Small group teaching: A trouble shooting guide*. Toronto: Ontario Institute for Studies in Education.

Tinto, V. (1987). *Leaving college: Rethinking the causes and cures of student attrition*. Chicago: University of Chicago Press.

To grade class participation? (1989, May). *The Teaching Professor*, p. 5.

Tubesing, N. L., & Tubesing, D. A. (1994). *Structured exercises in stress management* (Vols. 1–4). Duluth, MN: Whole Person Associates.

Twotrees, K. S. (1994, June). *Medicine wheels and organizing wheels: A tribal perspective on learning*. Workshop presented at the 9th annual conference of the American Association for Higher Education Assessment & Quality, Washington, DC.

Urbach, F. (1992). Developing a teaching portfolio. *College Teaching*, 40(2), 71–74.

Van Maanen, J., & Barley, S. R. (1984). Occupational communities: Culture and control in organizations. *Research in Organizational Behavior, 6*, 287–365.

Ventimiglia, L. M. (1994). Cooperative learning at the college level. *Thought & Action*, 9(2), 5–30.

Wales, C. E., & Nardi, A. H. (1982, November). Teaching decision-making with guided design. *IDEA Paper No. 9*. Manhattan: Kansas State University, Center for Faculty Evaluation & Development.

Wales, C. E., Nardi, A. H., & Stager, R. A. (1987). *Thinking skills: Making a choice*. Morgantown, WV: Center for Guided Design.

Walvoord, B. F. (1986). *Helping students write well: A guide for teachers in all disciplines* (2nd ed.). New York: Modern Language Association.

Weiler, K. (1988). *Women teaching for change: Gender, class, and power*. New York: Bergin & Garvey.

Weimer, M. (1990). *Improving college teaching: Strategies for developing instructional effectiveness*. San Francisco: Jossey-Bass.

Weinstein, C. E., Goetz, E. T., & Alexander, P. A. (Eds.). (1988). *Learning and study strategies: Issues in assessment, instruction, and evaluation*. New York: Academic Press.

Weinstein, C. E., Schulte, A. C., & Palmer, D. R. (1987). *Learning and study strategies inventory (LASSI)*. Clearwater, FL: H and H Publishing.

Weinstein, C. E., Zimmerman, S. A., & Palmer, D. R. (1988). Assessing learning strategies: The design and development of the LASSI. In C. E. Weinstein, E. T. Goetz, & P. A. Alexander (Eds.), *Learning and study strategies* (pp. 25–40). San Diego, CA: Academic Press.

Weinstein, G., & Obear, K. (1992). Bias issues in the classroom: Encounters with the teaching self. In M. Adams (Ed.), *Promoting diversity in college classrooms: Innovative responses for the curriculum, faculty, and institutions* (New Directions for Teaching and Learning, no. 52, pp. 39–50). San Francisco: Jossey-Bass.

Wexler, D. B. (1991). *The prism workbook.* New York: W.W. Norton.

Whitman, N. A., Spendlove, D. C., & Clark, C. H. (1986). *Increasing students' learning: A faculty guide to reducing stress among students* (ASHE-ERIC Higher Education Report No. 4). Washington, DC: Association for the Study of Higher Education.

Widick, C. & Simpson, D. (1978). Developmental concepts in college instruction. In C. Parker (Ed.), *Encouraging development in college students* (pp. 27–59). Minneapolis, MN: University of Minnesota Press.

Will the school year ever end? (1989, May). *The Teaching Professor,* p. 6.

Williamson, B. (1993). *Playful activities for powerful presentations.* Duluth, MN: Whole Person Associates.

Winston, S. (1978). *Getting organized.* New York: Warner Books.

Wlodkowski, R. J. (1985). *Enhancing adult motivation to learn: A guide to improving instruction and increasing learner achievement.* San Francisco: Jossey-Bass.

Index